Minding My Own Business

Marjorie McVicar & Julia F. Craig

Minding My Own Business

"...a wonderful 'workbook' for any woman wanting to begin her own business. My congratulations to Marjorie McVicar and Julia Craig. Obviously, much time and work has gone into the preparation of this 'how to book.' "

MARY KAY ASH,
CHAIRMAN OF THE BOARD,
MARY KAY COSMETICS

"...this is one of the most comprehensive and accessible guides to starting and nurturing a small business...An eminently practical manual—in a class with Albert Lowry's *How To Become Financially Successful by Owning Your Own Business.*"

KIRKUS REVIEWS

"...this book offers a multitude of possibilities, amply illustrated by the experiences of numerous women entrepreneurs."

LIBRARY JOURNAL

MINDING MY OWN BUSINESS

Published simultaneously in the United States and Canada by Playboy Paperbacks, New York, New York. Printed in the United States of America. Library of Congress Catalog Card Number: 82-80425. Reprinted by arrangement with Richard Marek Publishers.

Books are available at quantity discounts for promotional and industrial use. For further information, write to Premium Sales, Playboy Paperbacks, 1633 Broadway, New York, New York 10019.

ISBN: 0-867-21149-0

First Playboy Paperbacks printing September 1982.

10 9 8 7 6 5 4 3 2 1

To women working together in business

Contents

Introduction

It was the day after Christmas, and we were sharing a letdown feeling. The magic was gone, the season's efforts had been either torn out of packages or eaten, and we were looking into the bottom of our coffee cups. We both cherished our young families, but at the same time, our lives seemed inundated with endless, often unsatisfying tasks. The exciting, unpredictable college years we had shared as roommates were gone, and although we had read about something called creative mothering, there didn't seem to be anything creative about washing a load of diapers for the hundredth time or wiping the morning mush off the walls. We shared an unsettling urge to do something apart from—and in addition to—the roles we had chosen. We shared a dream of expressing ourselves through the creation of a business.

This book is the result of that dream. We decided to talk first to other women who owned their own businesses before starting one of our own. We may have lacked business expertise and financial backing, but what we found through our efforts to organize our venture was a resource far richer than any banker and more profitable than a business-school degree.

We found a community of women business owners eager to share what they had learned with other women who were just starting out on their business adventures. Through them, we learned what a woman's business is really about. Their stories were infinitely more meaningful than any statistics or business guides ever could be, and the advice they gave us was so personal, and yet apparently so universal, that our purpose when talking with these women gradually changed. Our "creation" took a different form than had been our original intention. The "business" of collecting and researching the information and advice these experienced businesswomen offered, and compiling it into this book, became our primary goal. Through this book, we can share the actual experiences of over one hundred women business owners who told us, in their own words, how they filled up their muffin tin with change, or bought their first property, or plugged in the machine that really gave their business its start. Every word they shared with us, and now with you, is based on their experience in doing what you aim to try: starting your own business.

Little did we realize what we were undertaking. It didn't take us long to realize, however, that women at home with small children aren't the only ones who shared our need for a sense of independent creative expression. In the course of our interviewing, we spoke to single women, married women, women with grown families, widowed women, formerly employed women—women at every stage of life. And never before had we met a more enthusiastic, intense, radiant group of people. Their excitement, joy, self-esteem, and willingness to share their secrets overwhelmed us. We were impressed by their immense satisfaction with whatever they were doing. Financial rewards were important, but the rewards they described in personal and emotional satisfaction far surpassed any financial reckoning.

Their effect on us was so electrifying that we put our most intense efforts into gathering specific information to assist other women in their business ventures. First we searched bookstores and library shelves for information on how to go into business. We found that most of the material available was so government-pamphlet boring or college-textbook technical that we could hardly force ourselves to read past the first pages. And while there was very little timely and practical advice on the subject, there was even less information directed specifically toward women. We found books which covered various elements of business—preparing a financial statement, choosing employees—but we found no book that told how to deal with the guilt you might experience when you worked sixteen hours at your new business, leaving your husband and three-year-old home to fend for themselves. Or how to deal with the banker who turns your loan application down flat as he looks at your twenty-year record of "unemployment" as a housewife and mother. Or how to respond to the customer who decides against having his car repaired by a woman.

We found business books that told you how to open a hardware store or cleaning service, but rarely did they cover the problems of licensing a day-care center, going to the fashion "market" for the first time, or establishing a business cooperative. In this book, we look at the process of opening and operating a business as well as the issues, challenges, and problems that are unique for women entrepreneurs.

In addition to our personal interviews, we wrote dozens of letters to businesswomen, asking for their advice. We enrolled in seminars, spoke to business teachers, lawyers, Small Business Administration officials, bank loan officers, and psychotherapists. Although most of the women we spoke to are from the Pacific Northwest, their experience and advice can be universally applied. When a fabric-store owner told us how she dragged some old furniture out of the alley trash and used it as her shop's first "fixtures," she was telling us all that you can start on a shoestring, if you've a mind to. When a woman told us that shopping was the thing she did best, so opening a shop was a natural for her, she is telling us all to be in touch with our own talents.

We include charts, checklists, questionnaires—everything to help you chart your own success story. It's up to you to decide what kind of business you really want. Something to help you market your particular creative talent? A business that gets you out, mingling with the public? Or a one-woman operation in which you can work at your own speed? Do you want to work at home, or to travel? Is the opportunity to develop an idea into a large corporation with big profits your goal? Or do you want your own business because it allows you to limit its size and your involvement? We've heard all these reasons, and more, from women who have taken their first steps in business.

We offer no one woman's advice as the only way to go. We tried to balance different opinions and experiences against others offered by women in the same field. There are endless choices available when you decide to develop a business. We wanted to provide you with as many as possible to use as your guidelines.

A note on the organization of this book: We've divided up our information into two parts. Part I concerns the preliminary groundwork you should cover before setting any of your business plans in motion. This groundwork includes personal analysis and the examination and development of your original ideas. You'll draw up a working business plan and learn how to make all the decisions that are involved in running a successful business, such as where to locate, how to advertise, what price to charge, and so on. When you've completed Part I, you'll be aware of all the business basics.

Then go on to Part II for more specific information on the operation of different types of businesses—retail businesses, service businesses, and manufacturing businesses. In the chapter that describes the type of business you are interested in, you will find the advice we have gathered that pertains to your particular field. Don't overlook the chapters on the other kinds of businesses, however. You will find helpful comments in each section that you can adapt to your own business situation.

At the end of the book, you'll find some conclusions we have drawn about businesswomen in general. And we also offer a glossary of business terms that we think you'll find helpful.

Most of the businesses in this book were a dream years before they became a reality. Use our book to start your own successful business today or to kindle your thoughts for your future success story.

Part I—Groundwork

1 The Idea

Testing Your Good Idea

Every business success story starts with a good idea. Where do these ideas come from?

"I love to cook, and nobody in my family eats very much. So when the local YWCA needed someone to open a lunchroom, I was first in line."

"I love antiques and have shopped for them for years. Because shopping is the thing I do best, I decided to open my own shop."

"I knitted and crocheted my way through the raising of six kids. I not only designed my own knitted dresses, but I also taught knitting in my living room to groups of friends. One day, in the middle of an afternoon, I found myself on my hands and knees, checking under my son's bed for something to clean up or put away. It was then that I knew I needed some kind of an out-of-the-home commitment, and it was then I began working on plans to open my own yarn store."

"I worked in a printing shop from the time I was fourteen to the day I graduated from college. When I became a teacher, I couldn't get over the low quality, high-priced printing the schools were paying for. I knew I could do it better for less."

"Since I was ten years old, I have been baby-sitting. I love children, so providing day care is a natural for me. I've only advertised once in the eight years I've been in business, so the need for my services is most definitely there."

"I am a gourmet cook, and I got tired of having to go to New York to get the cooking utensils I wanted. So I opened my own gourmet kitchen shop in my own town."

How do you know if your idea is really a good one? In our conversations with businesswomen, we found that a good idea is usually comprised of two specific elements:

1. A good idea includes both your special personal talent, interest, or past experience and your burning desire to pursue it.
2. A good idea fills a need.

It is interesting to see where some women's personal talents, interests, or experiences have carried them in business. One woman who enjoyed shopping and ministering to the needs of others set up a shopping and errand service for the elderly in her community. Another woman who had enjoyed living with a European family while she was studying abroad decided to organize an agency that houses traveling Americans in British homes. Gail is a young, attractive woman who developed her own home-remodeling business in Portland, Oregon. Her story clearly illustrates the development of a good idea.

When Gail was in high school, she helped her father paint and remodel his rental properties. When she went to college, she found herself fixing up each apartment and old house she lived in. She thought of her fixing-up skills only as a hobby until she decided she wanted to own her own business. At that time, she began to realize that her past experience had equipped her for a business that was an exciting extension of her personal talents.

"I could see what was happening with new housing—it was getting more expensive, and there was less land available to work with. The idea came to me that I wanted to work with housing in the inner city. There was really no one I knew of who was specializing in restoring older houses on a speculative basis—professional rehabing. And I just hit on this idea—it overwhelmed me—that *that's* what I'm going to do!"

"I planned to take houses that were derelict, that weren't livable or habitable, and fix them up. I would provide houses to buyers who normally wouldn't look in the city because they couldn't find houses that were fixed up. Maybe they'd like to live there, but they couldn't fix a house up themselves. Or they would completely overlook the house because it looked so gross! I felt that some of the work that was being done by other remodelers was substandard, that they were trying to make new houses out of old houses. I was trying to renew the old houses, to recover their integrity, to take *off* what other people had done over the years."

Thus part one of Gail's good idea was satisfied. Her business could develop along the lines of her own talents and interests. And part two of her good idea was also satisfied. Her remodeling business would fill a community need.

Recognizing Your Personal Goals

You have a good idea. Next you must very carefully define your personal goals. What do you personally want to achieve by owning your own business? Financial independence? Recognition for being an expert in your field? An outlet to express your creative talents?

Why own your own business? Why not work for someone else? Although the answer may seem obvious, put it into words, like Gail did:

"My long-range personal goals are to achieve a position of power and authority through my business with which I can make an impact on my community. If I can achieve a position of power through the business, then I can attain *more* of my specific personal goals than I could have before. For example, before, when I did volunteer political work, I would go to a campaign headquarters and lick stamps. But now, through what others might accept as my 'success'—and I mean a kind of institutionalized success, such as a banker might take notice of—I feel very competent to tell the mayor what *I* think about the city's housing problems. Would he ever listen to me if I were tucked away in my neighborhood with no credentials? It is the achievement of *authority* that helps me achieve those long-range personal goals. I feel that I'm personally involved. Establishing the business and making money and being recognized as successful is all part of it. And I think it's important that we women have to stand up and say, we don't want to just do a *good job* in life, we want to be *recognized*. We want the *rewards* of success. Just recognizing that we want these rewards is a new phase for most of us."

What are your personal goals? Put them down in writing, so that your good idea can take on some definite direction:

Throughout our interviews we noticed that "money" was never mentioned as a driving personal desire, and although it was certainly part of everyone's goal, it was rarely at the top of the list of personal priorities. We can all benefit from one woman's hard-earned advice:

"When I was in college, two friends and I came up with what we thought was a wonderful scheme that would make us all millionaires. My partners and I invested our respective life savings into the new company, which was supposed to provide discount merchandise to factory workers. Within a year's time, we lost everything. We realized later that we knew next to nothing about salesmanship and much less about running a sales business. It was a hard lesson. But today, ten years older and wiser, and after several years of begging and borrowing for survival, I am a successful photographer. Photography is and always has been my true love. I should have followed that direction from the beginning."

Do you have an idea for a dream business of your own? Is it an extension of your own personal interests? Does it fill a specific need in your community? Will this business help you attain your personal goals? If you've answered yes to these questions, you've made a good start in your business planning. If you've answered no to any one of the questions, you'd better go back to the drawing board and do some further thinking. Only by following your interests, filling a community need, and being in touch with your personal goals will you have the kind of success that makes all your efforts worthwhile.

Defining Your Business Purpose

A good idea is not enough, however, to make your business dream a reality. You must be very specific about what you are setting out to do. Everyone gets sidetracked from time to time, but in business, your best track to success is a straight one. The only way to know where you are going is to define your idea and create a very specific business purpose at the beginning of your venture.

One illustration of the benefits of a clear, well-defined business purpose makes this point impressively. Ask yourself this question: What is the basic business purpose of the IBM Corporation? Making computers, you say? Developing office machines? Designing cards that provoke bending, stapling, and mutilation? Wrong. Those may be aspects of the business, but not its basic purpose. Each of those answers places a limit on the extent of IBM's reach.

As conceived by the founder, IBM's basic business purpose is twofold: "data processing and word processing." The concise, simple statement of purpose has helped this business achieve incredible success by defining its goals without restricting its potential. An international giant is probably different from the business proposition you have in mind. But, in this case, what works for one is also imperative for the other! You, too, need a clear, well-thought-out business purpose to help you reach your goals.

How does our remodeler friend, Gail, define her business purpose?

"My purpose is to provide renewed, affordable housing in the inner city." Her purpose is concise, precise, and unrestricted. Take plenty of time to formulate your purpose. When you feel you have a "tight" yet flexible goal, put it down in writing. We'll even supply the space:

Pat, the owner of fabric stores in Oregon and Idaho, offers this bit of advice that is both unique and very sound:

"List your business purpose on a 3-by-5 card. Actually write it down, and carry the card with you always. Get the card out occasionally and look at it, to avoid getting sidetracked. And don't seek the approval of others for your goal. It is yours and yours alone."

Several other women told us about their very specific business purposes and how having a purpose has helped them maintain their original direction. Linda and Gretchen grow and sell packaged herbs, potpourri, and herbal products. They told us:

"The purpose of our business is to promote the use of herbs and to educate people in the medicinal, aromatic, and culinary uses of herbs. We've watched another herbalist in our town grow and grow, providing herbs to discount stores and now even to nationwide mail-order houses. We've reached the point where we, too, could expand in such a way. But we have chosen to maintain our original course, as becoming bigger and bigger and more and more detached from our customers doesn't serve our business purpose."

Their purpose is clear and straightforward. It is definitely not merely the production of guest-room-closet sachets, and neither is it the promotion of quantity wholesale and mail-order herbs.

Setting Your Business Goals

Now that you have a good idea, are in touch with your personal goals, and have a well-defined business purpose, you are ready to begin listing some specific business goals. These goals are the commitments you make to yourself in order to achieve your business purpose. Listen to how Gail develops her goals in her remodeling business:

"All along I have had a one-year plan in my business. At the beginning of every year, I say, what do I want to have accomplished at the end of a year? Then I work backward and say, what do I have to have accomplished at the end of six months to reach that goal in a year? What do I have to do in the next three months to get to the six-month goal? What do I have to do next month? Next week? What do I need to start doing tomorrow? You set your goals, and then you move backward. I think a lot of people make the mistake of just trying to move forward without that firm end in mind. If you don't know what your specific business goal is, then how do you know how to get there?

"I set very firm time lines. Whether or not I achieve it, it gives me the goal to work on. Just saying that I would do it made me do it! I have always made strong commitments to myself, and it is interesting for me to read back over these goals—I keep them all in a file—because I look at them and see that every year, I actually do *more* than I set out to do. At the beginning of the year, it seems so impossible, what I wanted to achieve. But when I looked back, I had done it, and *more*, because just knowing what I wanted to accomplish, I knew what to work on. And when I did it, I had time left over to do something else."

Pat, the fabric-store owner who suggested that you carry a 3-by-5 card with your business purpose printed in bold letters at the top, also suggests that you use this same card to list your ever-changing business goals. At first, your goal list will seem endless: create a business plan, find a building to rent, attain a business license, get a baby-sitter, find a lawyer, order stock . . . But later, when your business is really underway, your 3-by-5 card may look like this:

Business Purpose:
To instill the methods of creative sewing in others.

Date Entered	Deadline	Goals
1–4	1–8	1. Enroll in community-college course on creative quilting.
1–4	1–10	2. Prepare a valentine display—design embroidered heart and sew calico valentine.
1–5	2–6	3. Contact new instructor and set up class times and agenda.
1–5	1–5	4. Reorder fabric numbers 246, 293, 682.

When you make up your card, include the date you entered the goal and a realistic deadline, which you may modify as you wish. The point of having business goals is to be constantly aware of them, always working to achieve them. Thus, your goal deadline may be for the week, the month, or even the year. And as you cross off achieved goals and fill up your card, start another card.

Keep the completed cards in your file, and when your business is really underway, you can look at these goals as mile markers to show you how far you've gone.

A bit of information may encourage you to take serious note of this advice on setting up your business purpose and your goals. The fabric shop owner who keeps her 3-by-5 card constantly updated has parlayed her $127 investment eight years ago into a million-dollar business today!

Gail, our remodeler, "couldn't stress enough the importance of planning day by day for success every day. Every night I write down the six most important things I have to do the next day. I number them in order of priority. Some of the things are personal things, and I try to focus on these one at a time. If I get distracted about everything in my life, then I can't get anything done. So I just work from one to the other, taking care of number one before I go on to number two on my list. A series of those successful days ends up with the achievement of the result.

"Sometimes I look ahead and say, how am I going to get through that next month? But if I refocus and just try to get through each day, pretty soon I will have gotten through a whole month of days, and my business is still going! Without plans, I would have ended up the month still stewing. Focus on goals, and take care of first ones first, without avoiding them. That's what will make it for any business owner."

Having a thriving business and a successful personal life as well proves that this method of planning for success works for Gail, and we feel that it will work for you, also. Gail mentioned to us that the result of careful planning and goal-setting for her is a business much wider in scope than she could have originally imagined:

"Each year there are bigger challenges, hurdles that I haven't yet faced. They seem just as hard as my initial challenges. But if I were to go back and look at where I was when I got my first house—right now I have about ten properties in various stages of construction—all the work and all the hassles I've had to face up to, I might have been afraid even to start. That's why I think it's good to keep *little* goals in mind. Because if you think of the *whole* thing, it may seem impossible to achieve."

Taking Time Out for a Little Self-Analysis

Every woman we talked to suggested one or more probing questions that she felt other women should ask themselves before they embark on their own business adventures. Before we go any further, then, we'd like you to take a little test. Ask yourself some questions, and be honest in your answers. The questions are compiled from the suggestions we gathered from other businesswomen. They represent points that these women felt were essential to the operation of a successful business, and in some cases, they are the result of lessons learned the hard way. As you complete your answers, you may be surprised to note abilities you didn't realize you possessed. You may also find your problem areas. Owning your own business will be one of the most rewarding things you've ever done, yet it definitely won't be easy. By answering these questions truthfully, you can take stock of the abilities and talents you possess and learn the areas in which you must compensate for your weaknesses.

After each question, we give you some of the answers, or solutions, that other women already in business have devised to cope with these specific issues. By knowing the reasons behind each question—the problems, the discoveries, the means that were used to rectify the situation—you will be able to benefit from other women's experiences. There is a movement today among businesswomen across the country to organize an old-girl network—a system offering assistance, guidance, information sharing, and morale boosting among all women in business. The basis of the network is that the established and experienced women will show the way to newcomers in the business world by serving as role models and by offering their experience and advice whenever helpful. Over one hundred women, from businesses as different as delicatessens and dance studios, answered our questions and proved that the network is functioning. Heed what the network has to share with you in clarifying and developing the points on our questionnaire:

Testing Your Strengths and Weaknesses

Question #1. Do you have the time it takes to run a business? You must be very realistic about how much time your business will take. We asked the respondents whether the business takes more time than they originally thought it would. The overwhelming response was *yes!*

"A business cannot be a sideline," one woman told us, "and once you start, your time is not your own."

A print-shop owner advised us; "We've always worked over forty hours a week. We are getting more business now—but we used to work this much because of our mistakes and our inefficiency! One goal I had when I started this business was to allow good political material to be published. Second, I wanted to print. I find that maybe 5 percent of my time goes into political printing; 10 percent into other enjoyable printing projects; and 50 percent into running the business—a prospect I had never imagined."

Several women involved in "creative" businesses caution that once your hobby becomes your business, you have little time left to pursue the craft yourself for the fun of it. A yarn-shop owner confesses to returning many partially worked stitchery kits to the shop for the salespeople to complete.

We suggest that you realistically chart a week of your time in the following chart:

	M	T	W	T	F	S	S
9–10:00							
10–11:00							
11–12:00							
12–1:00							
1–2:00							
2–3:00							
3–4:00							
4–5:00							
5–6:00							

Now, decide where you can make some big holes of time in your week by deleting activities of lesser importance than your business. If you are unwilling to give up your exercise class or the baseball team you play on in the summer, you'd better reconsider. One shop owner told us quite frankly:

"A business is like a new baby—it requires as much of your

time. I've been in business for several years now, and I've seen women's businesses come and go because some women are not willing to give up enough of their time."

Question #2. For those who have family obligations—do you have the time to devote to both family and business?

"Men don't have to worry so much about integrating their lives. They never stop to think, am I going to have a business or am I going to get married and have a family! I am striving to become an integrated person, where I don't have to separate my life. I am trying to take some of the things I have learned about managing my business and apply them to managing my private life as well. I am trying for some kind of balance. I made up my mind that I would not succeed in business at the expense of my private life. That's where I think a lot of men go wrong. They are successful only in their businesses."

Whether you are married with no children, married with children, or single with children, balancing the time you spend with family and business is one of the most pressing problems you must face.

A Corvallis, Oregon, woman has done everything in the operation of a small business from sweeping floors to managing government contracts. Jean is a partner in a consulting engineering firm and manager of a manufacturing firm. She notes that "the demands of small business, small children, and a husband often drive a woman up the wall and back into the kitchen!" In order to avoid this, Jean suggests making definite time commitments for your husband, your child, and your business—and then sticking to them! "You've got to recognize your different life phases, enjoy them, and not fight them. Do what you have committed yourself to doing, don't look back, and then go on to the next thing."

"Avoid becoming a 'role hypochondriac,'" Jean told us. "Don't worry about everything all the time. Just do your own thing, in your own managerial style."

Family obligations were mentioned time and time again as a difficult obstacle to overcome when organizing a new business. But where there's a will, there's a way, and there are many ways to manage a family and a business, too. We noted three different methods that women commonly choose.

Accustom your family to changes. Get out your time chart and study it carefully. As a family-oriented woman, your activities probably reflect a good deal of family responsibility you have assumed. Many of us have accustomed our families to laundry, cleaning, and meal services. But life is full of changes. Why not provide them with some? Replace your Saturday-morning bread-baking sessions with a frozen, thaw-and-bake counterpart. Put more responsibility on the shoulders of other family members. You will be amazed to see how well your family can do without you.

Above all, lower your standards. Everyone knows that the world is not going to come to an end if the house isn't dusted or your family has to rummage through the laundry room one morning for some clean underwear. One woman told us:

"My husband has the illusion that if the bed is made and the dishes are done, the house is clean. That is a good enough guideline for me. It takes me twenty minutes each morning to 'clean the house.'"

Finding day care for small children and arranging transportation for school-age children with after-school activities is always a problem. As another woman said,

"Your child has Brownies and dancing lessons. But you can't very well hire someone to come in to mind the store so that you can run your kids here and there. Those are things that you have to work out—and it can be done.

"I can remember a time when I thought to myself frantically, how am I going to get a baby-sitter? Just *that* was too much for me to take. Because whoever came to baby-sit had to be perfect. I thought it was impossible, but I found out it's not. You pick up the telephone, call the newspaper, place an ad, and you might have to interview fifty people—but you will find somebody. Then that's over with and you go on to tackle another problem. Those things used to seem monstrous to me. They are now just little things compared to the newer problems that are always cropping up."

Another woman suggested that you locate your business near your child's school so that you are accessible after school. This brings us to our next way to manage family and a business, too.

Set limitations on the infringement of your business on your family life.

"Before we started, we set limits on the business development.

We agreed to end the venture when it either infringed on our family life or when it wasn't fun anymore."

Another way to avoid too much interruption in your family life is to get together enough partners to spread out the hours to everyone's satisfaction. We spoke to several three- and four-member partnerships that did just that. Three women who operate a quilt shop together offered:

"None of us puts the shop before our family, and we each arrange our schedules so our family life is uninterrupted." One member of a four-partner needlepoint shop told us that they each work one day a week, plus one Saturday a month. They hire a woman to be there every Friday, and thus they are able to keep the shop open six days a week.

Still another alternative to putting your family on the sidelines is to establish business hours that are suitable to both your family and your customers. An antique-shop owner converted an old guest house on her property into a store:

"All of my customers know my hours are Wednesday and Thursday from 1 to 4. They know I will always be there at those times, or if I must be away, I will arrange for someone to watch the shop. And if a customer calls me ahead of time and asks to come on a different hour or day, I'm always flexible."

Not everyone can have her shop right next to her house or has such low overhead that she can afford to be so flexible. But if you do choose to have limited hours, make sure you establish yourself in a business that does not require you to maintain specific, regulated hours. For example, mall shops are usually required to maintain certain hours and in many cases, to be open on Sundays, too.

Taking work home at night is another way your business can infringe upon personal and family time. Two owners of a "soft porn" shop discussed the difficulties they encounter in avoiding doing business at night. One of the owners complained, "The other night at a party, someone started to discuss sex. I just had to say, please, let's not talk shop!"

Make your family part of the business. The perfect way to avoid concentrating on your business to the exclusion of your family is to combine the two. Not only will you educate your children to the ways of the business world, but you will gain some confidants who share your experiences and relate to what you are doing. A restaurant–gift shop owner told us how her combined family effort was literally the foundation of her business:

"My business has never interfered with my family life, because the entire family is involved in the running of the restaurant. We live in a room off the dining room, and we use the restaurant kitchen as our own after we close.

"This has been a family project from the beginning. We owned this old barn, and we had used it for 4-H projects as the kids were growing up. After my divorce, I decided to open a business in it.

"Before we poured concrete for the foundation, we had to scoop the manure out with a tractor. I'll never forget the day the cement truck came to pour the floor and foundation. My older son was gone, and I watched in horror as my eighth-grade son and his friends spilled wheelbarrows full of cement all over in an attempt to pour the foundation. By the end of the day, we were covered with cement, but the foundation was laid."

And the owner of a day-care center tells it this way:

"My children have grown up with my business and they've never complained about it, probably because it's all they've known. Every day they help with the other children, the dishes, and the cleaning up after the younger children leave. My girl has always had a baby crib in her room, and my boy has always shared his toys with the other children. And my husband, Rick, is very understanding. He's very helpful, and when he comes home after a hard day's work, he really doesn't mind the mess—play dough all over the floor. . . . I think it would be very difficult to do what I'm doing without my family."

Such family participation as this, however, is not always possible, due to the ages of your children or your family's own interests or abilities. Guilt about spending less time with the family is often not easily soothed away. There will always be a self-righteous mother-in-law or neighbor who doesn't believe in "baby tenders." You love your family, but you must also be in touch with your own needs. Children learn by copying, and as they see you pursue an interest of your own, they, too, may learn to follow their own independent interests.

One woman told us how she soothed her guilt feelings.

"I let one thing set a precedent over my shop. When one of my sons is in a ball game, we close up everything and go!"

We asked how other women handled these feelings.

"I realize now, through the help of a psychiatrist, that the guilt feelings I had about neglecting my family led to a great inconsistency in my methods of discipline. To compensate for the time I spent away from my boys, I let them get away with murder. My psychiatrist gave me one great bit of advice: 'Never feel guilty for doing something you want to do.'"

"I suffered pangs of guilt that first year. I couldn't imagine how my family could manage without me. To my amazement, they managed quite well. My husband and children were very supportive, and they all learned to handle most of the things I thought only I could do."

Question #3. If you are married, will your husband give you the support you need to operate a business?

"My husband has always been very supportive. I consider him my full partner because he let me put a mortgage on everything we owned and let me take all of our savings when I started my business."

An overwhelming majority of the women we spoke with credited their husbands with being a contributing factor in the success of their businesses. Aside from offering moral support, many husbands assisted their wives by running the household, doing the bookkeeping, and even tending shop occasionally. Yet some women complained bitterly about their husbands' lack of interest and support.

Husbands may not appreciate being classified as problems, but the women we spoke with mentioned them often enough that we can't ignore the comments we heard or the general impressions we formed. Though feelings on the husband's role in women's business varied in shades from "rosy glow" to "maniacal magenta," one woman put it memorably when she commented:

"My husband wasn't very happy when my business began taking more and more of my time. But no one likes giving up a slave."

As more women opt for a business of their own, they—like others who choose to combine marriage and family with a career—are often faced with the question, does a successful career spell the end of a marriage?

In our discussions with career women, we learned of many changes that occurred in their marriages, some causing problems, others allowing for a beneficial growth in the family role of each partner. Nearly all of the married women we spoke with began their businesses with support and encouragement from their husbands. Many husbands even contributed to the establishment of the business, either financially or physically (hammering, hauling), as well as offering tremendous emotional support. Yet, surprisingly, it was often these most-supportive mates who soon grew to resent their wives' business involvement.

"At first, my husband was all for it. I sincerely think he thought we would go under, but now that we are a success, he does not and cannot share my enthusiasm. I think it infringes on his ego. I absolutely love this, and I hate housework. You can clean the bathroom and clean the bathroom—and it will still get dirty tomorrow. I think that if I were as excited about my cooking and cleaning as I am about the shop, he wouldn't mind it so much."

Let's look at some of the things that were mentioned most often as causing changes in the marriage:

Time was often cited as a problem, or, more accurately, the lack of time: time that used to be spent, for example, ironing husband's shirts or taking spur-of-the-moment weekends at the coast.

"My husband complained about the time my crafts business was taking. But the first time I paid for something out of my earnings that really helped him out—I had our new yard landscaped—my 'craft' suddenly became my 'work,' and he stopped complaining."

A psychotherapist told us that marriages work well when both partners recognize the need of each to pursue personal interests. Your interests don't need to be the same; it just *helps* if they are.

"My husband gave me a lecture this morning—the same one I've heard dozens of times. He was making a list of things to do today, and he said if I would only sit down and make out a list, I might accomplish something, too, like he does. The thing that he can never understand is that without a list in hand, dictating what to do next, he might have time to stop and talk to some of his patients. I like to react to people, talk to them. We have a regular ministry going here at the shop with all the women who talk to us about their problems. He doesn't have time for that."

A successful business and a divorce don't necessarily go hand in hand. But, as one woman explained:

"I don't feel that success in your own business necessarily leads to a divorce. But I do feel that your own financial success, and security, will help dissolve a relationship that wasn't satisfying before."

Women who seek to change their personal life-style drastically through a total, even excessive, involvement in business may possibly be reacting to a husband who has always put his own interests and his career in a role of utmost importance. Author Marilyn French, in *The Women's Room,* has described such husbands and the wives who serve them:

"How convenient to have a whole class of people who give up their lives for other people! How nice, while you're out doing things that serve your ego, to have somebody home washing the bathroom floor and picking up your dirty underwear! And never, never cooking brussels sprouts because you don't like them."

With newfound personal and economic freedom, a successful woman may be tempted to look for someone to serve *her* ego for a change (not to mention cook her brussels sprouts!). And if a power struggle arises between a husband and wife over whose career is the most important, some kind of change is inevitable. Hopefully, the changes will be the kind that will enlarge and enhance the relationship.

A divorce which takes place while a business is struggling to establish itself can be devastating. We received some good advice along these lines from voices of experience:

"I don't think I would be in business today if it weren't for my ex-husband. He saw my potential and pushed me all the way to use it. But our divorce was the beginning of untold problems. My first and foremost advice to any married woman who is in business and considering divorce is that if you have any debts together, make sure they are paid."

And, "Starting a new business is fun and exciting when you have a husband's salary behind you to carry the family on while you make your first mistakes. But a divorce at the time my business was just beginning forced me to be on my own, to support myself and my children. It is one thing to do something for fun, and another to make a living at it. It takes a lot of $5.95 and $6.95 gift-shop sales to make a day's wages."

We've mentioned these problems because our conversations made us unable to ignore them. This is certainly not to say that all businesswomen will suffer marital problems. Far from it. Many beautiful relationships grow even better when "the baby" arrives.

"When my business was first getting started, I was working out of my own home. I often found myself up till all hours, slaving away in my kitchen, completing the next day's orders. And while I was slaving, my husband was in the basement being an 'artist.' I resented it very much. Now that I'm really in business with a bakery that's not my own kitchen, and making a good living, I find that this pressure is off. It doesn't matter anymore if he works or if he doesn't. I'm making enough money for us, and it's soothing to come home at night to my family. I think I'm falling in love again!"

What? A note of optimism? Of course! The changes that are coming about with the women's movement and the rise of women's businesses across the country are bound to offer many rewards. Women who are successful and independent, both financially and emotionally, are free in some ways to change their expectations of men in general and of their husbands in particular. By achieving satisfaction and security on their own, aren't they a little less likely to demand these things from their mates? And when husbands no longer feel obligated to be the pillars of family strength, security, success, and prosperity, then maybe they will be free to develop, too—in new and satisfying ways.

Question #4. Can your family survive a financial failure?

Any new undertaking will involve additional expenses, and you can't count on income from the new business to offset them, at least for quite awhile. As one woman said, "It's hard to start a new business and expect to live on it!" Many others echoed this woman's remark. In fact, in nearly every business we surveyed, we found the profits were reinvested *entirely* for at *least* the first two years, and often much longer. One woman, in business for twenty years and now working on her "second million," confides that, in retrospect, the first fifteen years in business were "educational," and that all the profits have been made in the last five years!

Plan for your business to survive for at least two years without any profits being removed. It takes money to grow a business, and if you take funds out for your personal expenses, you cut off the nourishment that a growing concern requires.

If you're married, better warn your husband to forget that dream of his of retiring early now that you've set up business. And if you're single and supporting yourself, plan to do what nearly all the woman we surveyed have done—take the smallest possible draw when you have to and reinvest the rest of your profits to build your business. By the end of your first two to five years, you'll have earned yourself the right to a salary (maybe even a bonus!).

Also consider that there is some risk involved in every business venture. You put up your money, and you take the chance of losing, or multiplying it. Several successful women told us that they never ventured more than they could afford to lose, and as their experience accumulated, so did their money. A rule of thumb to consider: Never put up more than you or your family can afford to lose.

The next series of questions concerns personal qualities that may help make or break your business.

Faced with the prospect that between 75 and 90 percent of all business ventures go bankrupt in the first three years (bankers and government advisers all emphatically stress these discouraging figures), it *can't* be considered a waste of time to do as much planning and evaluation of *yourself* as possible. In fact, we've learned that 42 percent of the businesses that fail do so because of what professionals call managerial incompetence—an inability to manage time, people, money, and records.

Answer the following questions very truthfully in order to assess your own special qualities and abilities. You may find that you are more businesslike than you think.

Question #5. Are you willing to work very hard?

Remember that "burning desire to pursue your special interest" that was an element of your "good idea"? During your first years of business, expect your life to be inundated with business details not only during business hours but after hours, as well.

"I met several Los Angeles designers before I started my own fashion-design business, when I was just designing fabrics. I'll never forget the strongest impression I got from all the women designers I met, and that was that they had worked, and were working, *very hard*. I've never met another cross section of people where it shows so much, in their faces and their eyes. I remember reading once in *Women's Wear Daily* where Scott Barrie, a

Seventh Avenue designer, was talking about the pressure of the fashion business, how it never lets up, and it's very difficult work. He said sometimes when he's sitting in his office, and a messenger boy comes in and brings him his lunch, or a package, he looks at the boy and envies him for the ease of his life, the calmness, the simplicity. Then Barrie laughed and said he would never give up the excitement or the creativity of his work. But I know what he was talking about—the messenger boy."

Other women reported to us the tremendous work that is involved in running your own business.

"I teach dancing six or more hours a day," said a young dancing school owner, who added insult to our already imagined aching muscles by saying, "I also attend classes myself to keep in the best possible physical shape."

"There really are no part-time businesses, even if open-for-business hours are limited."

"As the owner of a business, you have to be prepared to sweep floors, work overtime to get the job out, manage people, collect past-due bills (not my favorite job), sell your product, and anything else that needs to be done."

Question #6. Are you able to organize your time?

No one can tout the merits of organization like two housewives who have made organization their business. They have developed a system of housekeeping that is based on their motto: We change lives with three-by-fives. Housekeeping chores, menus, and other responsibilities are all systematized in a card file. You are a prime candidate for their course if you spend a lot of time doing what you like to do and not what you need to do. You might find it useful to spend some extra time on organization. Here are some tips:

a. Try to figure out for yourself what your time is really worth, in terms of dollars and cents, in your business. Then you will be able to allot time for different projects according to relative importance.

b. Plan to tackle your most difficult problems at your peak time of the day. For instance, if bookkeeping is your downfall, don't put it off until the end of the day, or the week, when you are already tired and not working at your best. Organize your time so that your bookkeeping tasks are handled when you are feeling and performing at your best—possibly first thing in the morning.

c. Vary the jobs that you plan to undertake each day. Nothing makes you tired faster than doing the same thing over and over again.

Question #7. Are you able to organize other people and delegate authority?

"I had never considered myself good at organization and organizing other people, and when I was first faced with scheduling employees and delegating authority, I thought I might not be able to handle it. Then it came to me that I had been doing these things all along at home—organizing a husband, a house, and six kids. Actually, I was pretty good at it!"

The owner of a bookstore told us, "Everything is going well, but I get very resentful that I am working so many hours. I need to work on delegating responsibility to someone else. I sell best, keep track of the inventory best, display best, etcetera, and I don't want to give someone else a try. But at the same time, sitting here all day and some days into the night can just about drive you up the wall. I don't think you should work more than five days a week."

The owner of a successful restaurant delegates responsibility in her business so that "everyone who works here feels responsible. I think that has led to a low turnover of help in my business. We don't have a manager, or any set chain of command. I think, as an employer, that it is really important for employees to feel that they have control of their existence at work. They have certain responsibilities; they are not just somebody's pawns. And when I am not available, I've found that my employees can make really good decisions if they have to. They enjoy taking responsibility when I am away."

The ability to delegate authority is essential. If you have never held a position where you've needed this skill, don't despair. In Chapter Four, on page 182, we offer some suggestions on handling this.

Question #8. Are you good at keeping records?

If you don't know the answer to this question, here's a quick miniquiz to help you find out.

POP QUIZ

	Yes	No
Is my checkbook usually a disaster of errors?	______	______

If you answered no, then you're probably a record keeper. And if you have been known to spend hours laboring over a five-cent error in your bank statement, then you are most definitely a record keeper! On the other hand, if your answer was yes, you need help. Either hire a bookkeeper or CPA, or find a partner who can answer no to the question (and, better yet, one who searches for five-cent errors in her bank statement!). Your business must have clear, accurate, and up-to-date records.

Question #9. Are you patient enough to deal with employees, customers, and suppliers?

Remember, the customer is always right, especially because it's the customer who is paying your rent and buying your groceries. You must be considerate and understanding of your customers and their needs.

One woman told us that "some psychic ability to read the minds of customers would be extremely helpful!"

How do you know if you will be able to handle these contacts successfully? Examine your past. We're sure you'll find you have had some experience in organizing and directing others, perhaps in a political group, on a committee, or in past work experience. Use all your experience to your advantage. If your previous job was that of a homemaker, you've had plenty of experience dealing with emergencies, directing others to do their job, and coping with more than one thing at a time.

Question #10. Are you able to meet deadlines?

Think about it. Were you always late turning in your school term papers? Do you run out to do your Christmas shopping the day before Christmas? You must be reliable at meeting whatever deadlines your business entails. One woman with a typesetting business advises others interested in entering her line of work: "Think it over. . . . It is a pressure industry, deadline-oriented, error-prone, requiring the ability to work with all kinds of people. It requires someone absolutely dedicated to doing the job right . . . if it takes twelve times!"

In order to handle deadlines successfully, you must be efficient at *allocating your time*. You must learn to:

a. Assess the jobs and deadlines that are ahead and place them in order of priority.

b. Know your own strengths and abilities. Handle the toughest jobs when you are at your best, and delegate other responsibilities to those who can handle them efficiently.

c. Avoid putting things off until tomorrow or taking work home that you cannot finish during working hours.

d. Budget your time carefully. If you find that outside activities or too much socializing are cutting into your business time, make the necessary adjustments.

e. Improve your efficiency by constant reevaluation of your achievements. Did you achieve last week's goals? Did you meet your last deadline? If not, why not? What can you do to improve next time? Can your schedule be adjusted, can your operation be simplified or consolidated? Are you bogged down with too many little details, attempting "perfection"?

Question #11. Can you make decisions?

As one businesswoman told us, "Business could be very simply defined as: one decision after another." Are you able to make quick decisions? Or does it take you a week of Sundays and the advice of six friends to help you come to a decision—and then you're still not sure you made the right one?

"The problems and frustrations in running your own business are great, and you must learn to think on the spot and become more assertive, rather than turning a problem over to the boss. There is no one to pass the buck to. But the rewards are also greater at the end of a good day or when you make the right decision on the spur of the moment."

Another woman told us, "You cannot succeed in business if you can't make clear business decisions. I went through about two months of turmoil about what to do with a key employee who was having personal problems and couldn't function in her job. She was hurting my business, but I felt very sympathetic toward her. Still, I was paying her a lot of money, and she wasn't doing her job. I had to face up to the fact that she had to go because my business was faltering. It was a real growing experience to deal with this problem in the most humane way possible. To realize that if I truly wanted to be successful, I could not allow a situation like this to destroy everything I had worked for was a very clear business decision. I think a lot of us women operate on a personality level; we are not task-oriented enough. We are person-oriented; we allow personalities to get in the way of achievement. You need a happy balance."

If you are not a quick decision maker and are wary of on-the-spot decisions, sit down and gather all the facts on the issue and make yourself a list full of pros and cons to show you your options in black and white. When you've weighed all the elements, make your decisions with confidence. You'll find that taking the necessary action is easier than worrying about the decision.

Question #12. Are you self-confident?

"I find that attitudes can really help you or get in your way. I believe that you can achieve whatever you want to achieve, and you are who you think you are. If you want to become successful, you've got to behave today as though you are the person you want to be. Behave as though you are already successful, and you will be. You must be confident. People don't achieve a certain attitude because they are successful. They are successful because they have a certain attitude."

One woman described the development of a sense of self-confidence like this: "It's like snow—it has to build up, layer upon layer. And sometimes when you have a three-foot buildup, it can melt away in seconds flat under certain conditions. But you just have to build it up again. Your knowledge of the field of business that you've chosen gives you that first half-inch of snow that you need to build on."

And one woman who confessed great shyness told us: "To me, the most important quality a woman must have when going into business is self-confidence. At least *act* like you have it, whether you really do or not. The salesmen you deal with, as well as your customers, will appreciate you and respect you more if you handle yourself with confidence."

Another woman told us: "If you have confidence in yourself, you have everything."

We mentioned earlier some advice that was passed along to us by Jean, a partner in a consulting engineering firm. Jean also told us of the image that she feels *limits* women in their accomplishments: "Be pleasant, be thoughtful, and obey the Girl Scout laws!" To achieve success, she offers five rules to follow:

a. Women can do anything they set their minds to do.

b. Everything you've ever done in your entire life is training for business.

c. You are never too old to start a new career or to add to an old business.

d. You are never too young to end one career and start a new one.

e. The best security is to adopt your own style—don't follow the trends of others!

(And forget about those Girl Scout laws!)

And, finally, we were advised, "Learn to say, 'I'm the best!' Of course, you want to hear of people who are better, so that you can learn from them. But it's important to tell yourself that you are good instead of being very demure and saying, 'Oh, now, it's nothing.' That old syndrome—'Oh, anybody could have done it'—is all wrong. Say, 'Yes, I *am* very good at what I do.'"

Question #13. Are you able to persevere?

We've learned that hand-in-hand with confidence goes perseverance. Most of the successful women we talked with had started with a dream, and until their dream came true, they would not rest. In the midst of all this persevering, many businesswomen have also had to cope with the problem of waiting. Orders that don't arrive, lawyers who go on vacation, skies that begin to drizzle as soon as the house is sanded and ready to paint! Running a business is fraught with delays, and the persevering businesswoman learns to turn her waiting time into useful and productive time. We heard many such stories.

When the building where their sandwich shop flourished was torn down, two entrepreneurs searched for a new location. When their classes reached a peak with four hundred enrolled for a special seminar—and they found the entire area was sold out of the file boxes they needed for each enrollee—two other business owners wired to the East Coast for an emergency shipment. And when the box of one hundred extralarge, home-baked, easily broken peanut-butter cookies was dropped on the way to the car for delivery, another female entrepreneur went back to her mixer and oven. But her flock of Rhode Island Reds pecked peanut butter cookie crumbs for a week.

Your perseverance may pay off in a surprising number of ways.

Question #14. Are you optimistic?

Self-confidence, perseverance and optimism go together. They have a positive effect on everything they touch. Business certainly can't always be good, but as one veteran businesswoman told us: "I've been in the hobby, mail-order business for thirty years, and had never had a true slump in sales until three years ago. Some less-experienced businessperson might have panicked, but I looked at the positive side. I thought about all the income tax the government was going to have to give back to me that year!"

Keep in mind that your own optimistic or pessimistic attitude is a good indication of the measure of success you will achieve.

Question #15. Have you had previous business experience?

We're told that previous business experience is a must, even if it is in a field totally unrelated to your new enterprise.

"Women's worst enemy in business is their lack of training as managers and their general lack of business experience. Still, everyone has more training than she thinks. Getting an entire meal to the table on time is the ultimate in scheduling. And knowing how to get along with people is your best training for personnel handling."

A bookstore owner advises: "On-the-job training is very important. A couple of years' experience in a bookshop similar to the one you wish to operate would be invaluable."

And another shop owner told us: "When I was a teenager I was forced to do all the record keeping for my family's business. I hated it. But I realize now that it was a wonderful forerunner to what I am having to deal with now."

In considering a business of your own, why not try working part-time in the field you are interested in? You'll get firsthand experience, and you'll be able to watch behind-the-scenes operations that you may not have been aware of. A banking executive advised that you should try to "be the most valuable employee in the place. Be curious. Learn the history of the business, why things happen, all aspects of the trade." When you've learned all there is to know in your particular department, this woman advises moving into another area of the business to further your familiarity with the operation. Working for someone else as you learn the business has two more advantages: First of all, you'll be getting paid while you learn, and you can save your earnings to put toward your goal. Second, and even more important, you may find out that the reality of this kind of business is not what you expect—you might hate it!

One apparent difference between women and men business owners is their education. A college degree is definitely not a prerequisite for owning a successful business. But many of the women offering their advice to us did have college diplomas, and many even had advanced degrees. Yet most of these degrees were in the liberal arts and not in business fields. We spoke with former nurses, certified teachers, librarians, women with law degrees—even the owner of a greenhouse–plant shop operation who, though she may think talking to plants can be beneficial, did not feel her degree in speech and hearing therapy was a special advantage.

Many aspiring and educated women are handicapped by their lack of financial know-how and their inexperience in banking, bookkeeping, and running a business in general. The traditionally male courses of study—math, science, and business—must become traditions in a woman's education, as well, if she is to compete successfully in the business community.

Question #16. Do you have a sense of what motivates people to buy?

"In the nine years I've been in business, I've learned to appeal to every fad that comes along in the antique business. Collecting old kitchen utensils, crocks, crates, old wooden boxes . . . I don't know what's coming up next. The recession, I guess!"

An artist told us, "Artists are often just familiar with the production of artwork. It is very hard to sell your product commercially when you are not used to peddling. That is why I think lots of arts and crafts shops come and go so quickly. Though the crafts are good, the owners of the shops are not good businesswomen. They don't know how to promote and sell."

Carol, the owner of a Gig Harbor, Washington, art gallery, learned from experience that, though the gallery catered to fine art, it was the craft items (added though her artistic husband felt they weren't really "art") that people were buying most often. Though crafts are not the primary focus of the gallery, the owner recognized that they were a good selling feature. "After starting the gallery with only two hundred dollars, the crafts became our bread and butter. They still are."

Motivating a customer to make a purchase is a major consideration in any business. Because business success depends on successful sales, we have devoted a large section of Chapter Four to the problems of sales promotion.

Question #17. Will your personality complement your business?

As one fabric-shop owner told us: "I only buy the fabrics that I myself like. I don't try to please everyone's taste, only my own. I figure if something doesn't sell, I may have to take it home and make curtains out of it, so I'd better like it!"

On the other hand, one woman who bought out another woman's delicatessen told us that the former owner could hardly muster up a smile; the frown on her face seemed to be natural. And when the new owner took over, she found that business picked up immediately. She told us: "The former owner trained me, so the sandwiches are no different. I get the feeling that my customers come to eat my sandwiches *and* they come to see and chat with me for a minute or two."

Will your personality complement your business? By knowing who you are and what your business is, you can be true to both. You don't change your life-style with every passing fad—don't change your business image, either. Your personality will be reflected as much in your style of doing business as in your choice of wares. One woman suggested that "anyone considering going into business should think long and hard about her own personality. Be careful about locking yourself into something that is limiting to your own personal freedom—a franchise, for instance. If you like something that is set up, spelled out, and that makes you comfortable, then maybe that would be a good thing. But if you like to play around with something, experiment a lot, then think about something that is not going to impose how's and when's. You need to know that about yourself before you start."

Another element of your personality may influence your business success. How well do you work with men?

When you consider that 95 percent of the businesses in this country are owned and managed by men, you can see whom you will most often be dealing with in your business—and who most of your competition will be. Bankers, attorneys, suppliers—they will commonly be men, and though equal opportunity has been legislated, it has not always meant a change in attitude. Your success will often be judged by the values that are set by men.

When your dealings are primarily with men, experience will enlighten you as to what is your best approach. Some advice that was offered:

"My best advice is, if you can do it, always be your own person. Always stand your ground, with an extreme amount of politeness. If you don't lose your temper—if you can be calmer than they are—you can work it out. I think a real problem is that women are often trying to *prove* themselves to men. You should try to overcome that impulse."

Another woman suggested, "Be either positive or silent. It's better to be neutral than to be negative. When you're playing men's games, you have to learn to bluff. But never demean yourself."

Another woman had a unique approach to the problem of dealing with men: "I have quite frankly used a man to do specific business transactions for me—phone calls to banks and attorneys, for example. I have him help because I know that a man can often be more effective than a woman. A man can often slide right through situations that a woman cannot. Aggression is expected and accepted in men. However, there is absolutely no reason a woman should not be every bit as successful as a man, if not more so. The majority of the customers I sell to are women. My advantage is that I am a woman, too."

One woman noted what she felt to be a man's natural advantage over women in business: "Men tend to look and say, see what I can gain. Women look and see what they might lose."

Although there are women competing in male-dominated fields who feel that a portion of the satisfaction they derive from their success is that no men were involved, there are others who disagree.

"Too many women in business make the mistake of feeling that they do not need to heed and follow the advice of men. They won't take a man's advice, even though men are the ones with the business experience. I think it would profit any woman to have a male adviser in her business. They always have a different point of view and are often less emotional. Women, I feel, have an advantage with their stamina and resiliency; they have lasting strength. But men have temporary strength—they have quick resources of strength. It would be difficult to beat a combination of both."

If you have chosen to start a business in a typically male field—carpentry, painting, automobile repair, trucking—your problems of adjustment may be just what you make of them. You may even encounter some advantages!

A woman house painter told us she got one job "because a man contractor wanted me for a minority program. I got another job from a woman especially because she was interested in helping women in nontraditional roles. Some people say to me, 'Do you make enough to get by?' I think a question like that is a form of discrimination. When a man says to me, 'Are you any good?' I say, 'Of course I am. I wouldn't be doing this if I weren't good at it.' You just have to hustle and feel confident."

"Dealing with men almost constantly is a disadvantage," the owner of a tavern told us, "because men are used to dealing with other men. When they find themselves working with a woman, they often try to 'protect.' For example, when I go to the bank and say I need $6,000, my banker will say in a fatherly tone, 'Now look, Sandy. . . .' He wouldn't bother with that if I were a man."

Again, recognizing your own personality, handling yourself with confidence, and doing your job well are most important to your business success. The quality of your work will receive much more notice than the fact that, "Hey, it's funny to meet a lady mechanic." Or a lady plumber. Or . . .

Question #18. Are you willing to take a risk?

Often the women we talked to said they were unable to explain how they had achieved success. "It was like falling off a log," one said. Another commented, "It was just one of those days when you go ahead and make that phone call." But, in listening to their stories, we found it was much more than chance that led these women to succeed; each of them had the ability to consciously—and confidently—take a risk; not risking everything, but risking something, with confidence in her intuition every step of the way.

"Basically, I'm a gambler. I like pinball. You have to be willing to take a chance. It's a game. Knowing when to lay your cards out at the right time. Knowing where and when to invest. You may have to lose money to learn, but once you learn, you're on your way."

"I believe in me—the only thing I know. I know I don't have to succeed. If I don't succeed, I can learn from my experience. You've got nowhere to go but the sky, and you'll never get there, or ever know if you *could* get there, unless you try. If you really want something, there is a way to get it. But it has got to come from you. Nobody is going to help you."

The owner of a weaving studio with twenty years of business experience expressed it this way: "It never hurts to try. Don't be discouraged. If you want it badly enough, you can win. And the more women in business who succeed make it easier for those who follow."

For a single woman without the advantage of a husband's backup income, the risk can be even greater. One woman we spoke with was on the verge of taking an outside job, not only to support her family but to support her business, as well!

Feel that the risks are too imposing? Look at them another way, as one businesswoman advised us: "To me, a business is like a new Cadillac. Thinking that way makes the whole business seem less serious. Because if you buy a new Cadillac and you wreck it, so what? It's too bad, but you can buy a new car someday. If you buy a business and lose it, so what? It does not leave a mark on you. It's too bad, but the important thing is that you tried. By even trying, you're ahead of the next person. It's a risk, but take it. The money that you've spent, and may lose, will not buy you that much in your lifetime. But it could *make* you a lot of money, and it can bring you a lot of personal satisfaction. A lot of happiness. Like a new Cadillac."

2 The Plan

You've covered some very important ground so far: You have analyzed your personal goals and have come up with a good idea. You've defined your business purpose and set some specific business goals. And you've taken time out for some very crucial self-analysis. Now you must formulate a plan that not only tells you where you are going but also what to expect when you get there! Two partners we spoke with drew up a fifty-three-page booklet of their business plan. Other women tried to make it with a plan just in their heads. But one of our advisers stressed to us, "A plan in your head is only an idea. It is not a plan until it is written down."

"I wrote down my original business plan, and I still have it, three years later. It's very basic, but it still is amazingly clear. I have not changed my basic goals or what I wanted to do. It still rings true. You have to focus; you have to force yourself to write it down. After I wrote down my plan, I showed my plan to people whose opinions I respected. They would give me feedback on it, and then I'd rewrite it. I perfected it until it was pretty tight."

No one knows the problems that lead to business failure better than a banker. And if you intend to secure a bank loan to finance your new business, you'll need to convince your banker that your business will succeed. A well-thought-out, neatly typed business plan covering every aspect of your intended operation will help convince him or her. Your plan need not be complicated. We've drawn up a guide to follow that is simple and to the point. It helps break down your plans into those five w's you learned in journalism class: what, who, where, when, why, and how, and how much.

MY BUSINESS

(Be sure to use business name)

WHAT: My business purpose.
Pull out the 3 × 5 card you filled out with your business purpose on it and copy it down here. Then describe exactly what you will be selling or what service you will provide. Also include here how you will organize your business—sole proprietorship, corporation, partnership, or collective.

WHO: The people involved in my business.
Here describe your background and qualifications as a business manager, as well as anyone else who will be involved: (1) partners, (2) employees, (3) advisers, (4) customers, (5) competitors, (6) suppliers, (7) investors.

WHERE: My business location.
Describe your intended location (home or storefront) and your reasons for this choice.

WHEN: My time schedule.
When do you plan to open your doors?

WHY: Filling a need.
Is there truly a demand for this product/service? List the features that will help you compete in the market. (For example: convenience of product—new size, high quality, low price.) Use advice of similar local businesses as well as government and trade-association studies and statistics on the market for this item or service. Show trends and forecasts.

HOW: Deciding on an image.
Describe how you plan to promote your business through advertising, publicity, and special promotions.

HOW MUCH: My projected budget and profit.
Provide a comprehensive financial projection, including charts or graphs illustrating operating costs, income projections, and a cash-flow statement. Also include costs of major investment items and your personal assets and liabilities.

As you gather information for your business plan, you will be collecting your thoughts to lay the foundation of your business. We have elaborated on the facets of this plan throughout this chapter in order to give you a clear idea of how to create your own plan. In Chapter Three, we give you some further information on how to put your plan into action. Read through these two chapters first, then turn back to the guide above and begin to outline your plans. Don't worry that your plans are not fixed at this time—they shouldn't be. But you are taking the first step to making them work. In Part II, we will look more closely at the three different kinds of business—retail, service, and manufacturing. Included there are more specific details aimed at different kinds of businesses, which you'll want to consider and adapt to your plan. At this early stage, however, your plan must be flexible. Alter it, change it, add to it as your knowledge of the field increases. Remember, the plan is a *tool*. Use it to construct a business that will satisfy all your needs.

What—Your Business Plan

In Chapter One, we offered guidelines for the development of your "What": first, define your business purpose; then, set some specific goals. Use the questions raised in that chapter as an exercise to help determine exactly what you plan to achieve in your own business.

Who—You and Your Partners

Begin with yourself and your partners, if you have any. Remember, you must convince potential investors of your experience. One woman who started a printing business with a partner provided this written proof of her expertise:

"I have an extensive background in photography and art design. As a high-school student, I won several art awards, including the Bank of America Award for art production and two first-place awards for design creation for the Los Angeles Rotary Club. I was art editor of my school yearbook and won two scholarships to the Los Angeles Country Art Institute, where I studied under an Italian artist.

"After studying at Linfield College in McMinnville, Oregon, and obtaining a bachelor of science degree in physical education and health with a minor in art and drama, I worked in a Salem print shop which specialized in yearbooks."

Employees

Next, you must explain how many employees you plan to have and how much you will pay them. If you have a particular person in mind, tell all about this person and list her qualifications. There is more specific information on employees and salaries in Chapter Three.

Professional Advisers

Then list your team of professional advisers. We recommend that you secure a lawyer, an accountant, an insurance agent, and a banker, or at least three of these. They will help you through many of the problems which lie ahead. As one woman told us, "I may not have much business knowledge, but I have the good sense to hire those who do." Another businesswoman with years of experience summed it up in this way: "I'm a believer in using professionals. If you use their experience, you'll save yourself time, money, grief, and lost customers!"

Be sure to include a *lawyer* in your adviser team. A note of caution from someone who learned better: "When I first started out, I hired the cheapest lawyer I could find. He gave me exactly what I paid for." And one lawyer advises us that if you can't afford the money for professional advice, you don't have enough money to start a business in the first place!

A young, fairly new lawyer, located conveniently nearby, is your best bet. (You can hire a high-powered New York attorney next year, when business is booming.) A personal recommendation is also helpful. Your lawyer will probably give you most of her or his help right at first—advising you on your initial leases, contracts, and the form of business that your operation will take (corporation, partnership, etc.). You may not need legal services very much later on. Then again, you may.

Preventive advice is beneficial for a new business. By learning the loopholes to watch for, as well as the pitfalls to beware of, you'll save yourself grief and expense. Your legal expenses will possibly be highest in your first year of business, but it's worth it to get the extra education as well as the peace of mind that a lawyer can give you with a short call or visit. Mistakes are much costlier than the price of a professional, we have learned.

One woman told us, "My business is located inside a mall, and when you are dealing with mall management, you either have to know how to read your lease carefully or get someone who can. That someone is a lawyer. I learned the hard way many times. In my lease, for example, there's a small line that says, 'If you want to renew your lease, you must send a hand-written letter to the company within 100 days prior to your lease expiration date.' I've known two businesses inside this mall who have lost their businesses because they didn't do this—because they merely picked up the telephone and said, 'Yes, I want to renew my lease.' Big business doesn't operate this way, and you often need the services of a lawyer to understand your obligation."

In trying to cut your initial expenses, many of you will be tempted to forego the cost of an *accountant* at least until you're showing some profit. Keep this in mind: Most businesses that go broke do so before they know it because of poor accounting records. You may jot down lots of figures in your stationery-store ledger book, but if you don't have a clear picture of where your business stands at all times, you will not have the knowledge that will enable you to make the right decisions in purchasing, hiring, expanding, extending credit, and so forth.

To find a good accountant, you have to ask around. Inquire at other businesses in your field and ask for their recommendations. We've heard that a good accountant is (1) interested in explaining things to you, and (2) interested in your personal needs. Be choosy and select someone you can relate to easily. One accountant told us that "accounting people tend to be people you wouldn't choose to head your dinner party guest list. They relate to numbers more easily than they relate to people. You need one that can relate to both."

Most accountants begin charging for their time when they've given you fifteen minutes of it. Their hourly wages range between fifteen and sixty dollars an hour, or more. Hire one you can afford, but remember that a cheap price often brings cheap advice. Consider that someone between the ages of thirty-five and fifty is your best bet. If you get one too inexperienced and young, she may make her learning mistakes at your expense. A long-established certified public accountant (CPA), on the other hand, may have "seen it all" and may even pass your "menial" bookkeeping on to some of her office help, not giving you the attention you think you're paying for.

Nearly every business we encountered, including some very small, home-based operations, relied on the help of an accountant in one way or another.

"Get an accountant early," one woman advised. "Have your CPA lined up even before you get any money together. Then, as soon as you get your money, start keeping track of all of your expenses, long before you open shop."

Your accountant may help you set up a simple bookkeeping system that you can follow yourself. Then he can merely monitor your books periodically. On the other hand, your accountant may be an integral part of your business, offering almost as many services as you can imagine (and charging you, of course, for them all). One woman explained the way she uses her accountant: "When I moved my business out of my home and into an office, I started paying rent and leasing some office equipment. I found I needed a more formalized bookkeeping system than that I was able to work out for myself. An accountant set up my books for me in a way that I could handle. Now I have hired my first employee, and I find that my quarterly tax estimates are more involved, so the accountant will do the tax estimates for me for the first few three-month tax periods, until I feel that I can handle it myself. When I feel competent enough to handle the books again on my own, the accountant will merely monitor them at the end of the year."

We discuss your accountant's role further in Chapter Three.

Your *insurance agent* can do more for you than sell you some policies. She can provide you with a lot of service. After checking the organization of your business, she can advise you on the best coverage she has to offer. This coverage ranges from "key-man" insurance on the company's founder, to partnership insurance (very important in the case of the death of a partner), to comprehensive fire and liability insurance. You should check on the need for insurance on the improvements you've made in your shop and on your inventory, equipment, and business automobile, as well as protection against theft. Possibly you will want bonding insurance for your employees. Also check on worker's compensation.

When you talk to your insurance agent, use the following guidelines:

Essential Coverage:
- fire
- liability
- automobile
- worker's compensation

Desirable Coverage:
- business interruption (payment for uncontrollable business closure)
- crime insurance
- glass insurance
- employee benefit coverage—group life, group health, disability, retirement income

When you are choosing a bank to handle the needs of your business, don't look only at the policies of the bank—look carefully at the *banker* whom you will be dealing with personally. Is she getting ready for her retirement party? Or is she too new to feel secure enough to take a chance on your new business? Then she might be a poor choice. On the other hand, if she is eager and willing to serve you, or if she is understanding of your particular business, you are lucky.

Two Portland, Oregon, businesswomen had a special "in" with their banker; he had been buying their homemade bagels for some time at the weekend open-air market. When they came to apply for a loan to relocate their business in a real bakery, he knew firsthand that they had a good product and that they were successful in marketing it!

Another businesswoman advised us that "some banks are much more conservative than others in lending, and it would pay to shop around a little before settling on one bank or another." This woman also mentioned that "it helps if the loan officer you talk to is somewhat familiar with your kind of business. My loan officer," she explained, "happened to know a little about the printing business, so she was able to understand what it was that I would need."

A banker advised us: "How do you select a bank? I'd suggest that you pick a small bank, because small banks tend to have more stable branch managers. Big banks have the problem of branch managers rotating. But always remember that the individual banker you speak to is far more important than the bank itself. You may have to speak to five different bankers before you find one you can relate to."

A Washington artist, speaking from years of experience, put the problems of banking into focus: "If you have something to offer, and knowledge behind you, the banks will listen! (And with ERA, they'd have to listen!)" "The market has changed," another woman in banking explained, "but the requirements for getting a loan are the same."

For further information on dealing with banks and bankers, see Chapter Three.

You have listed who you are, who your partner(s) are, who your employees are, and who your advisers are. Next you must list who your customers will be.

Customers

We found that if you can answer five specific questions about your customers, you will be on your way to satisfying—and keeping—those customers. Ask yourself:

1. Who are my customers? Or possibly, who should they be? (If you are already in business and you don't know who your customers are, ask them. They are your most valuable resource.)
2. Where are my customers? (You may find locating your day-care center next to a retirement village is poor judgment. Likewise, a gourmet catering service in a low-income neighborhood is out.)
3. How do my customers shop? (Is there still a thriving mom-and-pop grocery nearby, or does a large shopping mall handle all the local business?)
4. What do my customers need most—quality, low price, speedy service, personal attention?
5. To my customers, what represents the greatest value—designer initials monogrammed on the pocket or athletic sweat socks that last through an entire soccer season?

We asked a number of businesswomen how they determined exactly who their customers would be. Two sisters who operate a "brown-bag" lunchroom in a downtown Portland location realized their potential customers from the start. "People don't need a sales pitch on buying lunch—they just need to know where to get it. A few days before opening, we went around to the closest large office buildings, where we would draw most of our customers from in the future. We passed out coupons for sandwiches and introduced ourselves. People were happy to have a new place to eat near their work." Centered in a midtown business district, they recognized their future customers to be office workers, on foot and in a hurry.

Mary Ann creates quality hand-crafted table linens. She is another woman who has learned the likes—and dislikes—of her customers, and she suits the selection of goods in her displays to the geographic location of the customers. "I learned that people in Salem and the surrounding areas not only spend less money, often commenting to me how they could make my items themselves, but when they do buy, their tastes run toward country simplicity. I could only get three bolts of this fabric before the mill quit making it," she said, showing us a scrap of orange calico. "If I could get twenty, I could sell it all in Salem." Mary Ann has shown her linens throughout the Northwest, and she has found that "people have different taste and buying power in different areas. For example, in Beaverton, people wanted contemporary designs and fabrics, or else elegantly old-fashioned articles, and they would not even flinch at buying my most expensive lace products."

Competitors

Next, make a list of your competitors. You should already be aware of the competition in your field, but if you aren't, make a determined effort of walking through the Yellow Pages and asking around until you know each and every one of them. Make your list of competitors part of your "Who." One woman we talked to who had just opened a beauty shop in her home invited all the hairdressers in her small town over for coffee. She wanted to get to know them better, but she also hoped to create an organized team effort in the beauty business.

Why—Filling a Need

You must demonstrate why your business will succeed by filling a need in the community. You will do this by (1) listing all the features of your business that will make it distinctive and in demand, and (2) listing government and trade-association studies that support the fact that there is a need in your community for your particular business.

What Makes Your Business Unique

In order to verify that you have something distinctly unique to offer or something that will create a demand, you must know who your competitors are, what they have to offer, and how they are succeeding. Your own personal survey of the competition will tell you these things.

Go out and talk to others in your field. Visit shops, buy something if you can, and strike up a conversation. Nearly every one of the women we spoke with was more than willing to share experiences and advice. And their energy and excitement was very catching. One woman, armed with a notebook, visited every children's-store owner in her state—outside a forty-mile radius from her own town.

"I wrote my goal on the first page—I was going to have a children's clothing store. I started saving my money immediately, and every day that I could afford to go, I drove to Portland, Seattle, the Tri-Cities, Tacoma, Vancouver, and I looked at every children's clothing store. I looked at all the racks and all their merchandise, and I asked to see the owner. I always told them what I was doing. Don't go into the area you plan to locate in. As long as you're outside of a forty-mile radius of your area, most owners will give you answers to specific questions that don't take up their time. I didn't stand there with a notebook—I had it in the car, and I went out and wrote down everything they said as soon as I left the store. One business owner will tell you one thing, and another will tell you something else. You have to write it all down and pick out what you think might work for you. Then write *that* down."

Suppliers

In Chapter Four, we devote a lot of attention to the problem of locating suppliers for your specific needs. Locating suppliers often requires a lot of detective work. Ask around. And, as one woman told us, if you find something you want to sell, don't give up badgering the store owner whose shop you found it in until you find out how to order it.

Where—Choosing Your Location

Here you describe your choice of location (home or storefront) and your reasons for this choice. You must consider parking, lease agreements, customer convenience, and many other factors. This is covered in great detail in Chapter Three. Weigh every consideration mentioned there, and then decide on a location that best suits your needs.

One woman's avenue may be another woman's dead end. A

needlepoint-shop owner told us about her needs: "We were torn between being in the new mall or in a more out-of-the-way, less expensive location. We decided on the out-of-the-way location, and we couldn't be more pleased. Ninety-five percent of all the people who come to us buy something. If we were in a mall, we would have to spend all our time watching a lot of browsers who happened into our store not necessarily intending to buy anything."

But, on the other hand, another woman had the opposite opinion. "I was originally in a shop outside of the main business district. I thought that since it was on a busy street, I would get a lot of customers, but I found out that the parking situation there was horrendous. I've since moved to the mall, and business is so good that I plan to open up two more stores in other malls soon.'

When—Your Planning and Organization Schedule

Allow yourself ample time for planning, organization, and investigating all aspects of your business. You will need time for consulting with advisers, ordering and receiving supplies, locating and drawing up a lease for space, arranging for hired help, formulating contracts, and so on. Be as realistic as possible. As a general rule, we found that allowing for six months to a year of planning time is being realistic. Set a date for opening and work toward it. If new construction or remodeling is involved in your opening date, be *very* realistic. One woman who was hoping desperately to open her fabric shop two months before Christmas asked us if we would like to come to her home to buy fabric, thread, or even a sewing machine. All her supplies had arrived, her loan payments were due, and the builders didn't even have the dry wall hung yet!

Gathering Some Statistics

The Small Business Administration (SBA), a government agency formed to assist small businesses, can also give you some help in determining if your competition is, at least statistically, handling all the business that the area can support. The SBA has compiled data that show how many inhabitants are necessary in a particular area to support various kinds of businesses. This information (available in *Starting and Managing a Small Business of Your Own*, 3rd ed., SBA, 1973) can be used in this way:

Let's say Alice wants to go into business in her hometown, population 12,000. She is considering as business possibilities her three favorite hobbies—flower arranging, record-album collecting, and cooking. According to the SBA guide, a florist shop needs 13,531 people in the town to support its business. Since there is already one florist in Alice's town of 12,000, another would not be a good bet.

SBA figures cite a population of 112,144 as necessary to successfully operate a record shop, so that is out, also. The town is too small.

Restaurants, however, need only 1,583 inhabitants to exist, theoretically. Although there are already three eating establishments in Alice's hometown, there is room for more (3 × 1583 = 4,799, and the population of her town, as we said, is 12,000). Voilà! Alice's Restaurant!

As Alice does to her chicken soup, though, add a grain of salt to these figures. Maybe the population of your town is growing in leaps and bounds. Or maybe your city is the wedding capital of the state and the florist is open twenty-four hours a day. The SBA offers average national figures. Use these figures as a flexible guideline.

How—Deciding on an Image

Before you begin to consider your advertising strategy, you must first decide on the image you wish to create. Write down in twenty words or less the image you want your products and your entire business to convey. We'll give you two examples; then you describe the image you're after!

> Good quality, low price, quick service foods in an informal atmosphere, suited to high-volume foot traffic.
>
> or
>
> Exclusive, high-fashion women's clothing featuring designer labels, unique accessories, personalized service.

Now yours:

List how you plan to promote your business—your advertising strategy. Include: (1) your business logo, (2) your paid advertising plans, and (3) your business-promotion plans and hopes for free publicity.

Your Logo

A small but significant element of your image is your store signature—the lettering design or logo (short for "logotype") that you select to represent your name. Your signs, shopping bags, cards, and advertisements will all carry this signature, so choose it with care to help carry out your theme. Gather your ideas together with your business name and take them to a commercial artist, as one woman did: "I knew what I wanted in the way of a store logo, but there was no way I could draw it up myself. So I went to an artist friend of mine, and she drew one up for me for a lot less than the going rate."

Another woman started out with one logo, but as her business began to specialize, she changed her name and logo to suit her new image: "When we started out I intended to have a fabric shop that offered personalized sewing for customers, and I called myself the Nimble Thimble. Then a restaurant in town asked us to sew their uniforms, and the word spread fast. After several other restaurants came to us, we decided to phase out the fabrics and the personalized sewing and go exclusively into manufacturing restaurant uniforms. Our new name and logo describe our image to a *t*—Classic Uniforms.

Paid Advertising

Paid advertising offers many possibilities—direct mail, newspaper, radio, television, home shows, and more. Your most effective advertising will reach the most people for the least expense. Note where the competition advertises and profit from their example. With experience, you will learn which method of advertising provides the best results.

Sarah Jean, who owns her own interior-decorating service, spent a lot of money learning that newspaper advertising does not pay for her business. "I am selling my talent, and you can't sell talent through a newspaper. I recently rented four spaces at the home show, and next year I plan to use eight spaces. Twenty thousand people went to that home show, and when could I ever get twenty thousand people to come through my shop?"

A fabric- and crafts-shop owner mentions that her "best advertising has been fliers." Sent to past customers and those on her mailing list, the fliers are hand illustrated to entice customers to sign up for new classes, sample new materials, and join other quilters at a shop-sponsored picnic. Fliers also include other store-related information and a class-registration form.

Under the next point in your plan, the How Much, you will make some financial projections. An average projected budget for paid advertising is considered to be from 2 to 5 percent of your annual gross volume of business. Keep this in mind when outlining the kinds of advertising you plan to use. We discuss further the specifics of paid advertising in Chapter Three.

Business Promotions

Another aspect of your selling strategy is your plan for free publicity and for promotions to create interest and awareness in your business. In our last illustration, we mentioned a fabric-shop owner's plans to hold a quilters' picnic. This is one example of a store promotion planned for fun as well as for increasing awareness of the shop and its activities. We discuss this kind of planning further in Chapter Three. Check pages 117 through 127 to get your thinking started on ways to promote your business at little or no cost.

How Much—Projected Expenses and Profits

"Have more money, more time, and more of everything than you think you need before you begin. We had about $3,500 to open our quilt shop; we should have had $8,000."

How do you decide how much money you will need to start a business? You'll have to do some smart figuring here. We've heard the sad tales of those who could have made it if only they could have hung in there just a little longer, till their idea really caught on. Don't be caught short in your planning for capital requirements. Money is important!

We'll include in the How Much part of your plan these items:

1. personal cost of living chart
2. the money I need to open my doors chart
3. projected profits chart
4. financial statement

One general recommendation we heard quite often: don't start out too big. Don't saddle yourself with tremendous debts when you are just getting your feet on the ground. You'll learn and grow as you go. A gift-shop owner told us: "I started out with only my small savings of two thousand dollars. But by putting all my profits back into the business for a year, I now have five times what I started with."

Your Costs of Living

In laying out your financial needs, you must start at home and be very realistic about how much it costs you to live each month. (Women who have an outside income or whose husbands' income is ample to carry the family expenses need not do this.)

PERSONAL COST OF LIVING

Regular monthly payments:		
house payments or rent	——	
car payments (include insurance)	——	
appliance-TV payments	——	
home-improvement loan payments	——	
personal-loan payments		
life insurance premiums	——	
other insurance premiums	——	
miscellaneous payments	——	——
Household operating expense:		
phone	——	
gas and electricity	——	
water	——	
other household expenses (repair/maintenance)	——	——
Family expense:		
clothing, cleaning, laundry	——	
drugs	——	
doctor and dentist	——	
education	——	
dues	——	
gifts	——	
travel	——	
newspapers, magazines, books	——	
auto upkeep and gas	——	
spending money and allowance	——	——

Food expense:
food at home ____
food away from home ____

Total monthly cost of ______living

If you aren't certain of your expenses, simply flip through your check stubs for the past year. Make a list of each of these expenditures, then divide by twelve to get the average monthly expense. The bottom line of the chart will tell you how much you need to live each month, which leads us to the next chart, detailing your business's financial needs.

If you are the sole means of support for yourself or your family, take your total monthly living expenses and multiply by six. You must have six months' living expenses in reserve to carry you while you start your new business.

Business Expenses

There are three basic kinds of business operations: service, manufacturing, and sales. The initial investment required to start your new business will vary, generally speaking, according to the business type.

Services (giving lessons, wallpapering, painting, sewing, housekeeping, etc.) often require the smallest initial investment of the three business types. Frequently a service business can be run out of your own home, saving you rent and office overhead. We've seen businesses started on a shoestring (a $10 shoestring, in fact), though investments ranged upward to several thousand dollars.

Light manufacturing businesses (and we are referring to the production of hand-crafted items in great quantities rather than the manufacturing of computer components, for example) are often next in line in capital requirements. Your greatest expense will probably be tools and materials. Less than five hundred dollars will often suffice if you have an extra room in the basement and already own your sewing machine, for instance.

Highest in their need for capital are the retail sales businesses, easily ranging from a two-thousand-dollar investment upward (toward the sky!). You'll probably have to rent a shop, and you'll have to stock plenty of inventory. Hired help will likely be necessary.

We have outlined the financial needs for each of the three basic kinds of businesses in later chapters. However, for now, consider this general expense ledger:

If you are running your business out of your home and have no employees, you will be able to simplify this chart by crossing off employee wages and such expenses that would be duplicated by operating in a separate business building (phone, utilities, etc.).

When you determine how much money you'll need, your next step is often determining how in the world you'll raise it! You may choose to work for someone else until you have saved enough for your own business. Or there are other options. (Check them all out in Chapter Three). Remember to consider loans from banks, the SBA, and other lending institutions, as well as your personal savings. And don't forget Uncle Charlie; relatives are often a helpful source of capital. But don't omit drawing up a note for a loan from a friend or relative. You'll need the note for tax and inheritance purposes, and you'll also want payment receipts. Don't be shy about asking for these things. You are running a business, and you need to keep all your records accordingly. Remember what Samuel B. Mayer once said, "An oral agreement is as good as the paper it's written on."

Making Profit Projections

You must also consider how much you can expect to make in profits. Though this is one of the last points we urge you to determine, it is our guess that you've been developing a taste for profits all along the way in your planning. As well as figuring *how much* profit you can expect, you also need to know *when* you can expect it. This can be critical, especially if your business is seasonal.

"All businesses are seasonal," mentioned one experienced

THE MONEY I NEED TO OPEN MY DOORS

Family monthly living expenses (from page 64)	____	× 6 months =	______
Remodeling and redecorating	____		
Fixtures, displays, shelves, necessary machinery, furniture	____		
Installation labor	____		
Signs	____		
Office supplies	____		
Merchandise and/or supplies	____		
Advertising (for opening promotions)	____		
Legal and CPA fees	____		
		Total	______
Monthly operating expenses:			
rent or mortgage payment	____		
utilities	____		
phone	____		
insurance premiums	____		
employee wages	____		
taxes	____		
Total	____	× 6 months =	______
			______
		Money I need to start	______

businesswoman. "It just takes a couple years' experience to determine what your seasons are and what the normal course of your business will be. No one buys at income-tax time, for instance." If most of your sales are made at Christmastime but your shop opens for business in February, you'll need to plan ahead to be able to hold out for nearly a year before cash comes rolling in.

"The wedding season is my busiest time of year," stresses a lady baker who specializes in decorated cakes. "From April to September, I am swamped with cake orders, averaging six weddings or wedding showers a week in addition to the regular small orders. In the summertime, I often start baking at four in the morning so I can avoid working in the heat of the day. Aside from the wedding season, when my highest profits are made, the business flows pretty smoothly, with Valentine's Day the only other really hectic time."

Another woman, a children's-bookstore owner, told us that she opened her store two months before Christmas, and although people told her not to expect to make money for a year, she began reaping profits the very day she opened, had a wonderful Christmas in sales, and has been doing well ever since.

Few of us can really predict the future, but with considerable thought and research, you can make a realistic profit projection. And as we mentioned earlier, the best way to determine the figures on the following chart is to (1) depend on your own experience, (2) talk to others in your field of business, and (3) consult a CPA familiar with your field.

PROJECTED PROFITS

	Jan.	Feb.	March	April	May	June	July	Aug.	Sept.	Oct.	Nov.	Dec.	Year Total
Anticipated cash receipts:													
1. cash sales													
2. collections on accounts receivable													
3. other income													
4. total cash receipts													
Anticipated cash payments:													
5. cost of goods													
6. payroll													
7. other expenses (including maintenance)													
8. advertising													
9. selling expense													
10. administrative expense (including salary of owner)													
11. building and equipment expense													
12. other payments (taxes, including estimated income tax; repayment of loans; interest; etc.)													
13. total cash payments													

Total projected cash receipts	
minus Total projected cash payments	
equals Total projected profits	

Your Financial Statement

If you intend to present your business plan to a lending institution, you must prepare a financial statement. A sample of such a statement follows:

FINANCIAL STATEMENT

I Own:

cash (bank accounts and other)	
securities	
real estate	
furniture	
car	
cash value of life insurance	
savings bonds	
money owed to me	
other assets	
I Own:	

I Owe:

current bills		
installment contracts		
appliances	______	
car	______	
personal loan	______	
other	______	
real estate		
other loans and debts		
insurance premiums		
taxes		
I Owe		

I Own	
(minus) I Owe –	
(equals) I am Worth	

Completing your business plan is a crucial step in the organization of your business. When you read this section for the first time, don't be overwhelmed by the amount of information the plan calls for that you feel you aren't sure of as yet. You are learning the groundwork you have to cover. Read on through this book, and you'll gather more of the facts you need to feel confident in developing your plan. When you finish reading our book and have given considerable thought to how you are going to turn your dream into reality, sit down with a pen and paper and begin, step by step, writing out the details of your plan. When you finish you will not only have a detailed map to follow, you will also have a most impressive presentation for potential investors. As one loan officer told us, "Although I see about three 'good ideas' a day, I usually see only one good plan that has real business potential each week!"

3 The Action

You've undergone a serious self-appraisal. You've learned how to organize your business ideas into a careful plan. And you've no doubt uncovered some problems that are better to know about now, rather than when you've signed a lease or invested your inheritance! Now you're ready for the action! You must next:

1. Get together your money sources.
2. Decide upon your business's legal organization.
3. Obtain a business license.
4. Choose a location.
5. Set up your business books.
6. Determine a pricing schedule.
7. Decide your advertising strategy.
8. Fix your employee requirements.
9. Prepare for taxes.

For starters, let's develop your money sources.

Money Sources

Money. Every woman we talked to needed money to develop her dream of owning her own business. And, almost overwhelmingly, no one had enough of it! In our survey, we found that it is not easy for anyone to borrow money for a business venture, and much less easy if you are a woman. For some women, it was not only difficult but grossly unfair.

"We wanted to open a print shop. We not only had a business

plan that was an inch thick, but we both had years of experience in the field and waiting customers to boot. We were turned down for a loan time and time again. At one time, a friend of ours set up a loan for us with an acquaintance of his. When we went to meet our lender, we realized the minute we walked in his door that the loan was off. His face dropped to the floor when he realized we were women, and he proceeded to fall all over himself explaining why he had no money to lend at the moment. Our parents were our last resort, and without them, we wouldn't be here today."

"No one would loan me money to open a gift shop. I had years of experience working in the gift department of a large department store, but I was a divorcée with four children and no substantial means of support. Nevertheless, I was bound and determined to have my gift shop. So I put my house up for sale and went to the gift show the week after a bid had been made on the house. I made a list of the gifts I wanted to buy and called the realtor every day to see if the sale was going to go through. The last day of the show, he gave me an okay; and I bought my gifts."

We found other women who had enough money of their own, and for some, getting a loan to start a business was not difficult at all:

"We simply borrowed on some bonded certificates we had in the bank."

"I had no trouble whatsoever in securing a bank loan to open my shop. My husband is a professional man in this town, and we not only grew up here but we went to school with several of the bankers."

Your particular financial hurdle may not be as difficult or as easy as these women found theirs to be. We suggest that you start at the top of our list of possibilities and persist until you've acquired the funds you need.

Your Savings Account

Women often begin their own businesses with savings of their own. However, many of them fail to realize how much easier it would have been with additional capital behind them. For example, one woman we talked to took the family savings in hand to show the banker her sincerity, and asked him to loan her some more.

"With six kids to raise on my husband's teaching salary, we never had any money. We had to move several times and managed to make a profit on one of the homes we sold. We had money in the bank for the first time in our lives—six thousand dollars. My husband encouraged me to take it and open the store I had always dreamed about. Furthermore, he told me that if I didn't do *something* with it, he was going to invest it in an apartment complex. The vision of me cleaning apartments was all it took. Our banker loaned us five thousand more (we mortgaged our house), and I set up shop."

Some experts tell us that even if you have enough in your savings account to begin your business, you will be better off in the long run to borrow even a small amount on a short-term loan in order to establish your business banking credit.

For example, if you need five thousand dollars to start your business, and you have six thousand dollars in your savings account, use only four thousand dollars of your own money. Borrow one thousand dollars from the bank. You'll not only learn the bank's procedures for business loans, but you'll show the bank how good you are at paying back a loan.

Perhaps you want to stock up on inventory at Christmastime and don't have the capital to finance it. Or you may run into an emergency expense like having to replace a furnace or repair a piece of equipment. Your banker will be more likely to help you out if you have dealt with him previously.

Friends and Relatives

We've all heard the adage: Never loan a friend money, and to go along with that, it's been said, Never borrow from a relative. We found that without friends and relatives, many women's businesses would never have gotten off the ground. For example, the members of one partnership told us: "No one would loan us money to open our fabric shop, so my parents came through. Although they had just retired, they decided to mortgage their house and loan us the money. If they had that much faith in me and my partner, I knew we couldn't fail."

Because banks want to see some of your own money going into your business venture, you may have to borrow enough from a friend or relative to let the bank know you are sincere. Or you could get a friend or relative with more collateral than you to co-sign a loan. And if you are really gutsy, borrow five hundred dollars from twenty friends and offer them stock, a percentage of the profits, or just an appealing rate of interest.

"I showed my business plan around to my friends, and one of them said, 'I'd like to invest in your business; I have five thousand dollars.' And my friend's mother-in-law, visiting from out-of-state, said, 'That's really neat. I'd like to invest in a woman's business.' So I decided that's how I would finance my business. All of my original seven investors were women with two or three thousand dollars in a savings account. I'd offer them a higher rate of interest than the bank was giving, and they would take an unsecured note. I still have many of my original private investors."

Creative financing is raising money from a variety of sources when a conventional bank loan is hard to obtain. It is an innovative way to finance a new business or to build an existing one.

Life Insurance Policies

Perhaps you have a life insurance policy that has been sitting around gathering dust. Many policies allow you to borrow on them, usually at a lower interest rate than a bank would charge.

Bank Loans

Despite what the 1974 Equal Credit Opportunity Act would lead us to believe and what some bank loan officers would like us to believe, loans for women's business ventures are few and far between. This is very simply because banks are in business themselves, and they don't want to take risks. Woman's role has not traditionally been that of business owner; therefore, women's business loans are considered risky. And to make matters worse, we found that single women are often discriminated against more than married women. Married women often have joint savings accounts and/or home-equity collateral to help them start a business or secure a loan. Many times single women have been so busy trying to support a family and themselves that savings accounts and collateral are minimal.

One prominent bank loan officer told us quite frankly: "It's illegal to discriminate, but culturally, we do. I'm sorry and wish it weren't that way, and I do try to shut that out when I'm considering a loan."

All About Loan Officers

The more you know about bank loan officers and bank loans, the better off you will be when you negotiate for a business loan. We asked several loan officers what they considered to be important on a business loan application. One bank loan officer gave us some insight: "I look at many things—background, success in what they've done before, ability to save money . . . Money-management experience is very important. Many people think that if they just *work hard,* they'll succeed. But in business, you don't make money working hard, you make money managing. You can work hard eighty hours a week and go broke, and you can work twenty hours a week managing and make a living."

And, "Everyone comes in with a good idea and very little money. They don't realize that they have to put up a good share of the money themselves before we are willing to back them. We certainly won't risk our money if they aren't willing to risk theirs. Our rule of thumb is generally one dollar of your money to one dollar of ours, but this varies greatly.

"Many times people have worked somewhere and think they could do it better on their own. But they have no idea of what business is all about. Perhaps you're used to five hundred dollars a week in salary and you work five days a week. When you go into business, you will have to work seven days a week and cut yourself down to the bare necessities—perhaps two hundred dollars a week. It will take five years for you to pay the loan back, and ten years before you can enjoy the success of the business. I look for an 'entrepreneur spirit,' someone who can not only organize and manage, but manage on a very limited budget.

"I might also add that most people come in here without the vaguest notion of how to present their business plan to us. We usually have to tell them how to go about creating a business plan." In summing up, he commented, "I think the most important thing I consider when a woman is applying for a business loan is her habits of thrift. I like to see her have something on her own, like a savings account. If she can manage money, she is a good risk."

Another banker said: "Everyone going in for a business loan should know the banker's three C's of credit: *character*, *capacity*, and *capital*. A banker may or may not give you a loan on the basis of your character, the personal impression you make on him. In evaluating your capacity, bankers are very unlikely to understand the technical aspects of your particular field. You must convince a banker that you know what you're talking about. And last, capital—a banker reacts very poorly to a plan without any of your own capital to back it up. A banker hates surprises more than anything else. Be honest from the beginning and *always overestimate your needs*!"

Another bank officer mentioned that she considers "community need" an important prerequisite for a loan. Though an idea for a new business may be a good one, if there are already several similar businesses in the area, the risk is greater. With this in mind, make sure to have some convincing evidence on hand to convince your banker of the dire community need for your particular business!

Types of Bank Loans

Now that you have a little insight into bank loan officers, you next need to take a few notes on bank loans in general. First, there are two kinds of loans: long-term and short-term.

Long-term bank loans. These are loans to provide money you plan to pay back over a fairly long time—a mortgage on a business building, for example, or payments on expensive equipment that you need to get started.

"I financed the business with a bank loan amortized over a five-year period, with the first payment due three months after opening. I had prepared a good business plan and a personal financial statement, and offered to secure the loan with a second mortgage on my home."

Short-term bank loans. You can use short-term bank loans to supply the money to carry accounts receivable (money your customers owe you), for building Christmas inventory, and so forth. A short-term loan is generally paid off within a thirty-to-ninety-day period.

"It's customary for retailers to borrow occasionally to build up inventory, particularly in the fall in anticipation of Christmas sales. Not realizing what a standard practice this is, I was ashamed the first time I had to do it, until my banker set me straight."

Collateral

This is another term you should be familiar with. Your signature may be the only thing the bank needs to secure a loan, but, more than likely, they will require you to put up some collateral, too. Collateral is a pledge of security to assure the bank you will pay the loan back. For example, we mentioned that one woman agreed to secure her loan with a second mortgage on her home. But home mortgages aren't the only kind of collateral. Consider some of the following:

1. Find an *endorser* to co-sign for you. If you fail to pay up, the bank will expect the endorser to make payment. The bank may ask your endorser to put up some security.
2. Get a *co-maker* to sign with you, creating a joint obligation with you to the bank.
3. Find a *guarantor,* one who guarantees the payment of a note by signing a guaranty commitment. Sometimes a manufacturer will act as a guarantor for a customer.
4. Banks also take commodities as security by lending money on a *warehouse receipt*. Say, for example, that you get a loan to buy a quantity of dinnerware at a special price, then you store it in your warehouse until the time of your big sale. You can give the bank the ownership papers of the merchandise until you are able to pay back the loan. Such loans are generally made on staple or standard merchandise, which can be readily marketed.
5. You may need a *chattel mortgage* if you want a loan to buy equipment such as a cash register or delivery truck. The bank loans you money and you give the bank a lien on the equipment you are buying.
6. Your *savings account* is another form of collateral for long-

term loans. In such cases, the bank gets an assignment from you and keeps your passbook.

7. Banks will lend up to the cash value of a *life insurance policy*. You have to assign the policy to the bank.

SBA Loans

If your application for a loan has been turned down by the bank (or by two banks in a city of 200,000 or more), you can seek financial assistance from the Small Business Administration (SBA). Government involvement in such assistance is extensive, the process is very time consuming, and the funds are limited. Still, the SBA does offer some possibilities. Here, briefly, is what is involved.

Before the SBA will extend any financial help, you must provide evidence that the funds you need cannot be raised by any other means. Be prepared to produce evidence of the other sources you have tried: loan refusals from two banks, for example, or proof that you cannot get a loan from credit sources or from other government agencies. Be able to prove that you are of good character (bring along some personal references), that your business plans are well developed (take a copy of your formal business plan), and that you have some management ability. Your entire personal credit record will be reviewed, as well as the ratio of your debts to your net worth. You must provide evidence of the sources of your income, all investment property held in your name, and any debts that you have (including installment purchases and insurance premiums).

After close scrutiny, if the SBA feels that your request for a loan is reasonable, they will first attempt to obtain for you a bank loan with an SBA guarantee. As much as 99.1 percent of all SBA loans are guaranteed loans. In this type of guarantee (available at over 10,000 of the 15,000 banks in the United States), the SBA promises to pay back the loan if you default. The SBA also has funds with which it can make direct small business loans of up to $100,000, but these are extremely limited. There are some funds reserved for borrowers in the "disadvantaged" category, but the fact that you are a woman starting a new business does not automatically put you in that category.

The SBA guarantee can amount to up to 90 percent of the bank loan, with a $350,000 maximum. Or the SBA can participate in the loan by putting up part of the funds (limited to $150,000), with the bank putting up the remainder.

The SBA is an organization for men *and* women, and despite rumors to the contrary, it does not have special programs for aspiring women business owners. The administration judges loan applicants just as any other lending institution does—on your ability to pay it back.

The SBA, of course, wants you to "make it" in your business, not only to secure the loans they guarantee but also to fortify the American economy. To do this, they offer *five thousand* pieces of literature providing helpful information on every imaginable aspect of business. This literature is available to anyone. Visit the office nearest you and find out for yourself—or simply write to them. They will send you a checklist of the material they offer.

Another note of discouragement: only 25 percent of the direct loans made and 5 percent of all guaranteed loans are used to start new businesses. The rest of the loans are made to small businesses already in operation. If the extensive red tape, limited funds, and government involvement put off your hopes for an SBA loan for now, you might keep it in mind for the future, when you may want to expand and develop your business operation.

The SBA supplies these guidelines for the preparation of your loan proposal to the SBA:

1. Prepare financial statement (balance sheet and profit and loss) no more than 60 days prior to when you turn in your loan application.
2. Prepare financial statement (balance sheet and profit and loss) for the three preceding years.
3. If your business is a corporation, prepare financial statements of all stockholders owning 20 percent or more of the capital stock. If a proprietorship or partnership, prepare financial statement of proprietorship or partners.
4. Prepare résumé of management personnel, showing all your past management experience.
5. Prepare loan proposal, outlining the use of proceeds and the time at which you want the note to come due, and outline collateral to be offered.

6. Prepare one-year profit-and-loss projection.

7. Bring this information to your banker or bank of your choice for review and recommendation.

8. If your bank feels loan proposal is feasible and requests SBA's guarantee, contact the district office nearest you.

9. If you have any questions, contact the nearest SBA office.

Choosing Your Business's Legal Organization

There are four basic types of business organization: (1) sole proprietorship, (2) partnership, (3) corporation, and (4) collective. You should know the advantages and disadvantages of each, so that you can choose the one that best suits your needs.

Sole Proprietorship

In this form of organization, you alone own the business. We found this to be the most common and simplest form of business organization.

Advantages: (1) There is little formality and no legal requirements; (2) There is no double taxation, as there is in a corporation (see p. 83).

You will have to pay self-employment tax, however, instead of social security.

Disadvantages: (1) You are personally liable for business suits. If someone slips on the carpet in your shop, your home and all of your personal assets may be at stake in a lawsuit against your business. (2) In the event of your death, your business is terminated. No one else has the legal authority to carry on the business. (3) All profit to the business is taxed, whether or not it is withdrawn. You may want to put some of the profits into a business savings account. This money would still be taxed. The profit can never be considered as a salary and is, therefore, not deductible as a business expense.

One woman we talked to expressed the general feeling of all the sole proprietors we talked with: "I like to be my own boss and run my own show."

Another woman said, "I work best by myself. I like being in control, and I *know* that I'm dependable."

Partnership

This is an agreement of two or more persons to transact business. There are two kinds of partnerships: general and limited. In a general partnership, all partners assume equal liability responsibility. No permission is required by the state to form a general partnership. In a limited partnership, each partner shares an agreed percentage of profits and liability. These must be registered with the State Tax Commission.

Advantages: (1) Like a sole proprietorship, you are only taxed once. Again you will have to pay self-employment tax instead of social security. (2) A partner may offer emotional and financial support that could prove invaluable to your developing business. (3) A partnership is generally less expensive to organize legally than a corporation.

Disadvantages: (1) You increase your legal liability when you add a partner. If a suit is filed against the business, the personal assets of both the partners are vulnerable. (2) If your partner should die, you may find yourself having to deal with one of her heirs—perhaps the brother-in-law that you never could stand. (3) You are not allowed the more liberal allowances of employee benefits that come with incorporating.

The women we talked to in partnership businesses had a lot to say on the subject:

"I think a partnership is the perfect solution for a woman who has to manage not only her business, but a husband and children, as well. One partner can mind the store while the other tends to personal matters, and vice versa."

"When I started my business, I had a partner because I only wanted to work part-time. If you can find another woman with part-time aspirations, you're set!"

Another woman commented, "I have found that it is better to base a partnership on abilities than on friendship. The pressures of doing business are often hard on a friendship. On the other hand, choosing a partner to complement your own personal abilities is a wise move. It may be that you have great business management skills but not much in the way of creativity. Pool your resources with a brilliant artist who is a flop in managing the books. In my own case, I wanted to open a weaving studio. I love the art of weaving and enjoy being involved with the craft. However, I am not a highly skilled artist. I chose as a partner a weaver who is well known and admired in the field. She adds credibility and skill, while I add the business sense."

"If you are the eternal optimist, choose a pessimist as a partner. Choose someone whose talents complement yours but whose background, business ideas and personal philosophy are a little different."

One woman learned from experience that having a partner to share the work load is a definite advantage. "My craft business has grown much bigger than I imagined in the beginning. Now much of my time is spent organizing and managing local craft shows as well as producing my own product. Last Christmas Eve was the last straw for me. I wasn't able to enjoy my family traditions because at the last minute, I was still rushing to finish orders that would make my customers' holiday complete. I decided that I would have to take a partner to help out with the craft-show aspect of the business. I did not want to share my profits with her on the accounts that I had developed on my own in the past six years, but we decided to split fifty–fifty on all the new accounts we obtained. I had worked with this girl in many craft shows and felt that I knew her very well before taking her as a partner. The fact that she makes and sells a craft item that is different from the one that I make is very important. I think it would be a big mistake for a craftperson to go into partnership with someone who produced the same type of craft. Now that I have a partner, I don't have to spend so many hours sitting at craft fairs, watching over my table and overseeing all the other tables. We can share this responsibility."

The members of one eight-year partnership told us that they planned to remain partners until their CPA decided it was to their advantage to incorporate.

Corporation

In this type of organization, you, the stockholder, are removed from any personal liability. You have only your stock to lose. The price you must pay for this freedom from liability is additional taxes, government regulations, and annual license fees.

Advantages: (1) Liability stops at the business level; it cannot go on to the stockholders. (2) Liberal corporate-tax-deductible employee benefits are allowed: Your health-insurance program may be totally paid for by the corporation, an entirely deductible business expense. (3) In the event of one stockholder's death, her heirs cannot automatically intervene. (4) Profits can be held within the corporation without being taxed if IRS guidelines are strictly followed (reinvesting them in the business, for example).

Disadvantages: (1) A corporation usually costs more to organize than other business forms. However, one woman we talked to suggested a way to avoid this cost. "A lawyer will charge you as much as $500 to incorporate. Why not do it yourself and save paying a $500 secretarial fee to have a lawyer draw it up? I took a copy of the incorporation papers from another business, penciled in the changes that would be necessary for my kind of business, typed it, enclosed a check, and mailed it off to the secretary of state. I was incorporated . . . and I saved myself a bundle of legal fees."

(2) You must make a yearly report to the State Tax Commission. (3) You are taxed twice on your profits. The corporation is taxed from 20 to 22 percent on profit up to $25,000, and 48 percent on all profits above $25,000. Then you are taxed on your wages, as any employer would be taxed. And speaking of corporate taxes, one attorney we talked to advised us to consider the following:

"When you are debating between establishing your business as a sole proprietorship or incorporating, consider carefully your tax situation. When your business is just starting, your initial losses and expenditures will be greater, and your tax write-off may be better, with the losses involved in a sole proprietorship. Also, if your husband is interested in using your struggling new business as a tax write-off, don't incorporate."

Again, we recommend that you confer with a professional adviser, such as a CPA or an attorney, who can help you discriminate the pros and cons of your particular situation.

Subchapter-S Corporation

Organizing your business as a Subchapter-S corporation is a way to avoid double taxation of your profits and yet take advantage of corporate protection from personal liability. To qualify under

Subchapter S, you must have less than ten stockholders and can have only one class of stock. Members of your family can be owners of the stock, and they can serve as your board of directors, too, if you like. Again, the advantages are that you are taxed only once on your profits and you are shielded from personal liability. The disadvantages are that you must set up appropriate records, hold regular meetings of the stockholders, keep minutes of the meetings, and send in an annual report to local authorities.

One partnership we spoke with went to a small-business seminar offered at the local community college, and went right home and filed for Subchapter S status. "We immediately realized that we were risking all our personal possessions to a possible libel suit by *not* incorporating under Subchapter S. We merely went to the State Tax Commission's office, got the necessary literature, read it carefully, and filled out the appropriate forms. We are now Subchapter-S incorporated, and if any of our customers wants to sue us, they can take us for all we're worth as far as our business is concerned (which isn't much), but they cannot touch our homes or other personal property."

Collective

After talking to the members of several different collectives, we decided that this form of business organization may be the answer for women who (1) don't have a lot of initial capital, (2) don't want to carry the full responsibility of a business themselves, and (3) want to become involved in something other than a nine-to-five job. Three Seattle, Washington, women described their collective as a "means of self-support and self-determination. Working collectively, we find time to pursue our own lives."

We are all somewhat familiar with sole proprietorships, partnerships, and corporations. But the collective form of business may not be as familiar to most of us. We visited a very successful collective in Eugene, Oregon. Starflower is a wholesale natural-foods warehouse and distributing company with about twenty-five members. It has been in operation about five years, located in a modern office-warehouse complex. One of the members explained the workings of the collective to us:

"In order to become a member of the collective, all the existing members must vote you in. Once you start working, you get the same pay that everyone else gets, no matter what your job is. You also accumulate equity in the collective, which you can draw out if you decide to leave, or you can borrow on it anytime.

"Our collective has a complex financial structure. Several individuals and concerns have loaned Starflower money. Starflower works from this capital and pays the lenders substantial interest. But there is a limit as to how much an individual lender can lend us, so that no lender has more power than another.

"The collective is divided into teams: office workers, warehouse workers, truckers, maintenance workers. . . . Each team meets weekly to make small group decisions and recommendations for the collective as a whole. The recommendations are brought up at the all-member meetings, and nothing can be done unless it is voted on by the majority of the members. For example, Margaret is our expert bookkeeper, but she cannot make final decisions on her subject area; she can only make recommendations. However, the individual teams do have smaller decision powers, such as their own working hours and days off.

"As a member you are part of the system, so you want to do everything you can to make it work. We have had to make allowances for extra pay for extra hours, so everything is not exactly cut and dried. And, like any other concern, we have personnel problems, like somebody not showing up for work. We usually try to find out what the cause of a particular problem is and work with the individual whose family or health problems are interfering with her work. We have only had to ask one member to leave.

"When we started out, we were working fifty to sixty hours a week, and the pay was minimal—$150 a month. Today, we work around thirty-five hours a week, and the pay is considerably better. In the beginning, we hoped to stay small. Everyone was supposed to do everything—take an order, collect it from the warehouse, do the billing, take part in the trucking and bookkeeping aspects. I was one of the first ones to say, 'Hey, I don't want to do the bookkeeping!' It just doesn't work well with everyone doing everything. Now, with the exception of new members having to work in the warehouse a month at first (to have an understanding for the warehouse worker's job), everyone is trained for a particular skill.

"We were once very idealistic and didn't want to get big, but capitalism doesn't work that way. You can't stop growing. If someone comes out with organic kosher pickles, we can't disregard them and say, 'No, we don't want to grow and make more space in our warehouse for them.' Someone else will, if we don't."

Another woman, a member of a collective of automobile mechanics, described the organization of their business, Mom's Garage:

"All of us who work at Mom's make financial and policy decisions about how the garage runs at shop meetings. Our purpose is to put making a humane working environment for ourselves and encouraging quality work at a fair price above making the highest possible profit. We don't have any hired employees and would not as a matter of policy.

"We are organized as a nonprofit corporation in the State of Oregon, though our method of operation is usually called a collective. As a nonprofit corporation, though, if we were to go out of business, our assets would have to go to another nonprofit, or tax exempt, organization. We have a board of directors, who do not work here. We, who work here, pay ourselves a percentage of flat-rate labor charges for the work we perform during the week. We do not have stockholders or pay dividends or make profits as such, or carry on business in a capitalist sense. When we do have surpluses, when there is money left over from parts markup or space-rental charges, it invariably goes to purchase tools or equipment that would be too expensive or inefficient for individual mechanics to purchase. In the future, we would like to apply some surplus to improving our working environment or providing some fringe benefits for the mechanics."

According to a member of a collectively run print shop:

"It was difficult to get the information that we needed about our legal existence. This was not because we are women but because we are a collective, and many people do not understand that form of doing business yet."

We recommend that you consult your lawyer about the procedures involved if you choose to organize your business as a collective.

Obtaining a Business License

The particular business licenses that you will need for your business vary according to local city, county, and state requirements. We recommend that you find out all of your licensing requirements early, long before you secure your first customer. Call your city hall, your county government offices, and the state licensing bureau. (If you are lucky, your state may have one number to call to learn which licenses are required, how much they will cost, what you must do to comply with regulations, and how long it will take to receive your license.)

Choosing Your Location

Working out of Your Own Home

In searching out a location, start by looking close to home—your home! We'll put aside the remark made by one of our favorite columnists, who says that she and the President of the United States are the only people who really do work out of their homes. In our survey, we've found successful decorators, seamstresses, artists, musicians, cooking instructors, landscape designers (and US Presidents)—all working at home. Of course, not every business is best operated that way. Some things neighbors won't tolerate, and neither will your customers. Here's a list of advantages we've uncovered from talking to women who do business at home:

1. The most obvious advantage: it's cheaper! You'll save money by not having to pay extra for rent, utilities, and furnishings. Look at it this way:

If your office rent	= $250	per month
Office telephone	= $40	"
Gas, electricity, etc.	= $25	"
Your total expenses are	= $315	per month

Add on your costs for commuting to your office (gas, parking, auto expenses, and the like, not to mention time spent commuting)

= $50

Total = $365 per month

Now consider your profit goals per month. Say you hope to make a profit of around $250 a week, or $1,000 a month. You've already saved $365 a month in office expenses by working out of your home. (A portion of this "savings" may be taken up by a slight increase in some home bills—phone, electricity, for example.) And there is another hidden savings from Uncle Sam. A percentage of your home expenses can be deducted from your income tax for your home office. However, this allowable deduction does have specific regulations, which you must abide by in order to consider it a legal deduction. For example, you must use the portion of your home that you deduct as a business expense *exclusively* for business. In other words, you may not deduct the office space in your den if you also use it for watching TV or as a guest room. If you do use a portion of your home exclusively for business, you may deduct that portion of your heating bill, home interest, taxes, and even depreciation. For instance, if your business office is 12 feet by 15 feet, or 180 square feet, and your entire home contains 1800 square feet of floor space, you may allocate 10 percent of your home heating expenses, 10 percent of the interest on your mortgage, 10 percent of your taxes, plus some depreciation. Here is how it works:

yearly heat bill:	$1,000 × 10% =	$100
interest on mortgage	$2,500 × 10% =	250
taxes	$1,000 × 10% =	100
depreciation	(figured below)	200
total home use deduction		$650

In deducting depreciation, you must exclude the property portion of your home and only consider the value of the building structure. Thus,

your home and property value	=	$50,000
the property alone	=	10,000
the home alone	=	40,000; 10% = $4,000

and $4,000 depreciated over, say, twenty years would be $200 a year.

2. By starting your business at home, your initial investment can be relatively small, and you can begin by working just part-time, if you want to. You can take your first steps slowly, letting the business grow gradually as you determine how much time you are willing to devote to it. You'll probably manage all the business yourself at first, so your overhead will be low. The opportunities for expansion will be completely in your control—you'll feel no pressure to expand to justify shop expenses, for instance.

"I worked in one furniture store after another, learning the interior-design business," said the wife of a career military man. "By moving around often, I had the opportunity to learn many different aspects of the furniture and design business. When I felt I had learned enough of the trade, I decided to set up shop in my own home. I decorated my entire house in furniture and accessories that I offered for sale. When I had everything in order, I sent out letters to all my friends and former customers, telling them of the interior-design shop I had opened in my home."

Like many other home businesses, this interior designer eventually felt the need for more showroom space and a desire for her home to return to its earlier role as a sanctuary from business pressures. But the years she spent operating the business from her home enabled her to become established and to build up her clientele without the added worries of office expenses.

3. If you have small children, running a business out of your home helps you be there when you're needed. It allows you to be more flexible in your working hours, so that your schedule can follow along more easily with your family obligations.

"When my babies were born, I took up oil painting as a hobby. Painting was great for my need for creative expression, but my children made it all but impossible for me to concentrate on painting for any length of time. Then I found needlepoint. I could design and paint my own small needlepoint canvases, then pick the piece up and easily put it down again before, between, and after naps, diapers, and feedings. The owner of a needlework shop noticed my designs and ordered some for her shop. Soon I was marketing them in many different shops. I also began teaching needlepoint classes in my home one day a week. (Next fall, I'm expanding to two classes.) I charge $12.50 for eight lessons, and I usually get a number of original-canvas-design orders from my students. My classes have benefited me in a way I hadn't anticipated—I'm meeting other women in my area who share my own interests, and by working at home, I can arrange my work hours around my family's needs."

4. For certain types of businesses, especially manufacturing and service businesses, a home office may be ideal. Many service business offices are not much more than a telephone number, since the services are often performed at the client's location. And if you manufacture a product and rely on a wholesaler or a retail shop to sell it to the public, you may not need a shop of your own (unless you don't have the work space that you need at home). An extra room, an attic, or your garage is often easily adapted to your needs. Many seamstresses, for instance, find that their profits are greatest when they produce their goods at home and sell them through established retail outlets or crafts fairs, eliminating the worries and expenses of running their own shop.

"I usually spend eight hours a day in my sewing room at home. I've learned to pace myself. Working at home by myself, I found that in the beginning, I often worked until I was too tired and grew bored with what I was doing. Now, when my back and shoulders are tired from sewing, I go on to packaging or labeling. I cut out my fabric pieces in the evening in the family room, so I can spend that time with my husband. When I have large orders to fill or when I want to spend extra time shopping for fabric or designing, I subcontract the sewing work to other women who sew in their own homes. I have a list of women I have trained to follow my patterns and instructions."

Sewing at home can have unforeseen problems, however, as one Portland, Oregon, window-shade designer learned: "In my basement, I have very strict rules: Wash your hands before starting work with the fabric, no smoking or eating while working, no coffee cups on the work tables. Everyone knows the rules. Everyone except my cat, I should say. He loved to sleep curled up on the shade material. He wouldn't learn from his mistakes, either. He's the only one in my workroom I've had to let go."

Service businesses are often the easiest type to run from your home, and, according to the statistics we've read, they are the fastest-growing type of business in the United States. More and more people are having things done now that they used to do themselves. If you perform your service at the client's location (wallpapering, cleaning, house sitting, for example), you have the added benefit of being out and about and not confined to a small room or shop.

"My first business venture was a junk shop. I bought up a few households for a small initial investment and set up business in a building I already owned. I opened for business, and in two weeks I knew I *hated* it—I couldn't stand being confined all day in the shop. I needed to get out and around. Luckily my investment was small, and I was able to get out of the business easily. My next venture has been a tremendous success. I have no office, no furniture, no employees. I opened for business by going around to paint and wallpaper shops and leaving my card offering my wallpapering services and my home phone number. For two months, I solicited my new business in this way. Six years have passed since I did this advertising, and I still average a call a day for my services."

This woman enjoys the benefits of a home "office," that is, no added rent, no employees, no overhead—yet has the added pleasure of a little travel and a variety of scenery. Her experience in the junk shop is one to keep in mind, though, with regard to having your own business operate from your home.

This leads us to the list of drawbacks to working at home.

1. As Erma Bombeck says, the big problem with working at home is that no one treats you like a professional. What business office have you ever been in where a voice from the back room is yelling, "We're out of toilet paper!" Schools, children, and friends find it difficult to resist you when they know you are captive in your home office.

Professionalism may sometimes become an issue in your home business, even though it shouldn't be. Other persons doing business—including a surprising number of women—often disparage those operating out of their homes, for whatever reasons of their own. The manager of several Northwest crafts shows puts it this way:

"Frequently I'll present the details of my own crafts business to the manager of a shopping center, and then I'll describe the elements in my plan for organizing a craft show in his center. When I have finished, I'll still receive the comment, 'Yes, my dear, but what do you really *do*?' Because I operate out of my own home and manage shows in a semi-part time fashion (that is, I don't hold a show every day), I am accused of not being 'professional.'"

A woman in the typesetting business told us: "When you are doing business at home, some people, especially men, feel that you are doing it just for a hobby. And since they think it is your hobby, they feel that your rates should be 'unprofessionally' low. Without having to pay extra rent for a shop, I *was* able to offer my customers a slightly lower price. I was also new in the business, just getting started, and it is usual to offer a very competitive price when starting out. But I was working just as hard as if I had been working out of a shop, and because of my residential location, I had to include the added expense of deliveries. Though I found that my women customers were generally enthusiastic and supportive of my home business, men often treated me as though I were not thoroughly professional. I think this is because men most often do their work outside the home, whereas women would often welcome the possibility of doing business at home."

2. "Working at home is both a blessing and a hindrance," says a craftswoman who whittles for a living. "Constant interruptions slow down my work, and I haven't been able to come up with a good solution to the problem."

Before taking on this kind of situation, perhaps you had better consider how well you work with interference—like crying, barking, TV noise, and friends who figure if you're doing it at home, you're doing it just for fun.

One of your biggest problems may be convincing your family and your customers that your hours are limited. The owner of a typing and editing business in Seattle, Washington, mentioned the difficulties she encounters when the phone rings after business hours and she answers it, not as an entrepreneur but as a businesswoman who is through for the day. "I just get nasty and say the office is closed, call back in the morning at ten. Then I repeat it again and again, like a recording, until they get the message."

This woman listed for us what, after two and a half years experience, she finds to be the biggest problems of working out of the home:

(a) Customers call as late as 10:30 at night or as early as 6:45 in the morning and on Sunday, demanding information and/or service.

(b) Errands to the bank and other businesses that are open only during normal business hours are always done at the risk of not being home when a customer calls. And, I've found that the majority of customers refuse to speak to an answering machine.

(c) The temptation to go for a walk on a sunny afternoon for an hour or two if there is no business must never be yielded to, nor can you get involved in an elaborate nonbusiness project of some kind. That phone will surely ring if you are midway through, say, kneading dough for a couple of loaves of bread. If you have bits of cloth and pieces of pattern spread out all over the floor, a customer will certainly be coming to your door unannounced.

3. We have already mentioned the problem of confinement. If you frequently look for excuses to get out of the house, think again before locating your business there.

4. Working out of your home may demand that you offer additional services that might cut into your profits and take much of your time. For instance, "Being located in a strictly residential area that is not zoned for business use, I had to be careful that the business did not draw too much traffic. So I offered pickup and delivery service for my customers. Eventually this delivery aspect of my business took far too much time and caused me and sometimes my customers great inconvenience. For instance, I had to make deliveries during the business hours of my customers. Therefore, I found myself doing my own work late into the night. At other times, I would have one order ready to go, but would have to make that customer wait for his delivery while I finished

another order that would go to the same general area. I often found myself working twelve to sixteen hours a day, trying to compensate for the hours I lost making deliveries."

5. Another problem falls under the category of motivation. Many women find it difficult to embark on the day's business enterprises when, from the corner of their eye, they spy dirty dishes, unfolded laundry, a fresh pot of coffee, and one last cinnamon roll. Women who have worked outside the home for a company and then decide to free-lance out of their homes often give voice to this problem. Says one: "When I had to be at work at eight every morning, seated at a nice clean desk, surrounded by other hard-working folk, I had no problem getting the day underway. Now it's eight-thirty before I finish reading the paper, I'm not even dressed yet when my neighbor calls to gossip, and my cat comes down with the runs. What am I doing wrong?"

They should heed the advice of a Beaverton, Oregon, artist who tells us: "I go into my workroom most days at 9 A.M. You can't wait until you have the urge to do something or you'd never get anything done."

A home office demands scheduling and routine, just as any other business office does. You must be able to overlook temptation and proceed with your work and ideas without interruption. Here are a few tips on organizing yourself in a home office. We've gathered them from various sources and offer them because many of the home-based businesswomen we spoke with mentioned their desire to learn how other women are coping with these problems.

1. Set specific hours for working, then try to stick to them.
2. Make a list of things to get done, in order of importance, then get to work on number one. Don't work on anything else until that is finished. Then proceed down the list, one step at a time. You may not cover a lot of ground, but you'll get the most pressing things handled first, and they'll be taken care of completely. Better to deal with your greatest problem entirely than to end the day—or the week—with ten projects half-resolved and nothing really done.
3. Avoid telephonitis, both in making and receiving calls. When you are making a business call, note on a card the facts you wish to

cover and questions you want to ask. Jot down the answers that you get on the same card, and you have a written record of your information. When you are receiving calls, try to be brief. If personal calls interrupt, you'll just have to be firm. State your business hours and suggest a call back after hours.

4. Working at home can be confining, sometimes lonely, occasionally frustrating. You'll have to pace yourself. If a problem or a job seems too big to tackle, try breaking it up into several little problems and work them separately. If you get stuck on something, double-check your facts, try to look at it from a different point of view (standing on your head?), then leave it for a while and come back to it again when it has rested in your mind.

5. Give yourself a little motivation—a personal bonus—a walk in the park, a date for lunch—when a job is completed. Or, if face-saving is your only prod, tell someone else what you're accomplishing that week. You'll be compelled to keep your word.

Just remember, discipline is vital when you work in your home. If you can't discipline yourself, best "get ye to the office" so you can get some work done!

Locating in a Shop

Enough news on the home front. How about setting up shop . . . in a shop? There are many aspects to consider in choosing your business location. First, let's listen to a sampling of the advice we've been offered. We'll begin with a sad tale:

"Because I couldn't decide on a catchy name for my carpet and floor covering store, I named it for the street it was located on. Last year the city commenced an urban-renewal project that proposed relocating all the businesses along our street and replacing the business district with low-cost housing for the elderly. Though they would pay relocation costs, who could repay my losses doing business as A Street Carpets on D Street. And if I renamed the business, I would suffer not only from a new location but I would lose the customers I had already serviced and won under the previous name."

Moral: Business name and location are two different things. Think carefully before you make them one.

Considering a second-story operation? Some small-business owners are tempted by lower rents to begin working in an upstairs office or studio. Listen to the warning from the owner of an Olympia, Washington, herb store and massage practice: "When I bought the business it was in a second-story location. Six months ago, we moved to a new location on street level, and the business has become more recognized as a therapeutic massage and healing center. The second-story location kept a lot of folks we wanted to attract away and attracted those we'd rather avoid. It is for this reason also that I would never operate a massage business out of my home, as some do. There are always some men who come just looking for sex."

Moral: To look like your business is on the up-and-up, choose a location that is downstairs.

"I chose my location in Old Town Portland because it was one of the few places I considered that did not require me to pay a profit percentage in addition to my lease agreement. The space had been vacant for twenty-five years, and the cobwebs were there to prove it. But the building owner gave me $1,000 to fix the place up, and I've been delighted with my location from the beginning."

"I found a small old house to rent for $125 a month," the owner of a craft business told us. "It needed fixing up, but it was close enough to my home so that I was available to my children when they needed me. I would advise others to fix up an old house for their business. Don't go to a mall and pay all your profits out in rent. People come to my business from miles around."

"My partners and I all live in the immediate area of our business, and so we feel locally motivated. Being part of the neighborhood, we feel our services are more personal than those offered in the shopping centers."

Moral: Don't start out giving all of your profits to the landlord. Small businesses are still thriving outside of the "plastic bubble" shopping malls.

The owner of three Seattle-area bridal and gown shops who has stores in both the downtown area and shopping centers explains: "The choice of a downtown or mall location would, of course, depend upon the area. I have done well in both. In a shopping mall, you have to maintain mall hours, which is quite costly. The rent figures are also very high. But you do get more shoppers. The downtown location can be run with less help and for fewer hours. All in all, though, it is the bottom line that counts, and I have had about the same success at both locations."

"Shopping malls are great," according to one entrepreneur whose stores are located in suburban malls. "But you have to make sure from the beginning that the mall expense will be worth it for your business. The mall must give you service as well as a place to locate. Sometimes the choice of locating your new business in a mall is not up to you. Many shopping centers screen new businesses carefully and will not accept you until you have proven yourself in business."

Moral: If you choose to establish your business in a shopping center, make sure you have justified this choice with the facts in your business plan, your financial projections, and your personal business goals.

Special circumstances may often determine your choice of location. The owner of a "soupery" lunchroom located in the Eugene, Oregon, YMCA explains her choice very simply: "I was trained in cooking, and the need arose at the YMCA for a lunch operation. The equipment was there, as was the need to feed people cheaply."

The story of a Northwest business legend seems appropriate here. Fred Meyer, the late founder of the grocery–department store chain which bears his name, operated a grocery store in downtown Portland in the 1920s. Police put a ban on parking near his store to prevent the traffic jams that formed at the popular retail establishment. They almost put Fred out of business. To keep the customers coming, Meyer paid out thousands of dollars in parking fines that customers received while they were shopping at the store. As he paid the dollar fines, however, he pinpointed on a map the addresses of the ticketed customers. It soon became apparent that most of his shoppers were coming from the residential Hollywood district on the east side of town. When he decided, a few years later, to move his merchandising empire to a suburban location, Fred knew just where to locate. The Hollywood store opened in 1931.

There is another possibility you might consider if you're still stewing over your choice of location. How about sharing space with another business? Not only will you have a little financial support in sharing office expenses, rent, and possibly legal advice, but you'll have an office mate who just might supply a little moral support while you're getting your feet on the ground. Many businesses complement each other nicely—antiques and flowers, children's wear and handmade toys, bookkeeping and secretarial services. It may even be possible for you to provide your space-sharing partner with some kind of part-time service in your field of business to cover your share of the rent. This type of communal operation is a kind of share-the-costs partnership, as opposed to a profit-sharing relationship.

We learned of another kind of location sharing that works nicely for a Bellevue, Washington, woman who creates beautiful dried flower arrangements. As her business grew, she needed more space than she had available at home, yet she wanted to avoid the high rent of a shop of her own. Solution? She leases the basement of a home in her area. The location and rent are good for her, and there is another benefit. Her landlady, an elderly woman, enjoys the security of knowing she is not alone in the house all day, as well as the small added income she receives in rent.

Another kind of space-sharing enterprise has developed in an eastern city. Finding it difficult to operate her small consulting business out of her home, one woman contacted several other small service-oriented businesses, and together they rented an entire floor in a large office building. They opened up The Workplace, and together they enjoy the benefits of an office without all the expense. Each entrepreneur can select the services she needs (including answering service, typewriter, telephone, secretary or researcher, etc.) as well as determine which facilities would serve her best. She may rent office space monthly, or simply choose to use a desk and phone for the day. Movable partitions divide the office space, with private offices also available. Costs range from a daily desk and phone charge of fifteen dollars to over three hundred dollars a month for private office space. Conference rooms are also available. Clients in this work-space-sharing arrangement have the advantages of mutual stimulation and moral support that are not available to those working alone at home.

In general, choosing the right location for your business is usually the result of a consideration of the needs of your particular kind of business. The owner of a handicrafts store spent months looking for the right location. "I needed plenty of parking, good visibility from the street, enough shop space, and, to top it off, reasonable rent!"

There is a rule of thumb for figuring out if the rent on a prospective location is affordable. Consider that 6 percent of your intended sales volume can be set aside for rent. If, for example, you intend to make $25,000 a year in sales:

$$\$25{,}000 \div 12 = \$2083/\text{month}$$
$$\$2083/\text{month} \times 6\% = \$125/\text{month}$$

Therefore, $125 is the highest rent you should be willing to pay.

We've assembled a checklist to help you find the best location. When you think you've got your niche, see if you've checked out all of these points.

Location Double Check

_____ Why did the last tenant move from this location?

_____ Is this location convenient for the type of customer I am after?

_____ Have I personally checked the flow of traffic at this location (watching the building in the morning, at noon, and at night as well as on the weekends)?

_____ Am I choosing this location solely because of cheap rent?

_____ Have I considered my *type* of business when choosing this location? For instance, clothing stores benefit from being close together, but two shops handling the same goods—records, wigs, sometimes books—often split the trade, for a mutual loss.

_____ Since 40 percent of the nation's retail business occurs in shopping centers, have I:

_____ 1. chosen to follow the trend? Even though the high rent necessitates a high volume of sales from the very beginning, I feel the high volume of traffic will secure these sales.

_____ 2. chosen to disregard the statistics? I will establish on my own without the interference of mall managers, high-pressure rents, and shopping-center promotions that won't promote my kind of business.

If I checked 1, have I considered the type of shopping center that will best serve my needs?

_____ a. a neighborhood center (lots of parking, close to a large residential area)

_____ b. a community center (usually contains one large discount or department store and several smaller, associated shops)

_____ c. a regional shopping center (big)

_____ Realizing that a high percentage of new businesses do not make it through the first five years, have I commmitted myself to purchase the building in which I am locating or signed a ten-year lease?

_____ Is the location that I have selected zoned for my kind of business?

_____ In this location, will I have easy access to the suppliers who service my business?

_____ Have I had this building examined by a building inspector (and if I'm opening a restaurant, by a health inspector) so I am sure I won't have to pay for unforeseen repairs to bring the building up to code?

_____ Has my lawyer checked my lease before I signed it?

_____ Have I checked the other stores in this area and determined who will be my biggest competitor, what price line they carry, how many customers they handle, and so on?

Feel ready now to put down some roots? Choosing a location is one of the biggest decisions you have to make. Take your time and consider a couple of alternatives before you make a final choice. And if you make a poor choice initially, all is not lost. Recently we noticed a quarter-page ad in our morning newspaper. "Grand Closing Sale," it announced. "Everyone who comes into our store," it read, "has found our merchandise exciting. Trouble is, hardly anyone comes into our store, so we're looking for a better spot." The bottom of the ad gave the store's address, "inconveniently located at . . ." Take heart. You can always move!

For Additional Help in Selecting Your Location

1. Ask your banker to recommend several people who are familiar with the problems of location for your type of business.
2. The Chamber of Commerce has statistics on the economic and business climate in your area, offers free brochures and some literature for a fee, and will counsel you on your project.
3. The Census Bureau publishes Census Tracts on Population that may help define the composition of the population in the area you are considering (available at your public library).
4. The local office of the SBA is willing to help, in classes and in personal counseling, with this element of your business as well as with many other problems you may encounter.
5. Trade associations may offer advice on locating your kind of business.
6. Professional women's organizations in your field of business may be able to offer some enlightenment.
7. Write The Workplace, Inc., 1302 Eighteenth Street, N.W., Suite 203, Washington, D.C. 20036 for more information on the space-sharing enterprise described on page 99.

Setting Up Business Books

Almost every woman we talked to would rather have discussed knitting sweaters, fixing cars, or papering walls than keeping the business books. Most women go into business because they are expert at something; usually it is not bookkeeping. But despite this, your business cannot succeed without an accurate set of business books and someone to interpret them. We found that poor record keeping has destroyed more small businesses than inferior products or marketing mistakes. Experts tell us that 80 percent of small-business failures stem from the owners' inability to recognize what a good set of records should disclose. In other words, you may know what your bank balance is, but do you know how much money you owe your creditors or how much money your customers owe you? Do you know how much money you have invested in merchandise and equipment? Your books will answer these questions and a thousand others. Your books are to you what a thermometer and a stethescope are to a doctor—they help you keep tabs on the health of your business. Several women we talked to learned this fact the hard way.

"There was a point when we were working fifteen hours a day, and because the customers were screaming louder than the books, we let the bookkeeping slide till we absolutely had to turn in our quarterly reports or pay the bills. Then we would have to work straight through several nights in order to finish them. We finally wised up and hired Joni. She has done wonders for our business. She not only keeps up on daily records, but she bills our customers the day they receive our service. We get our money quickly and then are able to pay our own bills."

And one aspiring interior decorator told us of her woes. "I made the mistake of carrying the figures of my business bookkeeping around in my head. I let too many contractors owe me money for too long, had to borrow money to pay my creditors, and thus lost all my profits. I have yet to see the money some people owe me, simply because I didn't bother to keep a record of it. I now have an accountant, who is trying to straighten my mess out. It would have been so much easier had I gotten him from the start."

Other women had a lot of advice to give on the subject. Mostly it came to this:

"The bookkeeping aspect of business is just as important as the selling aspect. You can be fantastic up front and fall down totally in back. You must keep records on a day-by-day basis. The tendency is to put it off. My advice is don't."

We might add that there are many advantages to keeping your bookkeeping current and doing it on a daily basis. A quick, efficient billing policy enables you to pay your bills on time and maintain a good credit rating. A steady flow of cash into the business will also enable you to take advantage of the discounts that many wholesalers offer. By saving $100 on a quantity discount, or by paying bills early and receiving a special discount, you can achieve the same level of profit as $1,000 in additional sales would provide.

Another woman had these words of advice: "Bookkeeping? At first, I had a SCORE representative come in and help me set up my books. (SCORE—Service Corps of Retired Executives—is an SBA-sponsored program.) It is free and a wonderful help. We now have a bookkeeping service do the complicated government stuff. My husband is a businessman, and he reads the information they send us and gives me some feedback on what I'm doing. He told me he was going to cut off my fingers if I didn't stop writing checks. I consider *that* feedback. My advice is: if you don't have a husband who can read and interpret the bookkeeping information, get an accountant."

Another woman told us: "I do all my own bookkeeping; therefore, I can keep my finger on the pulse of what is happening in my three stores. Bill paying takes many hours, sometimes fourteen to sixteen hours in one day. Still, I feel that this is time well spent."

We can't give you a college course in accounting, but we can familiarize you with some bookkeeping basics. Remember, there are three good reasons to keep your business records accurate and current:

1. Uncle Sam. We really needn't say much more, except that we've heard that he loves to slap penalties and fines on people who carry their bookkeeping around in their heads—just to make sure he isn't getting cheated out of anything.

2. If you ever plan to get a bank loan, you'd better have some business books handy to show the banker your impressive track record, both before and after you secure your loan.

3. And, as we mentioned before, keeping accurate books is the only possible way to keep a tab on the health of your business.

Your business bookkeeping system should answer the following questions:

How long has my merchandise (my money) been sitting on my shelves?
How much money did I make yesterday, last week, last month, last year?
Who owes me money and for how long?
Is my bank account flush?
How much money have I put into my business?
How much do I still owe the bank on my business loan?
How much do I have to make each day to cover expenses?
How much must I pay in taxes?
Am I making enough money to open another shop?

We could go on endlessly, but you've probably got the idea.

Whomever you choose to do your business books, heed the advice of one boutique owner: "The bookkeeper must have a penchant for detail." She explained that she learned this from past experience. Her father and his partner had absolutely nothing in common. Yet one was an excellent salesman and the other an expert bookkeeper. In her opinion, this was the perfect formula for success. We noticed many such partnerships.

"Susan is the whole shop personality, the saleswoman, and I am the bookkeeper. She sells the stuff and I keep track of where we are financially. Neither of us could make a go of it without the other."

When you decide to get outside help with your business books, you will pay for the services of a CPA or a bookkeeping service, or both. We got varied advice on the subject.

One SCORE representative we talked to strongly advised small-business owners to spare the expense of an accountant and use a bookkeeping service. Another woman expressed much the same sentiment: "I prepare the necessary documents—employee hourly records, taxes, accounts receivable, inventory, and so on for the bookkeeper, and she takes it from there. All the CPA does is sign the IRS forms at the end of the year and authenticate them. This is the least expensive way."

Overwhelmingly, however, the women who have an influential CPA behind them would have it no other way.

"After eight years in business, I still don't understand all the accounting terminology, but my CPA is always there to answer my questions and explain everything I want to know until I do."

"My business was just going along ho-hum when I had a bookkeeping service doing my work. When I changed to a CPA, his advice helped me so much that business skyrocketed."

If you are determined to do as much of the bookkeeping as you can, we still advise you to have a CPA if for no other reason than for figuring your taxes. The members of one partnership told us that from their experience, this could never be overemphasized:

"We both had well-paying government jobs before we went into business for ourselves. But our first year in business, we earned next to nothing. Our accountant told us about income averaging, something we'd never heard of, and he actually got the government to pay us back over a thousand dollars from income taxes we had paid in past years. Considering the money he saved us, our CPA was well worth the fees."

It's your CPA's job to be up on all the tax laws that pertain to you and your business. And these laws change every day.

Another point on the subject of CPAs and taxes: if you are operating a small business out of your home and report a loss of income the first year, your tax return may be examined and your losses may be disallowed on the grounds that you don't operate with the expectation of making a profit. The government investigator may charge that you do business as a hobby. You will need an accountant to prepare you for such an event and to help you organize evidence of your profit-making intentions.

In Chapter Two, we discussed how to select an accountant. When you've made your selection, you can expect your accountant to:

1. set up your accounting system
2. help you with loan applications before you go to the bank

3. keep you current on tax laws, prepare your taxes, and represent you before the IRS, if necessary
4. periodically review your books and prepare a financial statement
5. help you make budgets and projections
6. help you choose an accounting period for purposes of reporting taxes

(One do-it-yourselfer we talked to decided upon a mid-year tax deadline rather than the traditional December 31, only to realize later that June, July, and August are the months she is away from home on store buying trips. She now has to fill out a volume of paperwork in order to get the deadline changed back to December 31. If only she had consulted an accountant first . . .)

Learning the Language

When you first speak to an accountant, it helps if you know a little accounting jargon. Here are a few terms you'll be hearing. To aid in defining them, let's pretend that you are running a peanut-butter-cookie factory out of your home.

Bookkeeping: the process of recording details—how much money your cookie sales brought in yesterday, how much that 50-gallon drum of peanut butter cost you, and how much you paid Sally for helping out last week.

Accounting: the process of putting it all together, taking all the totals from the bookkeeping and making an analysis of how your cookie business is doing. Taking all into account, what can you do to improve business?

Accrual and cash basis of reporting income: you have to tell Uncle Sam on which basis you are going to report your income. The *accrual* method reports all income and expenses incurred during your tax period, whether or not the income has been received or the expenses paid. The *cash basis* reports all cash transactions. It does not show unpaid credit sales and purchases and may present a misleading picture of your business. For example, you may show $100 in received income for last month and $500 paid expenses, simply because your credit customers haven't paid you yet. Doctors often use the cash method because they have very little inventory and some of their patients may never pay. You'll probably be better off to use the accrual method.

Cash flow: New York City brought this particular aspect of their city financing into national headlines. They couldn't pay their workers, not because they misbudgeted but because the taxpayers hadn't gotten all their tax money in yet. So it's not how much money is owed to you that is important here, it's how much money you have in your hand at the time the bills are due. If you owe $25 to the gas company and Mary Brunk owes you $30, her unpaid account won't turn your ovens back on.

Journals and ledgers: the *journal* is a business diary in which you record every business transaction that occurs—the flour you bought, the money you received, the taxes you paid. And the *ledger* is a rerecording of all this information into a more usable form. It is made up of accounts: one account for supply expenses (flour, sugar, peanut butter), one account for equipment expenses (ovens, mixer, bowls), one account for income. You may have three accounts or three hundred, depending on how big your business is.

You may either: (1) Combine your general journal and ledger, as in the example that follows:

General Journal					Ledgers		
Date	Check #	Description of Entry	Account to be Recorded in	Amount	Supply Expense Account	Income Account	Utility Expense Account
1-2-81	1	M.C. Market	Supply Expense	15 —	15 —		
1-3-81		Jennie Reese	Income	40 —		40 —	
1-3-81	2	Portland Electric Co	Util. Expense	20 —			20 —
1-8-81	3	M.C. Market	Supply Expense	40 —	40 —		
1-9-81		Joey Timm	Income	40 —		40 —	

Or you may: (2) Keep them separate by transferring the journal entries to the specific accounts in the ledger:

In order to use all this information you've recorded in your journal and ledger, think of each as a piece of a puzzle, and think of your accountant as a master at putting your puzzle together. You give your accountant all the pieces to create the whole picture of your business for you. Your accountant does this with financial statements and balance sheets.

General Journal

Date	Check #	Description of entry	Account to be Recorded in	Amount	Transfered
1-2-81	1	MC Market	Supply Exp	15 —	✓
1-3-81		Jennie Reese	Income	40 —	✓
1-3-81	2	Portland Electric Co	Util Exp.	20 —	✓
1-8-81	3	M.C. Market	Supply Exp.	40 —	✓
1-9-81		Joey Timm	Income	40 —	✓

Income Account

Date	Description of Entry	Amount
1-3-81	Jennie Reese	40 —
1-9-81	Joey Timm	40 —

Utility Expense Account

Date	Check #	Description of Entry	Amount
1-3-81	2	Portland Electric Co	20 —

Supply Expense Account

Date	Check #	Description of Entry	Amount
1-2-81	1	M.C. Market	15 —
1-8-81	3	M.C Market	40 —

Financial statement: a summary of the records of your business, compiled so that you will be able to tell at a glance the overall health of your business. It will include an income statement (how much you made or lost during a certain period) and a balance sheet (explanation follows). Using these, your accountant will help you determine trends, recognize danger signs, and analyze the business. How often do you prepare a financial statement? It depends on how often you want to see how your business is doing.

Balance sheet: a statement prepared to show the financial position of your business. It shows the various assets of your business and the claims on these assets. And speaking of assets, when your accountant is talking balance sheet to you, her or his speech will be peppered with words like . . .

Current assets: things you buy for your business that will be liquidated to cash within a year (the 500-pound sack of flour in your storeroom).

Fixed assets: long-term items—your ovens, cookie sheets, and mixer.

Intangible assets: assets having no physical nature—your trade name, your secret recipe, or a patent you may have on your automatic fork press, the machine you invented that fork presses a hundred cookies a second.

But this system does have disadvantages:

1. This system provides a record of your income and expenses, but it does not provide a complete record of such things as inventory, equipment, and loans—the money you paid for your cookie mixer or the money you still owe the bank for the loan you took out. Nor does it take into account the 500 pounds of bargain-priced sugar you have sitting in your storeroom.

2. It is frightfully easy to make mistakes with this system, because you only have to write down the amount once. The Phoenicians invented the double-entry system to eliminate that problem.

Double-entry system: simply means that you make two entries for every amount you spend or receive; each transaction is recorded twice. For example, if you spend $100 for flour, you

Choosing a Bookkeeping System

Your accountant will suggest the best system for you, but here are a few of the possibilities:

Single entry system: the simplest system, it really should only be used by the very smallest businesses—businesses that deal on a strictly cash, no-credit basis. You simply record all money spent or taken in.

At the end of the month, total both columns to see if you made a profit or a loss.

Date	Check No.	Issued to or Received from	Item	Expense	Income
1-2-81	#108	MC Market	100 lb. flour	$15.00	
1-2-81	Invoice #307	J. Reese	20 doz. cookies		$40.00
1-2-81	#109	Electric Co.	Utility bill	$15.00	
1-8-81	#110	MC Market	10 lb. peanut butter	$10.00	
1-9-81	Invoice # 92	Joey Timm	10 doz. cookies		$20.00
January Income: $20.00 profit				$40.00	$60.00

enter this in two places—as a debit (increase) in your supply expense and as a credit (decrease) in your cash account.

The terms "debit" and "credit" are confusing. What determines whether an amount is to be a debit or a credit? It all depends on the type of account and on whether the transaction will decrease or increase the account. We won't try to teach you this procedure here. It's not difficult, but it takes a bit of study. With your own business accounts in hand, the guidance of a good business teacher or your accountant will enable you to keep track of debits and credits.

We've mentioned that a ledger is comprised of accounts. Here are some examples of typical accounts:

- Current assets:
  - Cash in bank
  - Petty cash
  - Exchange account
  - Accounts receivable
  - Allowance for bad debts
  - Merchandise inventory
- Fixed assets:
  - Land
  - Buildings
  - Allowance for depreciation
  - Delivery equipment
  - Furniture and fixtures
  - Leasehold improvements
  - Allowances for amortization
- Current liabilities:
  - Accounts payable
  - Notes payable
  - Income taxes
  - Social security payable
  - Sales tax payable
- Long-term liability:
  - Notes payable—long-term capital
  - Owner's capital
  - Profit and loss

Pricing

Pricing is, of course, a critical factor in running your business. Your selling price for an item may be merely the manufacturer's suggested retail price, or it may reflect a more complex estimation of the entire costs in production (including fixed and variable factors), coupled with your profit needs and your educated guess of what the market will bear.

Determining Your Best Price

Your CPA will be able to help you with pricing, but if you're interested in a general rule:

Determine the exact cost of labor and materials for each item. Multiply that figure by the number of items you hope to sell in a year. Add to this your *entire* overhead for the year (don't forget rent, insurance, equipment payments, utilities, delivery expenses, etc.), plus your intended profit (how big a carrot is needed to urge you on in this endeavor?). You can determine your best price by dividing this total by the number of items you expect to be able to sell.

Let's see how Carole uses this formula in her home sewing business:

Carole is an expert seamstress with lots of energy and three young children. To earn just a little spending money, she enjoys working in her sewing room a few hours a week. She puts together an irresistible assembly of sewn-and-stuffed characters from A. A. Milne's stories: Winnie-the-Pooh, Tigger, Piglet, and Roo. She shops for fabric remnants on sale, whenever possible, as well as for bargains on stuffing and felt trims. She arbitrarily set a price for her characters by using a kind of "reverse deduction" method of her own. She decided first how much she thought *she* would be willing to pay for one of her characters if she saw it in the handicraft shop where she planned to market them. She then deducted 40 percent from this price, which she knew the shop owner would take as profit, and that left her with the price she felt she could charge the store for her work. One day she finally sat down and figured out how much she was earning for all her efforts, and the figures were distressing. If she was making a dollar an hour for her work, she was lucky.

Her method of pricing took an immediate turn. Using the standard formula we noted, here is how she refigured her prices.

For each set of four characters:

1. Labor (at \$2/hr) = \$8
   Materials = \$4
   \$12

2. Direct costs (\$12) × number of sets sold per year (approximately one set per week, or 52) = \$624.

3. \$624 plus yearly overhead (sewing-machine repairs, costs of delivering items to shop each month, utilities), or \$100 = \$724.

4. \$724 plus profit (at \$25/week), or \$1300 = \$2024

5. \$2024 divided by number of sets expected to sell per year (52) = \$39 per set

Carole's best price per set, then is \$39. When the retail outlet adds to this their 40-percent profit margin (or \$15.60), each set of four characters will cost around \$55. At first, Carole felt that this price for children's toys would be prohibitive. She has learned, however, that handmade toys (especially for one's grandchildren) are in demand. If the quality is high, the customer is willing to pay the correspondingly high price.

All thumbs get whacked now and then, and this pricing rule of thumb will be no exception. Your best price not only has to bring in a profit, but it has to bring in the customers, too.

Figuring the Price-Volume Profit Relationship

There is a price-volume profit relationship through which a store owner can determine the best price for an item. By comparing selling price with number of items sold, the owner can determine which price would raise the greatest amount of revenue, after subtracting direct costs to cover overhead and profit. Let's see how this works:

Pat and her daughter own a small manufacturing business in Salem, Oregon. They produce small, laminated, hand-lettered signs—metric conversion charts for the kitchen, famous quotations, and the like. They sell their signs at West Coast gift shows and through a nationwide mail-order business of their own. To determine the best selling price for one of their signs, they must consider both their price and their projected sales. The selling price they set, less their direct costs (materials and labor), gives them the amount of contribution that each sale will provide. The contribution is used to cover their manufacturing costs (machinery depreciation, print-shop maintenance, etc.), nonmanufacturing costs (salaries, advertising, etc.), and profit. If they can produce a design for $4 and sell it for $6, the amount of contribution from each item sold is $2. To determine their best selling price, however, they must consider both price and volume of sales. Here is how they would project the contribution figures of their $4 design at different selling prices, with different projected sales:

Selling price	$6	$5	$5
Projected number of items sold	1,000	3,000	1,500
Total sales revenue from projections	$6,000	$15,000	$7,500
Total direct costs (at $4 per item)	$4,000	$12,000	$6,000
Contribution	$2,000	$ 3,000	$1,500

According to these figures, the $5 selling price would be the best price for the item, providing that 3,000 could be sold. If the women decided, however, that the market for the item would only be half that estimate, the $6 price would make the greatest contribution toward their manufacturing and nonmanufacturing costs, as well as their profit.

Many businesses that use this pricing formula find it necessary to work out a contribution percentage that remains constant for all their pricing. By researching past sales records, the business determines what the percentage of contribution is that will ensure that the price set will cover all expenses and profit needs adequately. In the example given here, for instance, if the selling price was $6 ($4 direct costs plus $2 contribution), the contribution percentage would be 33⅓ percent. After a contribution percentage has been set, it is important to check it against the records from time to time, to make sure that the revenue it supplies is sufficient. With inflation, new equipment purchases, or added inventory, it may become necessary to adjust the percentage to ensure adequate profits.

"When you are manufacturing a product," one crafts artist told us, "you have to analyze costs every step of the way, especially if you plan to sell your product at a discount to a variety of shops. Usually a shop will take an item on consignment and keep 30 percent of the sale price. Or they may buy the item outright at a 40-percent discount. Pricing, therefore, is vital, for even a couple of cents' error can ruin your profit if you're selling an inexpensive item."

As we mentioned, though, a steadfast rule for pricing is impossible. For services rendered or lessons taught, a variety of pricing methods are employed:

"In my house-plant business, my fees are dependent upon the materials I use and the amount of time I spend. If I have to make a house call, I charge a minimum of $15 an hour, figuring that will cover my gas and general wear and tear on my vehicle and on me!"

"In catering parties, I plan to make a 40-percent profit on every job, plus $2 an hour wage for myself for the time that I spend on the job. I have heard that a rule of thumb in the catering business is to multiply the total costs of the job by two."

Says a dancing teacher, "My fees are based on competition in the area."

And the owner of a typesetting business informs us, "Our fees are based on an hourly rate ascertained by total cost of doing business divided by number of business hours. We do use a special factor to equalize the output rate of trainees vs. experts." In other words, the customer pays the same amount whether the job was done by a trainee in two hours or an expert in one hour.

The most important fact to remember, according to many women, was emphatically stated by a Salem, Oregon, seamstress: "*Never undersell yourself*. Pay yourself well for the time that you spend." A licensed massage therapist put it this way: "My partner and I had been giving a discount to students and senior citizens, but we decided today that we were poorer than most of our clients. We're discontinuing discounts."

Adds a wallpapering expert, "My fees are high compared to most—but I know, and my customers know, that I'm worth it!"

Other Elements in Your Best Price

You may strive in your business to offer goods only in a certain price range. In this way, you are limiting potential customers to those of certain tastes, be they dimestore or Mercedes Benz. Experts caution that though 99¢ may be appealing on a price tag to a budget shopper, a mink jacket will sell better at $3000 than $2999. There is an element of prestige involved in the price of an item, and sometimes an exceptional bargain on an expensive item will make a shopper wonder where the flaw is.

Some other words of wisdom to consider when you are thinking of raising your prices: "I agonized for a year about raising the price of my most popular item from $1.00 to $1.25. When I finally decided that I had to raise the price, not one customer ever commented on it."

This woman was right to consider her price change very carefully. Your image of providing fair prices and good values is far more important than the few dollars or cents that may be gained through an arbitrary increase in your price.

Deciding Your Advertising Strategy

The time to begin planning your advertising strategy is now! Every businesswoman we talked with mentioned word-of-mouth advertising as the best possible way to gain new customers. No newspaper column or radio ad speaks as loud as a satisfied customer, it seems. But developing your clientele through the grapevine takes time. What's the purpose of paid advertising? It helps speed up what would have occurred by word of mouth anyway. It establishes your name, creates an image, familiarizes the public with your "logo" or business symbol.

As we mentioned in Chapter Two, your budget projections for the year should include from 2 to 5 percent of your annual gross volume for advertising. Service businesses may easily spend more than this, while retailers may get by with less. If your product has an exceptionally high markup or if your suppliers offer "co-op" funds for advertising (we'll explain these later), your budget could be as high as 10 percent for ads. Of course, the first year is the toughest—and most crucial—to predict. You don't know what your gross volume of business will be, but you're going to have to make a guess.

A Portland advertising executive advises small businesses to advertise in this way: "When you are small, you have to be clever. Try to establish a consistent advertising theme, so that your ads will have a cumulative effect. Then spend enough to have a definite impact on the market, even if it is only for a short time. If you've created an image, future advertising will have a kind of residual effect."

There are many different ways to advertise. Let's consider again what is available to you:

paid advertising: newspapers, television, radio, magazines, billboards
publicity
promotions

Paid Advertising

With paid advertising, there are two rules that you must consider when determining where and how to buy. First, we've said that you must find the way to reach the most people with the least expense. Some advertising is deceptively, and unnecessarily, expensive in these terms. For example, an ad in a free shopper newspaper may seem to be very cheap advertising, compared to the cost of advertising in your city newspaper. But how many people is your advertising really reaching? Many people don't bother to read a "freebie," while most people who pay for their newspaper read it. You may be paying $3 to reach 500 people in the shopper ad. That's $6 per 1,000 people. If you pay $20 to reach 100,000 people by advertising in your city paper, that's 20¢ per 1,000 readers. The city paper advertising is cheaper.

Second, you must make sure the people you are reaching are potential customers and have an interest in your product. For example, if you've developed a cure for postnatal depression, don't bother advertising in the sports section of the Sunday paper or on a late-night radio talk show. Advertise in the women's section of the paper or in a new-mother magazine or with a billboard situated on top of a maternity store. Most of the different media advertising agents have information on different types of businesses—lists that show who buys a specific product, when they buy, and so on. By noting established trends, you can put your money where it will do the most good. This information can also tell you what seems to work for other businesses such as yours—including your fiercest competitor!

Also, keep tabs on the advertising you have tried. "I have always kept a scrapbook of the advertising we have done. The file includes paid ads, feature stories that the newspaper has written about us, fliers, and any promotional schemes we have tried. I record what worked and what didn't. I keep notes on what the weather was like when promotions were held and what the competition was doing at the time."

Try the scrapbook idea yourself; don't trust your memory for all the details of a successful ad campaign. Here's a list of the different ways you can advertise:

1. In the newspaper. Most retailers choose newspaper advertising to reach the greatest audience. Newspaper advertising representatives can help you develop your ad and help you establish your image. As the manager of the advertising department of a large newspaper told us:

"Most people don't realize that we give free photography, layout service, and copy service along with our advertising fee here at the newspaper. Just come in, and we'll set you up with what you need. And the more feedback you can give us on what you want, the more we can help you. And by all means, deal with us directly; don't go to an ad agency. Many times ad agencies charge you for their service, then come to us and take advantage of our free photo, layout and copy services."

This advertising manager also went on to say, "The best advertising a small business can buy is 'institutionalized,' where we run an ad with the business name or logo in the paper two or three times a week, keeping the business before the public eye, familiarizing the public with your name and location. One very successful flower shop has been running a small two-by-three-inch ad three times a week in the women's section, with a different short quip each time. The owner is paying around $30 a week, and it has been well worth it, as she not only has a lot of customers, but a lot of people who are actually looking for her ad."

An advertising representative can also let you in on some of the secrets of the trade, such as the fact that a quarter-page ad is nearly as effective as a half-page spread, and costs half as much.

Some women we talked to complained that newspaper advertising costs were prohibitive. "I ran four 3-by-3-inch advertisements in the newspaper last month, and my bill was $350. The response I received from these ads could in no way pay for their expense," according to a wallpapering expert. (A much cheaper and more effective way for this businesswoman to advertise was mentioned earlier. By merely distributing her business cards to paint and wallpaper stores, another woman gained all the papering jobs she could handle. The lesson here is clear: Aim your advertising only at your prospective customers. Newspaper ads are read by young and old, owners and renters, doers and sleepers. Customers in a paint store are there for one thing—redecorating.)

We recommend that if you choose to use newspaper advertising, try the institutionalized method. Use small ads often, displaying your logo or shop name, rather than infrequent, expensive, large ads.

2. In the Yellow Pages. Nearly every businesswoman we interviewed listed her business in the Yellow Pages. This listing is primarily for the customer's convenience, and according to recent research, three out of four adults turn to the Yellow Pages to find the products and services they need. Half the people who use the Yellow Pages do not have any particular business name in mind. Yellow-Pages advertising is effective, but it's also expensive. Prices vary according to the size of your city. One Portland, Oregon, woman related her Yellow-Pages advertising experience to us.

"I had thought that paying the business rate on the telephone would entitle me to a free Yellow Pages listing, but I found that there is an additional small monthly charge for the basic listing. Also, I would like to use a larger ad, possibly incorporating the logo that I use on my business cards. I was shocked at the rates for such an ad, however—a 2-by-3-inch ad can run as high as $150—and that is per *month*! I have to try to determine if the added monthly expense will be justified by the number of new customers."

Moral: Give your ad some careful thought and work closely with your phone company ad salesperson, so that you know what you're getting and what you're paying for it.

To help you get your thoughts together before you speak to a salesperson, here are a few tips on Yellow Pages advertising:

a. Make your ad neat and uncluttered, but different.

b. Start your ad with a headline that tells prospective clients how you can supply their needs. Your name is important, but should not come first.

c. Give such information as hours, location, and extras that you offer, such as payment plans, credit cards, special hours, or free delivery.

d. Be sure to include your logo or business signature.

3. On the radio. Radio station advertising representatives will help you direct your ads to the age groups you want to reach (age of the listening audience varies at different times of the day and night). Ads are relatively expensive, depending on the time of day you choose and, of course, the radio station that you choose. An average-size advertising campaign includes about twelve "spots," or commercials, over a five-day week. For example, in a city of 100,000, a thirty-second spot may average around $40.

$40 × 12 = $480 for one week's advertising.

Also consider taking advantage of co-op dollars in radio as well as other advertising media. The manufacturers of some products will sometimes share 50 to 75 percent of the costs of an ad when their product is featured. In some cases, you may produce the ad yourself, including the name of the specific product, or you may choose to run an ad prepared by the manufacturer. In a manufacturer-prepared newspaper ad, the product is the primary feature, and there is a blank space left in the body of the ad in which the name of your business, or your logo, is inserted. Co-op advertising is beneficial not only because the cost is low, but because a manufacturer-produced ad has a professional quality.

4. Magazines. Trade magazines and special-interest or local magazines are a good bet for a specialty business or service. Often their ad rates are quite reasonable. Many of the businesswomen

we spoke with utilize feminist publications and women's business periodicals for their advertising, with reportedly mixed results.

5. Direct mail and handout techniques. This type of advertising includes the fliers that you receive from your favorite shops announcing special sales, the opening of a new art exhibit, the addition of a new line of merchandise. Under this heading we also include leaflets that you pass out or distribute through various outlets, giving notice of your new business, revised class schedules, enlarged menu or the like. If you need help in planning this kind of advertising, there are professionals listed in the Yellow Pages under Mailing Services who can assist you. Better yet, follow the five steps we outlined here and produce your own direct-mail fliers.

a. Decide what you want to say—announce your opening, a sale, or a new product.

b. Type your message on a plain sheet of white paper or your business stationery, using a carbon ribbon or new black nylon ribbon.

c. Add to your typed copy any additional hand lettering, illustrations, or paste-on artwork that you wish. Use a nonreproducing blue pencil to draw your guidelines.

d. Take your "pasted-up" flier to a "quick printer." It shouldn't cost you more than $15 for 500 copies (that's 3¢ a copy).

e. Next, hire a kid to deliver your message to the doorsteps of your neighborhood, deliver them yourself, or buy envelopes and stamps and mail the fliers to your customers. Mailing your message is by far the more expensive route, but then again, you will be reaching the people most interested in your business—your customers!

Business cards are another handout technique. Several of the women we interviewed, including many in service businesses, used business cards as their only form of advertising—with tremendous results. "A bag of bagels and a business card," is the way one of Portland's favorite bakeries promotes its product to restaurants and delis all over town. Make your cards distinctive and print them up early—they give your business an air of legitimacy. Expect to pay from $10 up for five hundred or more.

6. On television. This is expensive. If you can afford TV, your business must already be thriving and you don't need us to advise you about it. However, cable or UHF television rates may be comparable to other advertising media. Also, think in terms of television publicity. Send a press release to your local television station, telling your story in two paragraphs brimming with public interest. We don't guarantee any free publicity, but it's worth a try.

7. Billboards. An easy way to repeat a concise message. From a sandwich board saying Eat at Mom's to a lighted billboard in the heart of town, your ad will catch the eye of the passing public. With the right approach, it just might work for you. Look in the Yellow Pages under Outdoor Advertising. Billboards are changed monthly, with rates significantly higher for a lighted one.

To these charges, add the cost of having your billboard printed or painted. The cost of printing twenty-five to fifty billboard layouts can run about $50 each, depending on the colors and design, and it would be, of course, much more to have a single board printed. The billboard rental agency handles and pays for all the pasting up and maintenance of your advertisements.

Those are the basic sources of paid advertising. (If you want to rent the Goodyear blimp, you'll have to do a little further checking on your own.) Of course, if you're enterprising, you'll think of lots of other ways to get your business name in lights. Several restaurant owners, for instance, have published collections of their most popular recipes in cookbooks. Every time the home cook pulls out the cookbook to try a new dish, the restaurant gets an extra dash of advertising. Yardage stores give out measuring tapes with their business names on them, bookstores slip a personalized bookmark into each book that they sell. All of these giveaways are a form of advertising that has proven effective as well as inexpensive. Let your imagination roll with ideas that particularly suit your kind of business.

Promotions

Promotions are planned events designed to make potential customers aware of your product or service, while offering them an opportunity to participate in your business in some way. They can be fun, educational, and profitable. For example, one very innovative owner of a lunchroom–gift shop has an art sale every year. Her dining room and shop feature consigned works of art and stained glass as part of the year-round decor, so the idea of a special art sale was especially compatible.

"Once a year, I invite about twelve local artists to sell their work here at a two-day sale. I send out around five hundred invitations to customers who have signed my guest book throughout the year, as well as to other friends, local residents, and business contacts. I take only 10 percent of the sale price of each item sold, which is much less than the usual consignment-type commission. But my purpose is not so much to make money on the art sales as it is to draw in new customers."

Other promotional events include contests, drawings (never drag them out longer than 6 weeks), and special holiday gimmicks. Perhaps you might want to hold a special evening sale and donate the proceeds to charity. When you plan such an event, keep these points in mind:

1. What do I hope to gain from this promotion? Recognition for your special expertise, increased sales, a more favorable public image?
2. Who am I trying to reach with this campaign? Old clients, new customers, business associates?

When you've decided those two issues, your next problems are organization and money. The purpose of a promotion is to inform the public of your business and to promote good public relations. A poorly run event could easily do more harm than good, so plan carefully. First check the legality of what you have in mind. If it's legal, make sure your insurance will cover it and that any contracts you draw up are clear and binding. If your star attraction fails to show up at your special event, you will look—and feel—worse than he or she will.

Promotions cost money, and before you get too carried away with your ideas, you should set some financial limits. After they're set, keep aside a little extra for last-minute details that you forgot to account for. Keep all the details of your promotion in writing. That way the information is at hand if you need it, and after the promotion is over, finish your write-up of the event, including all of its successful and unsuccessful aspects. This will help you in planning future business promotions. Keep your records handy in a file.

One woman advertising executive offered this advice to those hoping for free TV coverage of their publicity-promotional gimmicks: "If your promotion is a truly visual one, go ahead and call the TV station. By visual, I mean an event such as two elephants dressed up as vacuum cleaners heading down Main Street." You are much more likely to get newspaper coverage, so be sure to call the newspaper and invite a reporter to your event. As one newspaper advertising agent told us: "There is no better advertising than mention of your business in a newspaper story."

Publicity

And speaking of publicity, paid advertising is not the only way to get your business in the public eye. Sometimes you can make yourself so newsworthy that the media are willing to feature you on their own. This kind of publicity is great. A feature story catches notice more quickly than a paid advertisement will, and it's free!

We've heard through the grapevine that newspapers are more likely to give your business a little free publicity if the business is not *entirely* commercial. That is, if you run a nonprofit organization (intentionally, by the way) or if your business has some educational aspects, you may rate a little extra space. Got anything you can teach?

"Nearly every shop in our village of women-owned businesses has rated a feature story—and these stories have all been free. We always let the media know when there is something interesting going on. One young restaurant owner sent out twenty-five invitations to a Hamburger Tasting. The recipients of her invitations were not just your ordinary hamburger lovers. She mailed invitations to Julia Child, James Beard, Craig Claiborne, and so forth. She may not have had many takers, but her idea was novel enough to make it newsworthy."

You can also create your own news release and send it to your local paper. When you are writing the release, remember to include that now-familiar "who-what-when-where-why-and how," and mention these elements of your event in the first sentence or two. After stating these most important details, each paragraph that follows should be of declining importance.

Use short sentences and paragraphs, mention exact dates ("November 23," not "next Tuesday"), and keep it short. A good news release is never longer than one or two double-spaced, typed pages.

Here is an example:

FOR IMMEDIATE RELEASE

Frannie's Flowers
111 E. Main Street
Ashland, Oregon
Phone: 583-8754

Frannie's Flowers will sponsor a "Give a seed a home" planting party for all interested Ashlanders on Saturday, April 10, at the community garden plot on Purple Plum Road.

To promote the growth of the volunteer project, which is now in its fifth year, Frances Moore, owner of the local garden shop, will donate a package of seeds to each participant.

"It is my hope that the people of Ashland will work together again this year to make the project fruitful, both for themselves and for the poor of our community, who share in our bounty."

For further information on the planting party, contact Frannie's Flowers, 111 E. Main Street. Maps to the garden plot are also available at the store.

Remember to highlight your news release with the unique features of your enterprise (your family has been in this business for 87 years; the President's brother will be on hand to sample the first bottling of your new brew; you've been teaching ballroom dancing for 15 years even though you lost your left foot 12 years ago in a freak tap-dancing accident). Whatever makes you unusual makes you news.

During the course of business, keep alert to the possibilities for additional free publicity. Anytime you have a well-known artist or authority visiting, publicize it. If your business wins an award, sets a record, or loses a valued employee to the plague, announce it. Is your venture ecological, recycleable, fat free? All these are popular subjects. As you can see, dreaming up publicity angles can be fun! Watch for the opportunities and take advantage of them.

Some helpful words from a woman who is experienced in the public-relations business: you will be more likely to secure free publicity in the newspaper if, when you contact the media, your innocence shows. If you have a tendency to come on like a bulldozer, this woman suggests that you'd be better off hiring a public-relations expert.

"You can hire an expert by the hour to organize the publicity for your new business. Let's say she charges you $25 an hour. That may sound steep, but for $100, you could have your publicity planned thoroughly, your news releases written, and all your contacts made by a professional. You are buying knowledge."

Setting Your Employee Requirements

Our next topic is employees—the hired hands that keep those wagons rolling. How do you find them? What do you pay them? How do you keep them? And how can you get rid of them?

Employees we have encountered in our survey have included parents, children, the skilled and the unskilled, the pleasant and the not so, and occasionally a man hired for the express purpose of lending an air of authority and dignity, for those customers who have misgivings about women-owned business. (A woman lawyer we consulted has a man on her payroll for this very purpose. He is able to make contacts for the firm over the telephone that have been denied to the woman who is really in charge.)

Figuring Employee Costs

Hiring a first employee is a big step for a small business. Several of our business consultants offered this advice: Before hiring any full-time employees, be sure that you have "contracted out" as much of the work that you can. A typical example of contracting out occurs in the building business. Most builders are carpenters, and it would cost them more time and money to hire and oversee an employee to do the plumbing, electrical work, and dry wall work than it would to contract the work out to professionals who specialize in it. That all you have to do is write checks for their services makes contracting well worth it in terms of both paperwork and expense.

Similarly, pay your employees by the piece, whenever possible. This is considered to be "contract labor," and in this type of employment, it is not necessary to take withholding tax out of the wage. Women who own small manufacturing businesses in which some elements of the work are contracted out to other workers may find this the easiest method of payment. Seamstresses who hire other women to do the basic sewing or the finishing details on their work also may find this system the least complicated.

Hiring part-time help from employment agencies is another way to save your own energy for your business and not expend it on secretarial work. You just pay the bill; they do the paperwork. Or, as another woman advised:

"Have as much work done *out* of your office as possible. If you run a small advertising business, for example, have your clients type up the news releases you write for them. Then you won't have to have the staff do it. It's a good way to cut down on overhead."

Bookkeeping and paperwork increase tremendously when your first employee arrives. (We're told there are 39 different forms to fill out when your first employee is hired.) Social security and income-tax records must be kept for each person in your employ.

And additional paperwork is not the only thing that comes along with your first employee. There is also the added expense. Many new business owners are surprised when they realize the actual cost of an employee, which you must consider as the wage *plus* from 10 to 60 percent of that wage. This amount comprises social security (6.13 %), federal and state unemployment insurance (3.6 % or more), and worker's compensation insurance (ranging from .45 % to 51 % of the wage, depending on the safety factor of the occupation). Here's a formula for figuring the cost of your employee (weekly wage is symbolized by $):

$$\text{Wage} + \left(\begin{matrix}\text{Wage} \times \text{social}\\ \text{security}\end{matrix}\right) + \left(\begin{matrix}\text{Wage} \times \text{unemploy.}\\ \text{insurance}\end{matrix}\right) + \left(\begin{matrix}\text{Wage} \times \text{worker's}\\ \text{compensation}\end{matrix}\right) = \begin{matrix}\text{employee}\\ \text{expense}\\ \text{to you}\end{matrix}$$

thus the formula:

$$\$ + (\$ \times .0613) + \left(\begin{matrix}\$ \times .036\\ \text{or more}\end{matrix}\right) + \left(\begin{matrix}\$ \times 0045\\ \text{to } .51\end{matrix}\right) = \$\$$$

Now, let's try out the formula. Suppose you're thinking of hiring a secretary for $4 an hour, to work forty hours a week. Start with the wage ($) of $160 a week, and consider that the worker's compensation rate for office work is .45 percent.

160	+	(160 × .0613)	+	(160 × .036)	+	(160 × .0045)	=	
160	+	9.81	+	5.76	+	.72	=	176.29

Now, on the other hand, suppose you wanted to hire a building-demolition worker whose worker's compensation rate is 51 percent; and you plan to pay $7 an hour for a forty-hour week.

$	+	($ × .0613)	+	($ × .036)	+	($ × .51)	=	
280	+	(280 × .0613)	+	(280 × .036)	+	(280 × .51)	=	
280	+	17.16	+	10.08	+	142.80	=	450.04

You must be aware of all the expenses involved in hiring an employee or you might end up hiring one for the price you thought you'd have to pay for two! To find the exact worker's compensation rate for your particular employee, call the worker's compensation insurance office in your town. It's sometimes listed under SAIF (State Accident Insurance Fund) in the phone book.

Also keep in mind that before hiring anyone, you must justify the salary expense by determining if a helper's assistance will enable you to do the additional business and raise the additional revenue that will cover your added costs. Don't make the mistake of hiring too many employees to cover the initial rush on your new business. When the newness wears off and business levels off to a steadier pace, you may find you've overextended your budget. And it's always wise to check with your accountant if you are considering adding new employees.

The salary that you offer your employees may depend upon their special training or experience. Often, pay scales are fairly consistent in similar types of businesses, and you may learn from your competition what the going rate may be. Employees generally respond well to any special incentives that you may offer. For example, the owner of a Newport, Oregon, chowder house makes this interesting offer: "Anyone who can stick it out during the summer rush, and who can save up a hundred dollars for food, I take to Hawaii with me for a week at summer's end. We have a wonderful time."

Another woman employs several young girls to help her fashion "dough art" creations. If one of the girls comes up with a good new idea on her own, she can make it and her employer will sell it for her at the many craft shows and fairs that she attends.

When your employees work on a commission basis, their incentive is apparent:

"I hire on a commission basis only. Masseuses get a percentage of the massages that they do. In this way, I avoid going in the hole and filing unemployment, health insurance, and the like on my help."

To minimize the expense of your employee(s), you should consider the state and federal employment programs that are designed to serve as "training brokerages." One such program that was highly recommended by a businesswoman who has profited by it is the CETA (Comprehensive Employment Training Act) program. CETA has received its share of criticism, much of it leveled at its seeming disorganization. Despite its problems, CETA has been useful to some small businesses in our survey. A federal program designed to help economically disadvantaged people who are unemployed and age twenty-two or older (they can be younger if they are "emancipated," that is, legally released from parental control), CETA has listings of individuals who are actively seeking employment and on-the-job training. By contacting the local CETA office, a small business can be matched up with someone who has an interest in that field of business. For providing job training for at least three months, depending upon the job, CETA will pay a negotiable percentage (up to 50%) of the employee's salary, with the stipulation that the employee is hired full-time when the training period is over. For one Portland businesswoman, this meant that her small business could hire a much-needed full-time employee that she had previously thought she could not afford. The employee not only helps out in the office and is learning to operate the complex machinery, but she brought to the business some design talent that will increase the scope of the business itself. Like many government programs, the CETA program is subject to change. Check with your local agency for the most current information.

Choosing Your Employees

One businesswoman suggested to us that when you are considering hiring an employee, you should play from your own strengths and hire someone who can balance out your weaknesses.

Another said, "I pick up employees when I *find* them, not when I *need* them." In this way, she avoids making hiring mistakes when she's working under extra pressure. Many small businesses use part-time help at first, drawing their employees mainly from the ranks of available students, homemakers, or retired workers. Starting an employee on a part-time basis offers you the chance to see if he or she will really satisfy your needs. If you make the right choice, you can double your productivity as well as enlarge your own areas of development during the "free time" that your employee is minding the store.

Wondering about hiring your own children to help out in the business?

"I hesitated to have my son work in the restaurant. Since I nag him at home, I felt he didn't need my nagging him here, too," said one woman we spoke with. If your kids are interested in working, let them—with pay. If they are involved in the business, they probably won't resent so much its competition with them for your attention. Another advantage is that you won't have to pay that 6.13 percent if you hire your children. And one woman commented, "I say, always include the kids! My son is nine, going on twenty-one, and he always helps out in the store. It's great experience for him."

As far as employer-employee relations are concerned, your own professional standards will encourage employees to follow your example. One executive offered this:

"Being professional means being more interested in your work than in how you relate to the people you work with." This does not mean that you should be totally impersonal, but rather that you concentrate most on accomplishing your job.

Maintain your professionalism, but also keep in mind that employees respond to careful guidance, praise, and a certain amount of freedom. Their response is greater productivity. Those of you familiar with TA (Transactional Analysis) may attempt to improve employee relations with a system of "stroking." With this approach, you will strive to deliver your instructions and "constructive criticisms" muffled in "warm fuzzies" rather than in "cold pricklies."

Still a little insecure about "bossing"? Maybe you haven't had your own employee before. Bet you've had some house plants. Think of them in the same way. Too much supervision (or watering, or pruning) can be as bad as too little attention (no food, crowded pot). Talk to them, offer them a little sunshine, feed them some praise and encouragement. And by all means go easy on the fertilizer (after all, it's just so much———). Don't make promises you don't intend to keep. Don't play one employee against another, or offer favors to one and not to all. And when one of your "plants" blooms with a marvelous, fragrant new idea, don't pluck it off and wear it on your own lapel. Let it glorify the one who produced it. Employees blossom with tender care. (As for those spindly few who just won't produce—onto the compost heap!)

Employees can be an important influence on your business's image. Said one woman: "Selling carpet and floor vinyl was not half as hard as getting professionals to lay them. I made the mistake of hiring men who said that they could lay carpet, and they couldn't. I ended up having to pay for more than one 'butcher job.' At one time, I was so desperate for good carpet layers that I hired another carpet shop to lay my carpets. That shop laid some of my carpeting and stole a lot of my customers, too. I'm older and wiser now, and I know how to screen good carpet layers, and I even have one expert layer on the payroll. I have certainly learned that the quality of the people you have working for you, representing you, will make or break your business."

She makes an important point: When a customer's first contact with your business is through one of your employees, make sure that person represents you in a way that is appropriate and consistent with your business image. One woman told us:

"You should treat your help like your children, with respect and kindness. But you should only have to tell your employees *once* how you want things done in certain situations. Make yourself very clear. Then if they don't do what you say the next time, they're out." Sound harsh? Another said it even more simply:

"Make sure *they* do it the way *you* do it. You never get a second chance to make a first impression."

Preparing for Taxes

Death and taxes are the only things we can count on, it is said, and if you are starting a business, you had better start counting on taxes from the very onset. Begin looking at your projected profits in terms of profit *minus* taxes, as an unexpected tax bill at the end of the first year of business has been known to bring more than one aspiring enterprise to the ground. The Internal Revenue Service (IRS) has been known literally to lock the doors to businesses with unpaid taxes, leaving the owners deep in debt and without a means to pay it. One woman's experience speaks for itself:

"Our biggest problem has been paying the taxes, because despite the fact that they say that no new business is going to make money for the first three years, in the first four months, we had made enough on paper that our taxes were horrendous. In fact, our taxes were so high that for my husband and me, it was disastrous. He's retired, and it jumped us four tax brackets. You see, for the past year, we have been putting every cent of profits back into the business, into our gift-shop inventory. Within a year's time, our inventory has increased seven times over what we had started with. So we have to pay taxes on the money we were putting directly back into the business, plus an inventory tax. We absolutely couldn't believe it when we found out. I had put a couple hundred dollars aside, and I thought that was going to take care of the taxes. But it was several thousand that we had to come up with. I'm in a partnership, and the amount of our inventory—the value—had to be split between us and put on our personal income tax. We've recently talked to a tax consultant, and at first, he didn't think we should incorporate to relieve ourselves of this tax burden. But after going over our books, he said, 'My God, you can't afford not to!' So he's getting us straightened out and, hopefully, the business will soon be paying its own taxes. If only we had gotten some advice earlier!"

The IRS has some free tax guides that can help you interpret tax laws. Ask for them at your local IRS office: Publication #334, *Tax Guide for Small Business*, and Publication #552, *Recordkeeping Requirements and a Guide to Tax Publications*. After studying the guides, make up a list of the questions you want to ask concerning your business. Then consult your own accountant about your questions and about how far you can bend the laws to your advantage. Although the IRS offers tax consultations, many women mentioned that their problems were handled more efficiently and to their greater advantage by their own accountants.

What Taxes You Must Pay

These are the basic taxes you may expect to pay (depending on your location and type of business):

federal income tax
self-employment tax
state income tax
sales tax
excise tax (for retailers on such items as beer, liquor, diesel fuel, etc.)
local taxes (counties, cities, towns, and boroughs often impose various taxes)

And if you have employees, expect to pay:

unemployment tax
social security tax (you match what they pay out of their wages)

And expect to withhold and handle employees':

federal income tax
social security tax
state income tax

Part II—Operations

So far, we've given you the basic background information that we feel is necessary for the successful organization and development of your new business. Now let's look at discussions of the three general types of businesses that exist—retail, service, and manufacturing—for advice we have gathered that pertains to each of them. Keep in mind all that we have covered in the preceding chapters as you read the next three, because the business basics hold true for any type you choose to operate. The following chapters offer more specific details for each business type.

We'll begin by looking at the retail trade. All of us have been on the customer side of the counter many times. Let's see how business looks from the other side of the counter.

4 The Retail Business

Consider the possibilities. You could be running a nationwide chain of lumber yards. You could have your own porno shop, quietly located in a suburban shopping center. Proprietress of a plant shop? Owner of a newsstand? Hawker of fresh vegetables at an outdoor market? Why not? Other women own and operate these kinds of retail businesses and hundreds of others, as well.

Operating a retail business can be as simple as selling daisies on a street corner, as complex as running a discount department store. You may be the sole proprietor of the shop of your dreams, you may purchase an existing retail business, or you may choose to carry on your retailing adventure in a number of other ways—from operating a franchise to selling door-to-door.

The opportunities and possibilities in retail trade are boundless. The expenses can be, too. If a retail business is your plan, there are a number of decisions to be made before you ring up your first sale.

Two elements of your retail business will play an obvious, and crucial, role in determining your success. These elements are your product and your merchandising technique—how you promote and sell your product to your potential customers. Let's consider first how to choose the product that you want to sell.

Choosing Your Product

Your desire to operate a retail establishment probably stems from your interest in and enjoyment of a certain type of goods, whether it is clothing, books, athletic gear, or candy. And this is the best way to begin. Many women stressed the necessity of truly liking and believing in your product.

"I only buy things that appeal to my personal taste," an antique dealer told us. "I never could get too excited about things I really didn't like. If you are going to be in business, you've really got to like what you are selling. Otherwise it will be a real grind."

Another woman put it this way: "If I love something, I can sell it." She added that her only problem is that "everything I buy at the market for myself, I sell out of my shop before I ever get it home!"

You need an interest in and a genuine rapport with your product to be able to sell it to someone else. When you consider the long hours, hard work, and minimal initial pay that are the lot of the beginning shopkeeper, you'll realize that it will take more than the hope of future profit to hold your product and you together.

Researching the Products You Select

When you decide what you want to sell, do some extensive research on the product. Take a trip to the library and read all you can find on the subject, making sure to cover these three areas:

1. *Subject Card Catalog and Subject Guide to Books in Print*. Check any books dealing with your field of interest and with related fields by looking up your subject in the card catalog. Also check the publication *Subject Guide to Books in Print*, which lists under different subject headings all books currently in print. There may be books on your topic of interest that your own library doesn't have. This guide lists publishing information, so you can order the books yourself if you feel they are valuable resources.
2. *Reader's Guide to Periodical Literature*. Look up the field you are interested in in the most current edition of the *Reader's Guide to Periodical Literature*, located with the reference books in the library. This guide lists, by subject, the latest articles appearing in magazines and journals on any topic.
3. *Periodical Catalog*. Check in the periodical catalog under the subject heading Trade Journals and also under your specific field of interest. (For example, if you are interested in information

about restaurants, look under Food; for fashions and materials, check under Textile Industry.) You will find listings for the magazines, newspapers, and journals that serve each of these particular industries—the "trade magazines." By reading these journals, you'll learn what's happening *now*, as the information they offer is timely and pertains to all aspects of the trade. A potential restaurateur, for instance, may read journals on the food trade that range from *Gourmet Magazine* to *Institutions Magazine/Volume Feeding*, a twice-monthly professional magazine for the food-service industry. Many trade journals also publish directory issues, which contain listings of the manufacturers of different products in their own trade. These trade journals may easily prove to be one of your most valuable sources of facts and trends, both now and when your business is underway. Familiarize yourself with them.

You can also research the product by talking to other businesspeople who handle the same or similar lines. Ask how the products are selling and if there are problems obtaining the merchandise, promoting it, handling it, and so forth. (For example, is the distributor unreliable? Is the item perishable? Does the quality of the product vary with each order?) After a thorough examination of the information available on the merchandise, you may find that the difficulties involved in marketing it outweigh its advantages. Or you may find that innovations are already dating an item that you thought would be "the latest."

Two more things to consider when selecting your products: The image you drew yourself on page 60 when selecting your product will help you determine the price range within which you wish your stock to fall. It is wise, at least in the beginning, to choose your items from within a price range that is not too broad. To represent your business effectively, your products should promote your style as well as reflect the interests and distinction that your chosen location and intended customers will demand.

Also, when selecting the items for your intended business, keep in mind: The large retailing firms cater to mass tastes with products that have mass appeal. Such products are standardized. Take advantage of your small size by offering a unique and different selection of merchandise that contrasts with the "average" merchandise offered by the bigger stores.

Locating a Supplier for Your Product

When you decide which products you want to sell, there are several ways you can locate a distribution source:

1. Check the Yellow Pages to see if there is a wholesaler listed who handles the merchandise locally. If you live in a small community, get the Yellow Pages from the nearest large city. Look up the product by name, and if there is no listing, check under the heading that best describes the product for the trade name.
2. If you have a sample of the product, the label may list the manufacturer's address. Write for further information on the product and for names of local distributors.
3. Trade directories, found in the reference section of the library, are a valuable source of product information. There are books that list manufacturers' names, addresses, principal products, and geographical sales territories. For example, *The Thomas Register of American Manufacturers* lists general categories of goods and the manufacturers that produce items in that category. *MacRae's Bluebook Directory* is also very comprehensive. There are also directories for individual industries—for example, textiles, toys, tropical plants—as well as catalogs to help you locate specific items. You'll find directories for foreign sources. *The American Register of Exporters and Importers*, for example, lists importers of nearly every kind of product. There are directories of individual craftspeople, and directories that direct you to other directories. Listings cover everything from tags and labels to flavor ingredients to buying from Asian sources. If the selection confuses you, ask the librarian to help you find the books you need.

When you've located a source for the product you want, either call or write, telling which items you are interested in. Ask either for a catalog with product information or to have a salesperson call to help you place an order.

Buying at a Retail Market

Another way to find new products and lines for your shop is to go to one of the manufacturers' markets. These "markets" are actually trade fairs at which representatives of the different manufacturers display their lines of merchandise. Nearly everything that is available can be seen at these markets, including anything that is new or trendy. Some store owners feel a trip to a large market is very helpful before you first open for business, to acquaint you with the variety and range of goods that exist in your area of interest. Others mentioned that they felt a buying trip is not necessary until business is actually underway. We'll have more to tell you a little later about what is actually involved in a buying trip. For now, be aware that they are a good source for new merchandise.

How do you find out about them—when and where they are held, and which markets would be right for you? First, you'll see them advertised in the trade journals, which *must* become part of your regular reading. Many industries also have a trade "rag," or newspaper, like *Variety* for the entertainment business and *Women's Wear Daily* for the fashion trade. You don't need to take these papers regularly—they may be too expensive—but be aware of them and include them in your library reading. They will keep you informed about upcoming shows.

Second, you'll learn about upcoming shows from the product salespeople who call on your shop to promote their lines. Since they are aware of the kind of merchandise you want to carry, they can direct you to markets that would be helpful.

And third, when you get to know other businesswomen in the network of your trade—you'll learn more about which shows are especially important and which cater specifically to your kind of business.

Selecting Your Inventory

When you've made the decision about what lines of merchandise to carry in your retail business, you come to the next problem—which items, and how many, should you buy?

When you make selections for your opening inventory, no doubt you will make a few purchasing errors. A little time will be the best teacher in letting you know what lines to carry.

"My baclava was selling so well that I decided to carry brownies, too," said the owner of a Salem, Oregon, deli. "But I noticed I didn't sell more. I just spread out the sales over the two items. So I eliminated the brownies to simplify things, and to keep me from eating them. I loved the brownies, but I can take or leave baclava!"

Knowing which products are selling and which are not is a vital element of running a retail business. We will discuss later how to keep an efficient inventory that will help you know precisely which are your best lines and which slow-moving items are taking up valuable sales space in your shop.

We have learned of small-business owners who hopefully add more and more product lines with the goal of increasing their range of customers. In fact, they are often just tying up valuable capital in costly, inactive merchandise that brings down their sales volume. Remember, when you add a new line to your stock, the growth must come from your profits and not your capital. Your sales volume won't double if you merely double your product lines—it may, in fact, be reduced. Instead of adding more lines, you should consider "trading up" to higher priced lines, possibly with an increased markup. This could be the best way to increase your profits. And be sure to watch all new items closely to see if they are really adding to your sales. If they are taking up too much of your time or your space, or merely cutting down your sales of another line, then eliminate them.

Learn what your most popular products are and promote them accordingly. Keep in mind this advice from the deli owner:

"I am trying not to make the same mistake the former owner made. She is from Germany, and she put a lot of money into meats that are unfamiliar to the people in this area. She lost $500 in meats because nobody would buy them. I wasn't that familiar with deli meats myself when I started—I had never even tasted pastrami before! But I learned fast what my customers wanted."

It will help to keep an up-to-date file (locate it in your handy 3-by-5 box!) of the merchandise you plan to carry, as well as your suppliers. You'll want to list:

1. Product name.
2. Supplier's name and address. Be sure to compare prices and credit terms when choosing your suppliers. (Also keep a record of alternate, emergency suppliers.)

3. Wholesaling details (for example, smallest quantity you can order, quantity prices, cash discounts, credit terms).
4. Delivery charges.
5. Delivery time. (Also note how soon supplier can deliver fill-in orders.)

"We could never have had such success without our exceptional delivery service. If I sold five copies of *The Very Hungry Caterpillar* one day, I could order and receive more books in just a few days," comments a Salem, Oregon, bookstore owner. "Your delivery speed is very important. Some products take months to arrive—yarns from Scotland, specialty gifts from France. We just happened to luck out on the commodity we chose to deal with."

Keeping your file current will save you time and much repetition when contacting your product wholesalers.

Going "To Market"

Before we go on to the elements involved in the promotion of your chosen products, let's take a closer look now at your first buying trip to one of the large retail markets.

Many businesswomen stressed that even the smallest shop can benefit from some out-of-town buying trips to such places as Seattle, Los Angeles, San Francisco, and New York. Advance registration is a must, so be sure to call or write to find out all you need to do to secure your reservation. The show itself is usually free, though of course your travel, hotel, and meal expenses are all your own.

Arriving with Your "Bible"

When you arrive at the registration desk, you will be given a packet of helpful materials directing you to the various manufacturers represented at the market.

"At registration, they give you a wonderful little book with listings of all the items at the show. I spent two hours before I even started out, going through and marking what I wanted to check out. There were over four hundred different lines at the show, so I knew I wouldn't have time to see them all. I studied that guide, and it became my little 'Bible,' in which I noted information I wanted to remember on the different companies—what they had, which items of theirs I particularly liked, when I might want to order from them in the future, and so forth. That little 'Bible' is invaluable, because you just cannot *buy* that kind of information."

Even with your "Bible" in hand, however, your first trip to the retailers' wholesale market may be terrifying, and it will certainly be exhausting!

"I had absolutely no experience in running a business or buying merchandise for a store. My first trip to the clothing market was hilarious. I just walked in one door, looked at the first line of merchandise that I saw, and started buying. Now, each time I go to the market, I feel more confident. One manufacturer's rep has told me, 'Katie, when you first came in here, you were chewing bubble gum and pigeon-toed. Now each time I see you, you are a little more sophisticated.' That's how I feel, too."

Another woman recounted the confusion and education a buying trip offers: "When I went to my first show, it was hard. I went to the Los Angeles show—it was the biggest show on the West Coast, and as big as any in New York. I didn't know anything; I didn't even know how I made my money. I just knew that I would buy some merchandise and then resell it. I didn't know what the markup was, or my discount. It was very confusing, because half of the people at the show have things marked at retail and half have things marked at wholesale. And I really spent a lot of energy running from one showroom to another. One price was looking so much better because it was a wholesale price and the other a retail price. But it did finally dawn on me, about the second day, what was going on."

Finding a Helping Hand

How can you avoid this kind of anxiety on your first buying trip? Perhaps you can't. But many women offered us their suggestions on how to make the experience a little less traumatic, and most of them mentioned first that you seek the aid of the manufacturers' representatives who work the markets. Some of them are more than willing to help you.

"It was a helpful manufacturer's rep who finally set me straight on how to select the right clothes for my market. I was buying half-sizes for my shop, but in a one-hour session, a rep gave me some tremendous advice. 'Do you really want to deal in half-sizes?' she asked. 'Half-size women are hard to get along with. They'll take some of the fun out of your business. They've got chips on their shoulders because they're too heavy to begin with, so they'll take out their frustrations on you and your merchandise. You should think about what kind of community you are doing business in. There is money in Gig Harbor,' she said about my community, 'so you should cater to monied tastes. Choose the predominant feature of your town and cater to it.'

"This sales rep went so far as to circle the lines listed in the sales catalog that she thought would be suitable for my area. She told me that not only were the lines good, but the sales representatives that marketed them were good, and that they would be helpful to me, too. I followed her advice, visited the lines she had circled, and got tremendous help from all the reps I talked to. I told them that I was new, and that I needed advice on buying—how much I should order, size varieties, and so forth—and I asked them about the markup I should use. They were happy to give me lots of advice.

"I've found that asking questions is the only way to learn how things are done. I also think that's one reason so many women can make it in business—they're not afraid to admit they don't know something. Men, on the other hand, don't like to admit that there's something they don't know."

Another woman, the owner of a children's clothing store, told us of her efforts—and the mistakes she made—in setting up her first trip "to market."

"I knew of a woman who had a big children's clothing business, and I asked her if she would help me at market. I didn't know that you just didn't *do* that, that I was asking a bigger favor than you should ask anyone, let alone a total stranger. Still, she said that she would meet me at the market and introduce me to the people she bought from. What I didn't realize at the time was that you don't have *time* to help someone else at the market. You are busy from eight in the morning until eight at night. You don't have time to go to the bathroom, to eat, you get indigestion, you worry about how much money you are spending, what you are buying.

"Now, two years later, I am horrified that I had the nerve to ask this of this woman, but at the same time, I would never had gotten my foot in the door if I hadn't. Because, you see, the sales reps won't sell to just anyone who wants to carry their line. For instance, if a local competitor carries $20,000 worth of a certain line, and I go in and ask to carry it too, the reps will say, 'Sorry, maybe another time.' Because why should they risk a sure $20,000 account for my piddley $500? Being introduced by this other woman got me through most of that."

Another problem to be worked out? Sure, but this same woman had this to say, "Usually, though, the reps at market are really very nice. If you're a new businessperson, they'll do everything they can to help you. They don't want you to go broke. Most good sales reps have been at it at least twenty years, and they take a small account and know how much you can afford and won't let you spend more. They know that in that way, they can build up your trust, and that you'll come back to them. I've kept most of the sales reps that I started with, and that's what most people do. You're stupid not to, because they do all kinds of things for you. You pat their backs, they'll pat yours."

Only one woman we spoke with was nearly put off by an overpowering sales rep: "Our first 'help' was from one of the representatives of a large crystal company. He told my partner and me, 'I don't know how much money you have, but if you don't have thirty thousand dollars to start with, take whatever money you have and go home.' We were very shook up, because we started this whole thing on a shoestring. It's Karen's money, my own money. We wanted no men involved. We didn't want to get a loan if we didn't have to, so we were starting very, very small. The rep discouraged us very badly. We went out to have some coffee and to talk about it. I said to Karen, 'Forget it, we're doing our own thing. If we fall on our face, we'll just have a big garage sale and we won't have lost much. And we'll have had a good time doing it.' So we just blithely went on that day, sort of casing the place and being overwhelmed by the amount of merchandise that is available. Then we decided what we were going to spend and in what areas we were going to spend it."

Using a Merchandise Budget

To make your decision making easier, go to the market with a merchandise budget in mind. Know how much you can afford to spend for the season that you are buying for. Have your budget broken down into departments, or types of goods, so you won't blow all your money on sewing notions, for example, before you even get to the fabric displays. In making up this budget, you can use a basic stock list or a sample inventory plan as a model. After you've been in business awhile, your basic stock list will be developed from an analysis of your past sales—your records of which items are profit makers. To draw up your first list, you will have to rely on your own judgment or on a sample stock list that your product manufacturers and wholesalers provide. In the future, your basic list will show each item by name, the minimum quantity you need to stock, and the quantity to be reordered at a time.

Figure out what percentage of your total budget you want to allow for each category on your stock list, and use this as a guide in making your purchases. After you have been in business awhile, your sales records will show you which items in your inventory are selling well and which are not. By keeping track of your success in buying from one year to the next, you will be able to adjust your budget percentages to accommodate sales trends.

"Before you ever go to market, you should have planned how much you want to spend on each kind of item. All of your transactions are discussed in dollars and cents and units. You have to have this expenditure plan on a piece of paper, so that when you get through with one company, you know what you've bought and how much you've spent. The best thing to do is take along a pocket calculator. Even though you *know* you've spent $500, you sit down and hit that calculator, and you find you've spent $530. Then you must figure, how much discount do I get if I pay the bill on time? How much of the merchandise I ordered am I really going to get? (You'll probably get 85% of what you order, so figure 15% that you really didn't buy.) [Note: This percentage pertains to this woman's trade in particular. In other trades, the percentage of goods that you will actually receive after placing an order may vary. Check with your manufacturer's representative before making any assumptions.] So then you say, well, I'll gamble. I'm going to spend $2,000 more than I should, because that 15 percent may not come in, and anyway maybe I'll make $4,000 more."

This woman's next remarks make great sense. "It's kind of like playing Monopoly, because it's not real to you. You never see any money change hands at a market. Everything is done on paper, or it's all done mentally up here," with a little tap, "in your head."

This woman added, "Every time you get done with one company, you have to sit down and regroup. You'll see people in bars, and you wonder, what's that woman doing there, sitting by herself. Well, she's going through all her papers, saying 'I know I bought thirty-five dresses in size 12, now I need fifteen more to cover it.' You see, it's not a simple thing of walking in a door and saying, 'I know I bought a lot of dresses and a lot of pants.'"

Making Decisions at the Market

Many women feel that the very fact that they *are* women (digging through sales tables, watching the ads, clipping coupons . . .) has helped prepare them for their first market experience.

"Buying is sort of an ego trip," one woman told us. "You think, 'Gee, they like what I picked out.' But the thing I do best is shop. I'm a compulsive money spender. I adore it. Buying for the shop sort of took care of my personal spending."

The art of buying comes with experience, we are told, and of course, with making a few mistakes.

"A major task in business is selecting the items for your store. I travel all over the country in order to buy from the gift shows. Buying from the shows is hard work, but it sure beats having a salesperson come in. I take inventory cards with me whenever I buy, so I know exactly what I already have, and what is selling and what is not selling. I used to take a briefcase filled with these cards; now I take a suitcase. There is such a tiny margin between success and failure that I must take every possible measure to ensure my success."

Another woman's buying trips are not so organized, but she feels she has worked out the best system for herself. "I am an impulse person, and I go by feel. If I feel something is going to be right for us, I will buy it, even if I think we have no business spending the money. For example, we did not intend to go into jewelry. But I noticed some necklaces in a gift shop that I thought were beautiful, and I asked the name of the person who made them. I called her and went right out to her house. I walked out of her place with three hundred dollars' worth of thimble necklaces. Now, a year later, we have bought, wholesale, five thousand dollars' worth of necklaces. We have people sending thimbles to us from all over the country to have necklaces made. They are one of our biggest items. I just *knew* that it was something that was different, and that it would appeal to a lot of our customers."

Goes to show you that the "market" just may be anywhere you find it.

Keep your eyes open!

Advantages of Shopping the Market

"Once you get in the door, it's absolutely fantastic. It's a whole coliseum completely jam-packed with booths, like the commercial building at the state fair. Many of the booths are simply tablecloth-covered plywood sitting on two sawhorses. Some are much more elaborate. And the thing I like about it is that anyone can set up a booth there, as long as he or she pays the price. One of my favorite booths is run by an old gold miner, who makes and sells little figurines that sit on unusually veined rocks that he's mined. Right next to him is a company that has huge warehouses full of merchandise back in Chicago somewhere. That's why I like it so much; it gives you a chance to judge a company and its merchandise not by its size, but by the quality of the merchandise it has to offer."

A trip to the retail market gives you a decided edge over other shops, which may be buying only from local salespeople or manufacturers.

"Being a small store, you can be much more creative in your buying when you have the large selection that the market offers and not just what local salespeople are pushing. People often say to me, 'I haven't seen anything else like this in town.'"

There are also many other advantages:

"Your advantage in going to a show is that you know then

exactly what is available. When someone comes in to your shop and says, 'I want printed corduroy that is reversible,' you can say, 'I was just at the show and there was none available.' Your customers will respect you for that."

"After seeing the lines at the market, I know what I can and cannot get. It saves me hours of time spent writing letters and making phone calls to see if I can find something somewhere."

A partner in a quilt shop told us, "There is a bit of status in going to the big markets. You begin to get on mailing lists—not junk mailing lists, but helpful ones that keep you informed of what's going on in the trade. You learn about the politics in the trade and how to use it to your advantage. I learned, for instance, that you can sometimes bargain a little with the different sales reps to get the price down a little bit."

"When you attend a market, there are often special sales going on there. They want you to buy while you are there, so sometimes they will offer you a 'beginners kit' to get you to try some new stuff. Whereas you usually have to buy six of each item to order something, with this kit, you may only have to buy two of each. And then at maybe 20 percent off. It is a good way for a small shop to get to try new items."

"One big advantage of attending a show is that you can talk right with the representatives of the companies, ask them questions, make complaints, make special deals or arrangements. It also helps so much to see things in person. When you get it in the mail, it's one thing, but to see it used or demonstrated enables you to make your decision much more professionally."

A partner in a small shop told us, "I have taken a buying trip to Los Angeles, and it was a gamble for such a small shop. But we feel it has paid off handsomely in many ways. Since we are a small business, the big companies often don't want to take the time to call on us. At the market, I can see everything. And even though I run a small business, I feel if I am putting this much time and money into it, I want to do it in a professional way. I wanted to see what others were doing and what I'm up against. If the big stores were taking advantage of the markets, I wanted to, also. It is also fun to meet other shop owners from other areas, to talk about our troubles. In one case, we decided to band together to make a complaint to a big distributor. We also decided to get a few shops together to exchange 'dogs' (items you've had more than six months or so that aren't selling). All your people have seen them at least once. I'll send one shop owner a hundred dollars' worth of my dogs, and she'll send me an equal amount of hers. To our customers, it is new merchandise, and just because it didn't sell at the other location is no indication that it won't sell at mine."

Special Tips for Your Market Trip

"Allow a little extra time when planning your trip. Sometimes sales representatives will suggest that you stop by their manufacturer's warehouse and buy products directly. If you have the extra time, you can do this and save additional money."

"Plan to visit other shops in your field when you are away on buying trips or even on vacations. People are usually very generous about sharing advice and ideas, especially when they know you are from out-of-town and won't be using their ideas locally. It is always helpful to get together with others in your line of business."

"I think it would be especially nice if your family could accompany you on your out-of-town market trips. After working so very hard all day, you really need to get out at night. Of course, there is always a lot of socializing in bars and such during the show, but it would be much more relaxing, in my opinion, to get out somewhere else with your family at night."

"While the market is on, you may find it helpful to meet with the other shop owners from your area who are also attending. I did, and I learned about some good sources I had missed, and I also was able to make price comparisons with other merchants who had made purchases similar to mine. When I found out someone else had gotten something for a price lower than I had been quoted, I went back to the rep, and he subsequently lowered his price."

One final but interesting tip: "You'll run into all kinds of propositions and insinuations from the salesmen, with plenty of offers. Some salesman will say, 'Well, when can I come up and see you?' You just say, 'Sorry, you're just not my line.' They'll respect you for it."

Before we leave your trip to the market, we'd like to mention another exciting way to shop—taking a buying trip abroad.

Sometimes importing your own items is the only way to get the one-of-a-kind products that you are looking for.

The owner of a specialty kitchen shop above Seattle's Pike Place Market described to us her reasons for deciding to import many items herself: "I've made three buying trips to Europe in my six years in business. My first year I went to the United States shows—Chicago, Los Angeles, San Francisco. Then I decided to go to Europe and import my own things. I visited factories in Europe, mainly in France, for five weeks. It was very difficult because I don't speak French, or didn't at the time. When you import, you have to do it in a large quantity or it doesn't pay. Three years ago, when I went to the factories, they had a two thousand dollar minimum order. Now it's five thousand dollars. So if you want onion-soup bowls, you have to get *a lot* of them. Then you need the storage room to keep it all in." Still, she feels that importing her own items is the only way she can maintain the kind of out-of-the-ordinary image that her shop demands.

Merchandising

Now that you've chosen your product, how are you going to go about selling it?

Merchandising. Marketing, selling, peddling, hawking. Whatever you call it, it's the backbone of your retail business. We'll tell you a story we heard about the owner of a small pharmacy. Every month, a number of new products would come and go, with very little attention paid to them by the pharmacist's patrons. Some of these products were quite good, some novel, some just nicely packaged. But none of them sold very well. Then the pharmacist hit upon an idea. Every time a customer stood at his counter waiting for a prescription to be filled, the pharmacist would hand him one of the new items to hold, while he worked behind the counter filling the order. He would rarely comment anymore about the product than to say that it was new. The pharmacist kept a record of the sales he made on these items after he began his new approach. Seventy-five percent of the time, the customer bought the item he was handed.

You've been to the grocery store, filled your cart with items from your list, and you're standing in the checkout line. In front of you, you spy a basket piled high with little orange cans with an unusual label. They've caught your eye, you reach over to take a closer look, and next thing you know there's a little orange can nestled on the top of your cart, right up between the milk and the four-pack of toilet paper. Merchandising.

"Buy early, receive early, display early." What person witnessing Christmas decorations at Halloween could be unaware of this retail maxim? But it's true. The store that is showing it first will probably be selling it first, as well. That's merchandising.

Promoting Your Product

"One sure way to sell an item is to mark it 'One to a customer'"

The ways to promote a product in your business range from a cardboard display rack by your cash register to a trip to a French cooking school for your best imported-cookware customers. You may be full of ideas on how to display and promote your wares, or you may feel that you'd like some expert advice. Look back for a moment to Chapter Three and reread the section concerning business promotions. And here are some more ideas.

Your Wholesalers' Services

If you feel you'd like some personal advice on the needs of your particular business, ask the wholesalers you deal with in stocking your store for ideas about promoting their products. They can give you some guidelines on efficient merchandising of their wares. Wholesalers vary as to the services they provide. We'll list some of them, but be sure to check with individual salespeople to see what they offer. You probably won't want to use all of their services, but be aware of them, so that you can profit from those you do need.

1. In order to promote their products, wholesalers may offer you featured items from time to time. These are items offered at special reduced prices in an effort to encourage customer interest.
2. Wholesalers may have promotional aids such as window displays, racks, stands, and the like, which will help you draw attention to products.
3. Wholesalers may offer advertising on a "co-op" basis, in

which manufacturers pay a portion of the advertising bill when you specifically mention their products in your advertising.

4. Wholesalers may offer a system of stock control for their line of merchandise, in which they will maintain your stock at a consistent level at all times. We've all seen the potato chip and Pepsi people at the grocery store maintain their stock and displays.

5. Other services may include financial aid in the form of trade credit or delayed billing, retail counseling, and accounting systems.

Wholesalers are also a good source of up-to-date information on market and supply conditions and any other new developments in your field. Note on the file cards you maintain on all wholesalers which of their services are of value to you.

In-Store Product Promotion

Within your shop, your merchandise arrangement can enhance or detract from the product's customer appeal. Called visual selling, your merchandise displays act as silent salespeople, and are responsible for one out of four retail sales. The idea behind your display is to make the customer stop, look, and buy. Here are a few points to keep in mind when planning your product displays:

1. A good display promotes both your business and your product. Remember your image, and use your display space to carry out that theme as well as to publicize popular trends.
2. Use your displays to educate your public and to offer a useful demonstration of your product.
3. Know which items have unusual eye appeal and display them where they will call attention to other products as well.
4. Make use of window displays, multitiered stands, and counter displays, and have a regular schedule for changing the items on display. (For example, large window displays can be changed anywhere from two times a week to every other week. Keep records to show how often you change your displays and what merchandise was shown.)
5. Recognize which of your items are "impulse" items and place them in high-traffic areas in the store.

6. Watch which areas in your store seem to be the best for displays, and use them accordingly. Consider, perhaps, using "corner shops" within the store, showing special merchandise in an area set off by a distinctive and different decor.

7. When the price of an item is important, make sure that the tags are clear and easy to read. Use show cards to stress the benefit of an item.

8. Remember that your displays are meant to stimulate sales and to create a demand for new products. Displays are especially useful in promoting bargain merchandise, holiday items, seasonal accessories, and the like.

9. Hire a professional display artist if your talents in layout and display are minimal. If you feel you need help, ask for it!

Selecting Display Fixtures

Your in-store promotions are important, so don't forget to budget for special display fixtures (lighting, shadow boxes, islands, shelving). Check with display-equipment companies to see what's new when you feel you need some different display ideas and props. Also notice which features of other stores' displays you find interesting or unusual and jot them down for future reference.

You will get some good display ideas at the trade shows you attend by paying special attention to the way manufacturers display their merchandise. And do a little experimenting yourself, trying different background colors and lighting effects, to improve your in-store displays. Design experts have noted that the decorative scheme of a store is composed of one-third color, one-third lighting, and one-third design. Keep this in mind when planning your layout and fixtures. Also realize that periodic remodeling of your shop can be viewed as a form of promotion. Goods will be rearranged, taking on a new look, drawing attention, perhaps, to previously overlooked merchandise. So choose your fixtures with an eye to their movability and rearrangement. Flexibility and easy maintenance are important to remember when you purchase equipment and fixtures.

Special Activity Promotions

Promotions in your retail business are activities that enhance your public relations as well as promote your product. For example, the owner of a kitchen shop that specializes in French cooking utensils took a group of customers to Europe on such a promotion. Sixteen members of the group spent a week in France in cooking school, then went on to visit other European cities. Not only was this nonprofit activity great fun, but it created a special kind of interest for the shop.

Many retail businesses gain notice and new customers by offering special classes through their shops. Whenever a musical-instrument store offers private music lessons or a yardage shop offers sewing courses or a cosmetics boutique offers a beauty class, you can be sure that the students profit not only from the instruction, but from the supplies that they purchase during the course of their lessons, as well.

"When I teach a class, I will show my students the type of seam gauge I feel is the best for quilting. I explain why I feel it is superior to other kinds of gauges. When anyone asks where she might buy one, I always say, 'I happen to have a supply right here.'"

Many women who offer classes through their businesses report that their students are often their best form of advertisement. Your classes may be free, or you may charge for them. Often, the materials that the students use in the class are included in the class fee. Hold your classes in the evening or in a separate workroom, so they do not interfere with the normal operation of your business.

Retailing promotions are as varied as the kinds of businesses they promote. Here's a list of some common methods that we heard mentioned by many shop owners:

1. Newsletters. A monthly or quarterly newsletter was one of the most popular means we learned of to promote your new merchandise, lines, services, and seasonal ideas. Send it to everyone on your mailing list (compiled from names of customers who have made purchases and anyone else who has asked to be on the list).

"When we run an ad for the store, it often costs about sixty dollars for a one-time shot—and then it is gone. When we mail out our newsletter, our cost is about eighty dollars per mailing (figuring about 43¢ for each letter), but from each mailing, we get a continuing response. And we use it to take our customers into our confidence. For example, I found a source for 90-inch wide, 3-ounce quilt batting, but I had to buy ten bolts of it to get a good price on it. So I wrote in my newsletter, let me know if you are interested in buying chunks of this batting, and if enough respond, I will get it. Then my customers would call in, and I got enough calls that I bought the ten huge bolts, and I knew I didn't need to worry too much, because I had three of them sold immediately."

2. Community Services. Anytime you donate an item or shop space for a community-service project, you are promoting your business as well as ensuring goodwill for your shop. You will probably receive far more requests for donations (in one form or another) than you care to handle, but remember that a sense of belonging to the community makes good sense. Participation in chamber of commerce activities, merchants' and civic organizations, as well as contributions to school and charitable affairs are all forms of promotion.

3. Direct Mail. Direct mail, including fliers, brochures, and catalogs, is a means of effectively promoting special events, sales, new merchandise lines, a new menu or chef. Use your own mailing list or obtain one that suits your market from one of the local mailing-list brokers listed in the Yellow Pages. (More on these mailing-list brokers in the Mail Order section, p. 214.)

Advertising

We have discussed advertising in an earlier chapter, but to make the most effective use of your advertising dollars in your retail business, you should take the time to reconsider these points carefully:

First of all, consider your type of merchandise and analyze its promotional qualities. Some products, for example, are most easily sold through demonstrations or personal approaches. Stretch your advertising budget most effectively by realizing which items lend themselves to media (newspaper, Yellow Pages, handbills, radio, TV) advertising and which do not.

Second, identify the particular market that you wish to reach in your advertising. If your market is small and easily identifiable (antique military memorabilia collectors, for example), direct-mail advertising might be most effective. If your target customer group is somewhat larger, you must determine which of the media will reach the greatest number. Study the advertising techniques employed by other successful retailers in your area, especially those used by the competition.

Third, don't feel that you have to be a "Madison Avenue marvel" to come up with a successful ad or promotion. Enlist the help of the advertising salespeople at your local TV or radio station or newspaper. They have the technical know-how to help you design your ad.

Check to see if there are any cooperative funds available for advertising from your suppliers. Also, your suppliers may run nationwide advertising programs throughout the year. Tie in your efforts with theirs for maximum coverage.

Finally, always attempt to measure the success of your promotional and advertising programs. Keep a record of each effort, noting which days of the week seem most successful or which seasonal promotions elicit the best response. By keeping records, you can look back to see if your ads appear fairly regularly and if your spending on promotions is justified by increased sales. In developing an advertising schedule, experience will teach you how much you need to spend to get the job done.

Drawing up a chart like this will help you see which type of advertising is your best buy:

Type of Advertising (newsletter, newspaper, radio, Yellow Pages, etc.)	Size of Audience it will reach*	Frequency of use		Price of single ad		Approx. $ Cost
________	________	________	×	________	=	$________
________	________	________	×	________	=	$________
________	________	________	×	________	=	$________

*Ask your media salespeople for figures on potential audience size. They also have other information on audience composition, such as age.

Finding the Right Location

In Chapter Three we gave you a lot of advice on choosing your business location. Yet, as one woman put it, the three main ingredients of a successful restaurant are "location, location, and location." This advice is applicable to other retail businesses, as well. What specific aspects of your location will affect your business?

First of all, is the area large enough to support this type of business and, if it is, is the competition already handling a large portion of the market? If you will be serving just a segment of the market, is it large enough to be profitable?

Second, are there changes occurring in the neighborhood—are incomes unstable, is population seasonal or fluctuating—that may affect your business?

Third, and very important, is the location convenient—with easy access, near ample parking and bus lines?

Finally, how are other businesses in the area doing? Do they appear to be successful, or is there a high turnover of new businesses? What about the business that occupied your location previously? Did it fail, or did it move to a better or larger location? Why?

In addition to checking with neighboring businesses to find out about your intended location, ask the wholesalers and manufacturers that you intend to deal with. They know how their products are marketed in different areas and if there is room in the market area for another competitor. (Look back to page 88 for more sources of help in choosing your location.)

A good location is vital to your retailing success. Be prepared to wait until the right spot comes along. When you feel you have found the right building for your needs, be sure to double-check these points:

1. Is the neighborhood prosperous, on the way up?
2. Is street and foot traffic fairly heavy? Are sidewalks in good repair?
3. Do passersby look like good prospects for your kind of business?
4. Is there street lighting and adequate parking?

5. What services will the landlord provide, and what are the terms of the lease?

6. Can the building be remodeled or redecorated with a minimum of expense? Will it be large enough when your business grows a little bigger?

Expanding

The last point anticipates a question that may come up sooner than you think. Having a successful business often leads to the temptation to expand. But be wary. Often the sound and capable management of your thriving enterprise is much more important than growing—and risking—with a larger store or a second business.

"One of the mistakes people make when they have a successful business is expanding. When I decided to expand my business, I told myself it was not exactly greed that made me do it. I tried to call it ambition. I planned to spend $50,000 on my new tavern, but I am already up to $150,000 in remodeling costs and I haven't even opened for business yet. I expanded once before, and one thing I learned is that it is more than twice as hard with two businesses. It is more like four times as much work. And you certainly don't have twice as much energy!"

"My shop is only seven hundred square feet, but I've got a very high inventory ($30,000) for the size. I feel that when my feet are really on the ground, in about two years, I will have to get a bigger shop if I want to be able to handle the amount of business that would really justify staying in operation."

It is hard for a successful small shop to stay small. A growing business requires a larger inventory, which in turn requires greater shop space and larger facilities.

"My primary purpose for expansion was more space. I have absolutely no flexibility in my display area. We put in the Cuisinart when it came out five years ago, and we were the first people in the Northwest to sell it. I didn't have a place to put it except the sales counter, and I want a place where I can demonstrate it when people ask to see how it works. I want a sink there. I have to excuse myself now and run into the bathroom to wash the bowls out and so forth. And if the bathroom is busy, I have to wait. It's a mess. Also, it takes four people daily to run the shop, and we don't have enough working room. On Saturdays, with four of us behind the little counter, we really get in one another's way. It's a wonder we haven't murdered each other!"

For this storeowner's dilemma, an expansion in shop space seems the only answer. Inconvenience as well as sales lost due to lack of display area override concern for staying small.

Another reason for growth is the need to add a new line or product. The problem, put simply, is that if *you* don't do it, someone else will.

A partner in a gift and art shop told us, "We just expanded. People kept coming in here saying, where are your antiques? We tried to find someone to come in and rent the vacant apartment upstairs and put in an antique shop, but when we couldn't find anyone, we rented it ourselves. Now the upper branch of the Rose Tree features the nostalgic look. We have four rooms. In the kitchen, we show kitchen things, in the bathroom, bathroom things, and so on. We have had to hire finders to locate things for us at estate sales, and we've had to hire help for the first time. We had just gotten to the point with our shop that we thought we could begin to pay ourselves back our initial investment. But we've sunk it all into the expansion. If we didn't have husbands to feed and shelter us, we'd be in trouble!"

Don't overlook the lesson you can learn from a tour of your local department store, however. The big stores have seen the beauty—and power—of the small shops, and they organize their space accordingly. They show their fashions in tiny "shops" or boutiques scattered throughout the large store facility. Each boutique features its own unique style, be it ski wear, lingerie, designer dresses, or disco clothing. Remember, before expanding, to consider your unique appeal. And don't lose that appeal in an effort to try to compete with the big retailers.

If you decide to expand your operation to a second location, there are two elements that will be vital to your success—communication and control. An expanded business requires that more and more responsibility be delegated to employees. The lines of communication between you, the authority, and your help must remain open and friendly at all times. Since you can no longer have your finger on every aspect of your operation at once, you must have established an efficient chain of command to take the responsibility for business operations. You may find that your role changes from shopkeeper to upper management. You will need to choose your staff carefully, employing special talents where yours are no longer available. If your shop has prospered because it is a personality business—and the personality is yours—will the appeal be as strong in a second branch run by a manager?

Along with good communication, you will need to exercise adequate control over your expanded operation, and you will need to ensure that those in positions of responsibility feel accountable for the operations they supervise. If you are successful in handling these two most important elements involved in expansion, your business will reflect the results. Your profit from the total efforts of a dedicated and responsible staff will be much greater than you could have achieved from your efforts as a single entrepreneur.

Services

In a retail business, it is your customers who control your success. Cater to them. As a successful Texas retailer says, "We have always believed that if we can please the 5 percent of our customers who are the most discriminating, we will never have any difficulty in satisfying the other 95 percent who are less critical." Be especially courteous to your repeat customers. It is easier to increase the purchases that they make than to attract new customers. *Always* guarantee what you sell. And always accept returned merchandise. This is where the department store has the advantage over the small shop in many customers' minds. Department stores are built on the premise of easy shopping and easy exchanges. How often have you bought something at a large department store instead of a specialty shop merely because you knew that if the purchase was wrong in some way, it would be much easier to take it back to the larger store? Don't lose prospective customers because of this.

"We always give special service," said the owner of a newspaper and magazine shop. "That's the only way small businesses can survive. You have to be humble, which goes along with honesty. Sometimes I make a special effort toward my men customers—they like a little mothering. I've worked to reach a kind of plateau of trust." Her friendly, chatty manner gives personality to the little shop, and her service—well, who else would open at noon on Sundays so homesick Seattle-area readers could get the Sunday paper from San Francisco on Sunday!

Types of Credit

Included in your services will be the kind of credit that you offer. We've already noted that credit is a way of life today. But before you decide to operate with a credit system, be sure to consider your type of business, your type of customer, the credit policies of your competition (if they are extending credit, you had better, too), and the amount of working capital that you have. Offering credit is expensive, because the money that you tie up in charge accounts cannot be used to cover your own expenses, and you'll need additional capital. There are other expenses, too. Charge accounts require additional bookkeeping and billing. There may be financing costs (such as the service-charge percentage deducted by banks for bank-card use), charges for credit investigations on potential buyers, and charges for collections of overdue accounts. When you extend credit, there is also an increased possibility of bad debts.

On the other hand, charge accounts are one of the best ways to increase your sales volume and to attract new customers. It's possible that you can't afford *not* to offer a system of credit.

Here are a couple of methods of offering credit, and what some shop owners have to say about them:

1. Store charge accounts. This system may be convenient for your customers, but is often a headache for you. As the saying goes, the sale isn't made until you get paid, and there's a good chance that, in carrying your own accounts, you may not get paid. Of course, you have got to take your type of customer into account. A small but regular and local clientele is often very appreciative of this service. If your customers are fairly transient, seldom come back for repeat business, or are of the "quick-shop" variety, cash may be your best term.

If you do decide to carry your own accounts, there are a few different methods of billing that you will want to consider. Weigh the advantages of each of these methods:

a. Thirty-, sixty-, and ninety-day no-interest accounts. The customer agrees to pay within a specified period of time, and no interest fees are charged.

b. Thirty-day account. The customer is billed thirty days after the charge. If he or she does not pay in full in the specified time, interest is charged on the remaining balance. Allowable interest rates differ in different areas. Check with your CPA for the percentages allowed in your area.

c. 2/10 account. A 2% discount is allowed if the total bill is paid within ten days of the billing date.

d. Revolving accounts. Customer agrees to pay at least a minimum portion of the bill each month, with interest to be charged on the outstanding balance. Again, check with your CPA on the interest rate allowed in your area.

2. Bank cards. As one adviser told us, "charge" ranks behind only "mama" and "dada" in the developing vocabulary of an American child. When a major credit card is used, the bank deducts a service charge from the total charged on your customer's sales slip. If charging is a way of life for your customers, paying this small percentage is well worth it for you when you consider the many additional sales this service may bring in. Nearly all the shop owners we spoke with agreed on this point. And many added that it can cost you a lot more to write off losses in your own charge-account system than to pay the percentage charged by the various bank cards. With major credit-card sales, you are *guaranteed* payment for your goods or services. With personal (and possibly bad) checks, you do not receive such a guarantee. Some stores add a small percentage to their selling price to cover the costs of the bank-card system. Others have offered discounts for cash sales, since in reality the cash customers are subsidizing the charge customers. It may be wise to wait and see what kind of sales volume you handle with bank cards before making any pricing adjustments.

Credit Bureaus

Check the Yellow Pages for the names of local credit bureaus. These agencies exist to exchange credit information on consumers. When a retailer becomes a member of such an organization, she can take advantage of such services as credit checks on charge-account applicants, "skip-tracing" to locate debtors, and notification of poor-risk accounts.

Personalized Services

The relatively small size of your new business will make it possible for you to offer personal services that are not available at larger stores. Make the most of this advantage by selecting products and lines that, through their exclusivity or the nature of their use, will bring you into a closer relationship with your customers. This will also encourage the repeat business that will help your venture succeed.

A Eugene, Oregon, clothing store located in a freshly painted Victorian house near the downtown mall exemplifies the idea of personalized service. Leaded windows, overstuffed furniture, and elegant chandeliers lend a sophisticated air perfectly adapted to the tastefully designed, high-quality women's clothing offered for sale. The three owners of the shop are each ten years apart in age. One of them explained to us how their merchandise is selected and promoted.

"We are a specialty shop; we buy for our customers. Our look is primarily tailored, and with our ten-year age differences, we are able to cater to women of all ages. When we get in a new shipment of clothes, we call the customers that we feel would be interested in specific items. In other words, we service individual customers. We have found there is a great need in the community for such service. Our women love being catered to. Being aware of the personal tastes of our customers, we are able to put together ensembles for them, eliminating for them the problem of shopping from store to store to complete a certain look."

In other words, by knowing who their customers are, they are able to avoid costly mistakes when selecting the merchandise that they will offer for sale.

The owner of a quilt shop explained to us how the element of personalized service can work to the shop owner's advantage as well as aiding the customer:

"We offer our customers special services that also help us stretch our inventory dollars. For example, they know we will order something special for them if they call ahead and say, will you buy me a bolt of this or a certain color of that. I will add it to my shopping list, and they will get a discount on it because we haven't had to put it into our regular inventory—we haven't had to put it out, cut it, and sell it. I do the same in ordering quilt books. They are expensive, and I can't afford to have too many on hand. So the customers can look at the samples I have in my own library, and if they pay in advance, they can save a dollar a book. When I have to send off my check to the book company, I've already got half my money from the advance book sales, and I just get a few extra copies for the store. I don't have to have that big dollar tied up in inventory. I do this to make our dollar go three times around the block, but it's also fun, and a challenge."

When your store is new and still relatively small, it will be you, the owner, who ensures the good customer relations that come from friendly, specialized, and personalized service. As your business grows, make sure that your employees are as conscientious as you are about personalized customer service.

Other Services

The other services that you offer through your retail business may be free to your customers, but they won't necessarily be free to you. To decide which services it will be necessary to provide as well as to determine which you can truly afford, you should list the services you are considering in order of their priority, and then list alongside them your costs in providing them. When you've made your list, do a careful survey of the competition to see if you have overlooked any important services they are already offering the customers that you want to attract. Can you offer additional services that will invite new customers to your business? If you find your beginning budget can't handle all the services that you would like to offer, start at the bottom and eliminate those that can wait until you have your feet on the ground. Just don't cut out anything that your competition is advertising as a great feature!

Here is a list of some of the services you may wish to offer your customers:

1. free parking (in your own lot, or with a parking token for a nearby lot)
2. delivery service (consider three possibilities: owning your own delivery vehicles; leasing vehicles; using a commercial delivery service)
3. free mailing to out-of-town customers
4. free wrapping for gifts or for mailing
5. extended store hours (will you stay open evenings, Sundays or holidays?)
6. return and exchange policies

Stanley Marcus, the head of the exclusive Neiman-Marcus department store, illustrated the importance of this last service in his memoirs, *Minding The Store*. He tells of a customer who returned a handmade lace ball gown she had obviously used and abused. When his father replaced it without question, Marcus asked how they could afford to replace it when the manufacturer would certainly not assume any of the cost. "She's not doing business with the manufacturer," his father said, "she's doing business with us. So tell her with a smile to be more careful next time. It costs us over $200 to get a new customer of this woman's buying potential, and I'm not going to lose her for the $175 this dress cost us."

In the years that followed, according to Mr. Marcus, this woman spent over $500,000 at the store. And he had learned one of the most important retailing lessons of his career. It is the *satisfied customer* who will make your business a success. Any policy or service that will keep your customers coming back is a valuable asset to your business.

Financial Analysis and Control

Start-Up Costs

The finances involved in retailing can be frightening, but don't let them discourage you. Some women comment that running a household gives a future businesswoman all the purchasing-agent experience she will need, as well as budgeting know-how.

One of the things you'll want to do first is estimate your total expenses for outfitting your store. Shop around for your equipment, watch the want ads for used items, and get several different bids before you make your decisions. Shelving, lighting fixtures, display racks, and such can be very costly, or very funky, as your budget allows.

"An old, residential hotel above my store was condemned right at the time I was working on my displays. They threw out old iron beds to be hauled away by the trash man, but I hauled them into my store instead, painted them different colors, and used them to display bolts of fabric."

When you have an idea of what you will need in merchandise, equipment, fixtures, and the like, draw up an itemized list of the expenses you will incur before you even open your door. Here is a sample:

This list will provide the basis for calculating depreciation later and will also provide information for fixed-asset accounts. Keep these lists up to date, especially for items used for a year or longer. Record the date each fixture or item of equipment was purchased, the name of the supplier, a description of the item, and its cost.

Operating Expenses

Keep an operating-expense chart. As a new retailer, you need to know how much money it takes to run the business each month. Draw up a chart of your own operating expenses so that you can see exactly where your money is going. The SBA has developed a helpful guide for figuring your monthly expenses as well as the total estimated cash you'll need to begin your business. Here is their chart to help you figure these expenses. (Under Starting Costs, for fixtures and equipment, use the figures you compiled in the chart on the facing page.

In the reference section of the library, there is a large book called *Barometer of Small Business*, put together by the Accounting Corporation of America. In it, you will find average operating ratios and trends for different kinds of businesses. Use their

	If you are paying cash, enter full amount	If you are paying in installments, enter *Total price*	*Down payment*	*Amt. each installment* (For initial starting costs, figure down payment plus at least one installment)
fixtures lights counters racks dressing rooms signs				
equipment cash register adding machine safe delivery equipment				
decor (including paint, paper, carpeting)				
one-time expenses for grand opening (installation of fixtures and equipment, ads, promotions)				Enter totals here for initial installment buying costs
beginning inventory				
accountant and lawyer fees				
rent and utilities deposit				
sales-tax deposit to get seller's permit (if required)				
licenses and permits				
cash reserve for accounts receivable				
cash to cover everything I've forgotten				
	Total	+		Total

average percentage figures as a comparison against your own to see how your expenses compare to the norm in your field.

For example, here is a sample operating-expense chart from a small retail business. Notice which expenses are listed as controllable, that is, which expenses can be adjusted according to your needs and your available capital. The items listed under fixed

ESTIMATED MONTHLY EXPENSES

Item	Your estimate of monthly expenses based on sales of $______ per year	Your estimate of how much cash you need to start your business (See column 3.)	What to put in column 2 (These figures are typical for one kind of business. You will have to decide how many months to allow for in your business.)
Salary of owner-manager	Column 1 $	Column 2 $	Column 3 2 times column 1
All other salaries and wages			3 times column 1
Rent			3 times column 1
Advertising			3 times column 1
Delivery expense			3 times column 1
Supplies			3 times column 1
Telephone and telegraph			3 times column 1
Other utilities			3 times column 1
Insurance			Payment required by insurance company
Taxes, including Social Security			4 times column 1
Interest			3 times column 1
Maintenance			3 times column 1
Legal and other professional fees			3 times column 1
Miscellaneous			3 times column 1
Starting Costs You Only Have to Pay Once			
Fixtures and equipment			Use totals you arrived at on chart on page 169.
Decorating and remodeling			Talk with a contractor
Installation of fixtures and equipment			Talk to suppliers
Starting inventory			Suppliers will probably help you estimate this
Deposits with public utilities			Find out from utilities
Legal and other professional fees			Lawyer, accountant, etc.
Licenses and permits			Find out from city offices what you have to have
Advertising and promotion for opening			Estimate
Accounts receivable			What you need to buy more stock until credit customers pay
Cash			For unexpected expenses or losses, special purchases, etc.
Other			Make a separate list and enter total
Total Estimated Cash You Need to Start With		$	Add up all the numbers in column 2

expenses are just that—fixed, with no possibility of monthly adjustment. The percentages that we list are averages for a small retail operation. The dollar amounts we have filled in for illustration.

Operating Expenses

		Average % of Gross Sales
Controllable Expenses		
Payroll	$1,250	25%
Supplies	$ 100	2%
Advertising	$ 100	2%
Bookkeeping	$ 50	1%
Miscellaneous	$ 200	4%
Fixed Expenses		
Rent	$ 300	6%
Utilities	$ 150	3%
Tax and licenses	$ 100	2%
Insurance	$ 50	1%
Depreciation of equipment and fixtures	$ 50	1%
Total Expenses	$2,350	47%

By comparing recommended operating percentages listed in the *Barometer of Small Business* with your own actual figures, you can see where you should cut down. By using such a chart in your business, you will also know which items you have the most control over and which may not be necessary for the successful operation of your business.

Estimating Net Profit

When you have determined your monthly operating expenses, you can estimate your net profit in this way:

In our sample retail business, the estimated total sales each month (gross sales) was $5,000, or 100%. The actual cost to the retailer of the merchandise that accounted for these sales (cost of sales) was $2,000, or 40%.

Therefore, the gross profit is:

the gross sales	$5,000	100%
less cost of sales	-$2,000	40%
equals gross profits	$3,000	60%

Out of this gross profit, deduct your total operating expenses to determine your net profit before income taxes:

gross profit	$3,000	60%
less operating expenses	-$2,350	47%
equals net profit	$ 650	13%

Cash Flow

Your cash-flow records tell how your money is coming in, where it is going, and when. Cash-flow problems arise not merely as the result of a discrepancy between assets (what you owe and what you are owed) and liabilities (what you owe). A pinch also occurs when suppliers demand payment within a specified period of time, and customers take several months or so to pay their bill. Even though, on paper, you are making more than enough to satisfy your commitments, if the cash isn't coming in steadily, you may not be able to pay your bills soon enough to keep your business afloat.

"I'm just beginning to understand cash flow," a bookstore owner confessed to us. "I am a person who loves to pay off bills! I've learned you aren't supposed to pay off anything until it's due. That money is mine until then."

Your cash-flow chart shows two of the elements involved in cash-flow projections—sources of cash and uses of cash. The third necessary ingredient, as we mentioned, is the schedule of cash, which will show you when and how much cash you will have on hand to cover expenses. By studying your sources and uses, and by keeping close records of all your dealings for the first few months at least, you can come up with a month-by-month projection for your first year. By knowing which times of the year you will be bringing in more or less money, you will be better equipped to handle budgeting problems as they arise.

Here is a diagram of the cash flow in a small business:

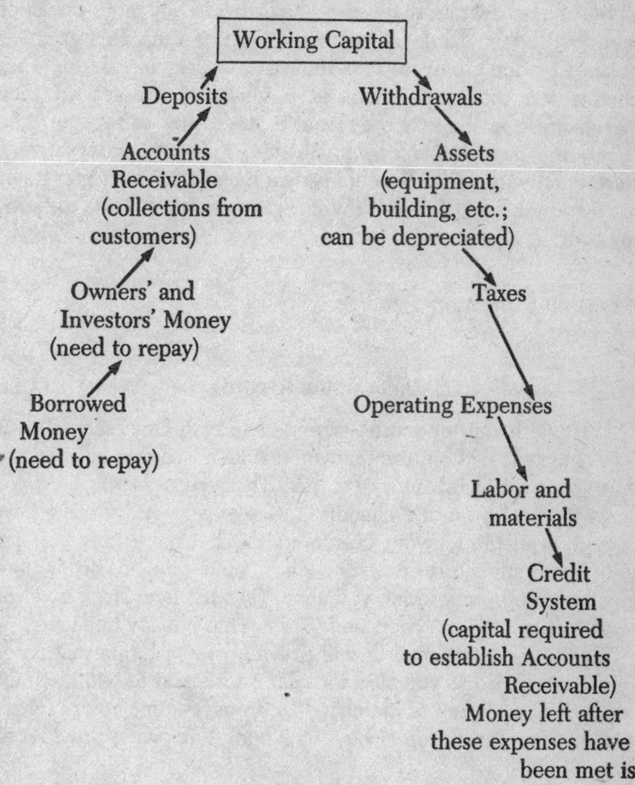

Notice that under Sources of Cash, we have included Borrowed Money. Most new businesses feel the need for some type of loan when first starting out. But a loan to get you underway may not be the only type of loan you'll need.

One woman expounded on this idea: "If you are a good businesswoman, you work off the bank's money. In other words, if you had twenty thousand dollars, you wouldn't use it; you would leave it sitting in an account, drawing interest, and you would work off the bank's money and hope you could pay it back! Almost all businesses operate that way—borrowing to buy more stock and then paying the bank off when the note is due. In fact, most businesses don't borrow two thousand dollars like I do. They borrow ten thousand dollars at a whack. They get all their merchandise in the way they want it, then they sell it, get their profit, and pay the bank back. But me, I'm very conservative. I started out with a cash flow of my own money. I like to operate on my own money. In fact, it's my main shortcoming. I like to spend my own money!"

Maintaining Inventory Records

Unit-Control Records

Along with your operating-expense and cash-flow records, your retail business will require that you maintain a comprehensive and up-to-date set of inventory records. These records will help you keep track of your merchandise, so that you will always have enough available for your customers but not more than you can sell. Your inventory records will enable you to order new merchandise by informing you about (1) what is in stock now, (2) what is currently on order, and (3) what has already been sold.

Your unit-control records will provide you with information on all the merchandise you offer for sale. These records will trace the progress of each unit of merchandise, from the time you purchase it to the time the customer buys it. A bookstore owner provides an example:

"I have devised a very special inventory system that enables me to keep the most exact inventory records possible. I keep a 5-by-8 card filed for every different item in my store. I enter the date that I purchase a certain book, for example, then I draw a line of little circles, one circle for each copy of the book that I put in stock. Ten books, ten circles. Then, as I sell the books, I fill in the circles with colors representing the month it was bought by a customer. Thus, I know exactly how many books I have on hand, how many I've sold and when, and how fast they are selling."

Another shop owner explained how these records provide valuable information about stock: "For every unit of stock that I carry, my records tell me when I bought it and how much it cost. When the item sells, if I see by my records that I had it for six months before the sale, I know that I didn't make the profit on it that I would have if it had sold immediately. I have had money tied up in it for too long."

Dollar-Control Records

Together with your unit-control records go your dollar-control records. These will tell you when and how much of a unit to buy. A fabric and quilting shop owner gave us an example of how she maintains these important records:

"I keep a chart that shows our sales in each line that we carry since the time we opened for business. The chart is divided into months and into different classifications of merchandise. Every year I add on another line at the bottom of the chart. If it shows, for example, that in June of the first year, we sold eighty dollars' worth of patterns, and the second year we sold sixty dollars' worth, and the next year forty dollars' worth, I say, hey, we're not carrying the material that goes with those patterns. Let's phase out patterns. The chart has shown the diminishing returns on the dollars spent on patterns, and so they go.

"On the other hand, we can see by the chart which months our sales are especially heavy in certain areas, and then we know how to order in advance accordingly. We used to carry eleven rows of small spools of thread and just a few colors on the large spools. Now we are down to one row of small spools. We found through our records that the bigger spools sell better for us, because we are catering to women who really sew a lot—quilters use a lot of thread. Now every time I go to market, I add more colors in the large spools. You have to keep track of the dollars you put into your inventory. If you put three hundred dollars into an item, and your return on the investment isn't for eight months, that wasn't a very good investment."

Computerized Inventory Systems

Your inventory must be handled efficiently in order to maximize your profits. Our examples come from shops with relatively small inventories. The number and type of records you keep will depend upon the type and size of your specific inventory. Manual inventory control systems such as we have described often work satisfactorily for small retailers; however, as the number of items and departments increase, it may be more desirable to utilize a computerized system of inventory control. Don't be intimidated by the idea of a computer. The existence of computer-service organizations and time-sharing concepts have made it possible for small businesses to take advantage of computer technology without the expense of owning their own computers. A service bureau, either owning its own computer or leasing time on one, can process your data and produce the reports your business needs. Bureaus generally have two kinds of service charges: one for designing the program that your business will utilize and one for processing. You must study carefully the initial and possible future costs of using such a service before you decide to convert to a computerized system. Weigh the costs against the benefits that such a system will provide (such as better record keeping, a reduction in clerical help needed).

One mail-order-business owner told us about her experience with computerization:

"Eight years ago, when we decided to computerize the business, the thought of spending twenty thousand dollars on a computer overwhelmed me. But when you consider that it paid for itself in two years (one office worker's wages, $10,000 a year), has given us worlds of information at our fingertips, and has saved us the endless hours we used to spend doing our inventory manually, I only wish we had computerized sooner."

Another way to profit from computer technology is through time-sharing. In this method, a terminal device is installed at your place of business and connected to the computer through telephone lines. You transmit information from your terminal to the computer, and the results are transmitted directly back to you, often within minutes.

With time-sharing, there is a monthly terminal rental fee, and there are additional charges depending on the amount of computer time used. As with a service bureau, you must be able to justify the cost by weighing the benefits. The SBA has produced a little questionnaire to help you determine if electronic data processing (EDP) is right for your business. With their permission, we are reproducing that questionnaire below and passing their criteria on to you:

DO YOU NEED EDP?

How many of these do you have each month?		Give yourself these points	Your points
Number of checks written	____	10 points for each 100	____
Number of employees (including salesmen)	____	1 point per employee	____
Number of customers' accounts receivable.......	____	10 points for each 100	____
Number of invoices you prepare...............	____	10 points for each 100	____
Number of purchases or purchase orders........	____	10 points for each 100	____
Number of different items you carry in inventory	____	10 points for each 1,000	____
Do you have very large items in inventory, such as trucks?	____	10 points if answer is yes	____
Do you need help in keeping track of your inventory?	____	10 points if answer is yes	____
Total points for your business			____

If you fill in the blanks honestly and your total comes to 100 or more, you would probably benefit from using a service bureau. Even if your total is less than 100, you might be able to benefit. But no simple test such as this can make the decision for you. Look into it carefully. Remember that EDP should reduce costs or increase income enough to repay every dollar you put into it.

Costs vs. Benefits

There are two aspects of your inventory that must be constantly weighed and balanced—the *costs* and the *benefits*. The costs involved in maintaining your inventory are not just those figures that represent the cost of the stock. There are also receiving and storage costs, insurance, taxes, and costs of keeping inventory records. Costs also reflect the amount of money you have tied up in inventory. A small business must realize that a slight change in the amount of capital tied up in inventory may result in a significant increase in the amount of working capital available.

"One big mistake I made was right after our big Christmas success. I had all this money, and I reinvested it in stock, stocking up the store to the hilt. Since then, I've had a beautifully stocked store, but the money has just been sitting on the shelves when I could have taken it and used it for myself during these slack times."

Because of its influence on your business's total cash position, you must consider carefully these aspects of your inventory in your business management:

1. Your selection of merchandise must be ample and appealing—but not *too* large.
2. You must aim for a high inventory turnover—but always at a good profit level.
3. You must take advantage of volume purchases to buy at the best price—but you must not overbuy.
4. Outdated merchandise must be eliminated—but not before good replacement items can be found.

Your Turnover Rate

On point number two, your inventory turnover rate: there are rough guidelines, published periodically by professional and trade organizations, against which you can set your goals and measure your achievement. Turnover rates show approximately how many times a year the merchandise in your store should "turn"—sell and be replaced in stock. Rates vary with each type of business as well as kind of merchandise, so refer to them only as guidelines.

"In a dress shop such as mine, the stock should turn four times a year. Mine is only turning two times now. This is bad, because if my sales are low in one season, it has a kind of snowballing effect on the next season's sales. I'm not getting the cash out of my investment to reinvest it in the next season's merchandise."

If your turnover is slow, a careful evaluation of your merchandise selection is in order. Is your merchandise varied enough to attract a sufficient clientele? Have you taken note who your regular customers are and suited your product to them? Can you afford to borrow money to invest in new merchandise that may help to turn this "slump" around? A low turnover rate demands immediate attention.

Employee Organization

Your retail beginnings may be small, but you'll soon find you need someone to help you out with selling, stocking, inventory, unpacking, and all the other things running a business entails.

Finding New Employees

Where do you find the right people to help you run your business? Your employees will come from six different sources:

1. friends, family, and acquaintances
2. unsolicited applications
3. public employment agencies, such as the state employment office
4. help-wanted advertisements
5. private employment agencies
6. student employment lists at local schools and colleges

When a prospective employee comes to apply for a position, you should use a standard employee application to get all the personal information you need. Here is an example of the type of form you should use. You can buy standard forms at stationery stores or draw up your own and have them copied.

EMPLOYMENT APPLICATION

Name
Address
Telephone
Husband's name
Children
Work Experience
    Present or last job

    Name and address of last employer

    Dates of employment
    Job title and work done

    Reason left
Education
References

Name	Address	Occupation

Employee Education

One important point that was mentioned by many of the women we spoke with concerned employee education:

"I try to keep my employees abreast of all our kitchen items and how to use them. It's like selling anything else that is a specialty, be it automobile parts or kitchen utensils. If your staff are knowledgeable, they are better able to serve you and better for the business. We spend a lot of time talking about food and food preparation. Last Tuesday night, we had all the employees and their friends over for dinner. We do that about once a month, and we usually cook something out of a new cookbook. I encourage them to read the new cookbooks, take them home if they want to, or take a break and go sit somewhere and read them. When I hire people, I always tell them they have to know how to cook and have to be interested in it. Even the person who does the stock must be interested. If a packing list has a soufflé dish on it and the person unpacking it doesn't know what a soufflé dish is, then I'm not going to get very much out of that employee."

One woman suggested using a set of note cards to help educate new employees: "I have a set of 3-by-5 cards which list all the do's and don'ts of the business. Every new employee I hire must study and learn the information on these cards."

You, the employer, may profit from a little employee education as well. Here's what one woman told us:

"I like the working relationship I have with my employees, who are mostly young kids. When it comes to teaching them and exchanging information, they often teach me, as well. They question procedure, they question something I've always taken for granted, and they'll come up with a better way to do it. That constant give-and-take, exchanging and using other people's information and testing my own—that's what makes the business exciting to me."

Here are some points to include in the education of your employees:

1. Make sure they know how to greet the customers.
2. Explain how merchandise should be shown and demonstrated.

"A lot of sportswear buying is done on impulse, so the clerks should put the merchandise out where it can be touched, where the customer can see what goes with what. It is important that a salesgirl know how to put the different parts of a new style together so they can be seen, so a customer can get the total look."

3. Explain how to do "suggestion selling." This includes suggesting related items—"this looks great with this"—as well as encouraging the customer to "trade up" to higher quality merchandise.
4. Make clear your policy on handling customer complaints, returns, and exchanges.

Delegating Responsibility

You will probably choose to do all the buying, record keeping, and ad preparation yourself, at least until the volume of business you handle forces you to delegate some of these responsibilities to your employees. The extent of your growth and development as an efficient employer depends a great deal on your ability to delegate authority. Trying to remember too many details, trying to do everything yourself because you're the only one who does it right, will only lead to ulcers and dissatisfied employees. You must realize which elements of the business are *really* your domain, then train someone else to handle everything else.

Delegating responsibility will help both you and your employees work to your and their full potential. And you will gain two other benefits. First, by relinquishing some authority and responsibility to your help, you will be able to see which of your employees are your most valuable—which employees are really worth their paycheck. Second, if ever an emergency arises and the boss can't make it to the shop, you will have sufficiently trained someone who can carry on in your absence.

The owner of a news and magazine shop put it best: "My employees act like they own the store. And that's just how I want them to act."

Draw Up an Organization Chart

We suggest drawing up an organization chart right at the beginning to show clearly where responsibility and authority lie. Even if the store is managed primarily by you, the owner, with the help of only two other salespeople, a chart defines exactly where the buck stops. It will eliminate confusion and a lot of finger pointing if something doesn't get done. Here's an example from a small, three-woman shop:

Look over your organization chart from time to time as your business grows. Add an assistant manager in a position between yourself and your salespeople when you feel you are able to delegate more of the business responsibility. Each time you delegate another of the chores that are necessary to daily store operation, you are freeing yourself or your top employees for more profitable endeavors.

EMPLOYEE ORGANIZATION*

Store Owner

Selects inventory
Plans advertising and promotions
Arranges shop display
Manages business records
Handles daily banking, mail
Helps customers

Salesperson #1	Salesperson #2
Helps customers Maintains store displays Straightens merchandise, cleans shelves and display counters Takes inventory Unpacks new merchandise, checking against invoices, and readying it for store display	Helps customers Maintains store displays Straightens merchandise, cleans shelves and display counters Takes inventory Unpacks new merchandise, checking against invoices, and readying it for store display

*In a small store, the customer is your primary duty. No customer wants to wait to be served while you complete a store-maintenance task. If the other salespeople are busy, put off what you are doing and wait on the customers.

Checks and Double Checks

All the best plans need constant revision, and your plans for your business are no exception. Keep up with trends, watch your percentages, evaluate, and don't overlook the human element in your scheme. Some mistakes are bound to happen, so don't hem yourself in so tightly that your seams will burst when you choke on your first problem. Allow a little extra money, time, and energy for all the things you have—and haven't—planned for! Here are some retailing pitfalls to beware of:

1. Don't pay your personal bills out of your business account!
2. Watch out for a drop-off of your old, repeat customers. They are the ones who will keep your business alive.
3. Check your back room. If it is bulging with leftover odd sizes or colors of merchandise, or slow-moving stock that is tying up your capital for next season's purchases, or picked-over sale items that your customers didn't even snap up when they were marked down, you've got a buying or merchandising problem.
4. Employees who don't know what goes with what, how to put together a total look or a workable order for a client, are losing business for you.
5. If you can't take advantage of all early-payment discounts offered by your suppliers, or if you are often penalized for paying your accounts late, you've got a cash-flow problem.
6. If you are not fully aware of all the aspects of your business and how it functions—an awareness that comes only from a careful study and understanding of your *business books*—you are not taking advantage of the tools that are there to help you succeed. Make it a habit from the beginning to check back regularly at the end of each month on your profit and loss, your sales and disbursements, the condition of your stock and your equipment, and anything else that is vital to the running of your business. In a small shop, a Monday-morning inventory is often a very wise idea. Remember, changes and adjustments are not always a sign of poor planning on your part. They show that your future is developing, and that you are aware of and allowing for this growth.

Now that we've given you some of the business basics, how about listening to a story that will show you where you can go from here? Listen to The Rime of the Rampant Bagel.

The Rime of the Rampant Bagel

"I've got the soul of a shopkeeper," mutters Helaine, stepping up to the counter to sack bagels for waiting customers while we take notes on the bagel boom that is emanating from her Portland bakery. Together with her partner, Sue, free-spirited Helaine is suffering what a friend termed a "materialistic regression." Her former home-kitchen bagel business is now a bona-fide corporation ("I'm the president of a corporation and I'm still mopping floors?"), housed on the site of Portland's oldest bakery ("We spent a fortune bringing it up to code"). In between customers and bagging up organic bagels for a health-food store, Helaine relates the story of how one coincidence after another led to the opening of her bakery.

When asked how she researched her market, she replied, "If you can call a friend and her three-month-old baby, my four-year-old son, and me in a van a research trip, I guess I took one. We tasted every bagel from Seattle to Los Angeles." Visiting West Coast bagel bakeries proved very enlightening ("If you're going to go commercial, you have to see how it's done—ask questions"). Helaine found that bakers were very open with her, "sharing everything but their recipes." She learned much about machinery, production, and general bakery operation, and "I think it was because I was a woman. I wasn't threatening to the men who were showing me around—and they probably didn't think I'd ever go through with the bakery idea, anyway."

Helaine wasn't researching a product that was unfamiliar to her, however. "I think bagels, work bagels, even dream bagels," she says. She had been making bagels at home for several years. "My marriage and my family were disrupted—literally *inundated*—by the smell of onion bagels!" She had been selling them at open-air crafts markets, and she knew the market was there for her product. She had hustled up a few wholesale accounts while still operating out of her home kitchen—"I was *schlepping* bagels all over town!"—and she had already learned two important business rules:

1. Keep the product consistent.
2. Get it there on time.

"To succeed in this business, you have to be willing to work yourself half to death," Helaine says, "but it was worse when I was working at home. I started there mainly to be home with my son.

But I had to be up at quarter to five—that right there upsets my biological clock! (In fact, the bakery business itself is not really suited to my life-style.) Some nights I'd still be working at midnight. I could make a living (my needs are fairly simple) at the Saturday Market, but I had to get the bakery out of my house. It was ruining my life."

Helaine went to see a lawyer even before her bagel "road trip." He, in turn, introduced her to an accountant. She was able to get an opportunity loan from the bank (the banker had been buying her bagels at the Saturday Market), and she offers this advice: "Get a few accounts lined up *before* you go to the bank, and get as much money as you can out of friends, family, and personal sources *before* you go. Then you can show the bank you're already underway."

She also advises starting out with as little capital invested as possible—"you can add the decor later"—Helaine jokes that she is pining for a little neon Star of David for their window, but it's too expensive.

Watching the want ads for used equipment helped keep costs down—they found used school equipment to be a good buy and are proud of their forty-two-year-old-mixer. Helaine moans, "California bakeries have $50,000 worth of equipment—you throw the dough in one end and it spits out bagels from the other end."

She feels that she and her partner have created the "archetypal bagel," hand shaped and higher priced—"but *better*"—than any others in town. "I set the price when I was making them at home. I felt it wouldn't be worth making them for anything less, and I've never had any trouble selling them at this price."

One day Helaine called up the food editor of the daily newspaper and told her that she was running a very newsworthy business—"I've got confidence in a great product," she said. The resulting feature story, with three large pictures, brought in droves of people to the shop. "Our retail business, since the article appeared, has grown to be 50 percent of our entire operation. Before, we were largely wholesale." While we perched on stools in the great-smelling back room of the bakery, we could hear nearly every other customer mention that they'd read the article, which had appeared in the paper a month earlier.

"When I went into business," Helaine says, "I told everyone I was going to be successful. I feel like your heart really has to be in it—you have to create an aura of confidence around yourself. It helps your success. Business is just like a game, anyway," she continued. "Money is just a way of keeping score. If you can keep the game aspect of your business going, you can help to keep it fun."

It seems as though the "Bagel Ladies" are having fun gathering "bagel artifacts" and offering a variety of six different bagels, including one "bagel du jour" and raisin bagels on Sunday. They still do the Saturday Market "for fun and publicity," and they're open Sundays for four hours "so the families from up on the hill can come down and get fresh bagels for Sunday brunch." (Still, Helaine laughs and interjects, "This is definitely not a hobby. I'm in it for the big bucks!")

Helaine feels that her business has more credibility now that it is located in a bakery. "There's not that air of flakiness of working out of my home," she explains. A large deli account that had turned them down when they were still baking at home came to them when the bakery was established in its present location. (The owners learned that all their help were buying their bagels from the "Ladies.") Helaine and Sue have set some short-range goals—"a walk-in cooling cabinet"—and some long-range goals for their business. Their partnership—"I'm the dreamer, the salesman. Sue is efficient, a fast worker"—has become a corporation for tax purposes. Their relationship works, Helaine says, "because we respect each other."

"I've never found it to be a disadvantage to be a woman," Helaine remarked. "Other businesspeople open up to us, workmen take pity on us! They never leave any work half-done figuring we can fix it ourselves. We fuss a little with our business, give it a woman's touch—we're not a real slick operation, like some others. Most other women seem to be really inspired by our success, too, and they give us lots of reinforcement."

"I think in the long run," Helaine philosophized, "when it comes to facing plague or famine, women will face it best. We can be independent, or a little bit of fluff—who will criticize us or object to it? Men have been so trapped into a role of provider-leader for so long. I think it's about time they got a break from that, too. Take the pressure off them for a while. We're as capable as they are in running a business."

"Sue's dad gave us his 'Six Words for Success' when we first started: *Find a need and fill it*. I think he was right. If you've got a good product and are willing to work hard, you can't miss. There is a large profit margin in bagels, and we know how to make them. You also have to trust in your own intuition. So much advice is thrown at you, but in the end, no one knows your own little business like you do."

For those starting out, Helaine repeats, "Ask questions! A couple of women came to see us saying they were planning to open a bagel bakery in Montana. I took them in the back room. I would have told them anything they wanted to know. They only asked a couple of questions, then went back to Montana. If that had been me, I'd have gleaned *every shred* of information out of us that I could get. That's the only way you learn."

The shop is closing, and as we take home a bag of bagels, we wish the "Ladies" continued success in their bakery. "Thanks," Helaine says, shaking her head and smiling. With a shrug of her shoulders, she says, "I still look around here and say . . . Wow!"

5 Restaurants and Other Food Services

Food businesses form such a wide and varied field that they are almost a category of their own. They are the number-one kind of retail outlet in the United States. And because there are so many new restaurants started each year, the failure rate is correspondingly high. What makes one succeed when so many others fail? Four factors were noted most often to us as being vital ingredients in a successful restaurant:

1. good food
2. fair price
3. pleasant atmosphere
4. convenient location

Statistics show that one out of every three meals is eaten away from home. And that means that about 33 cents of every food dollar is spent on food that is eaten out. There's the proof you need that there is a market for this type of business! Women's roles in the restaurant business are undergoing a gradual change. From waitress, to cook, to owner—the prospects are interesting and encouraging. Let's look at some of the different aspects of entering the food-services business.

Location

"Uncle Roy said you can put a restaurant up anywhere. If you've got a good product, they'll come to you."

Looking at the failure rate in the restaurant business, it appears many potential restaurateurs have shared Uncle Roy's opinion on the importance of a good location. The majority of the *successful* restaurant owners we spoke with felt otherwise. They cited several aspects of location choice that warrant special consideration:

1. Your restaurant should be in an area that is densely populated. Before your reputation is firmly established, it is difficult to attract new customers if your location is remote. If you choose a rural location, select an area that is already showing a demand for such an establishment—near a recreation area, perhaps, or an artists' colony—a place where travelers are already heading.

2. Areas where there are large concentrations of single adults—near universities, in the business district—are ideal locations.

3. An area of heavy foot traffic is a good choice, especially if your style of dining is informal. A dinner house, on the other hand, requires a location with *ample* parking.

4. Study the competition in the area before you make a definite decision. If there is already a popular eating establishment on the block, you may have to exist on its overflow customers. Remember, though, that other shops and businesses in the immediate area will increase your visibility.

5. A busy corner was mentioned most often as the best place to locate.

6. If you can locate in a building that formerly housed a restaurant, you can save remodeling expenses that are required to bring the site up to code. Health-department regulations can be an obstacle when opening a new restaurant, and a building that has already been approved will be quite a plus. Know what improvements will be required *before* you sign a lease, by having the health-department inspect the building you are considering.

If you do choose a former restaurant site, however, don't fail to find out why the last tenant is no longer in business. You need to know *now*, not after you sign the lease.

The style of the restaurant that you plan will also influence your choice of location.

"Mine is primarily a neighborhood restaurant. We close every night at seven, except on Saturday, when we close at four. And that is for our comfort and convenience. I had a philosophy from the beginning that I wanted to deal with local suppliers as much as possible. It's partly a time-saving device, but buying locally also supports my neighborhood. The money goes back into the neighborhood, and I like the aspect of a business that supports the people *right here*. I feel a great amount of loyalty to this particular space and to the people who come here."

If you plan to concentrate your menu on a specialty item (soup and salad, cheeseburger and soda), keep this in mind when determining the size requirements for your site. Be realistic in figuring how many people will want fondue for lunch every day, for instance, and don't allow seating for an army! You can enlarge the place later, but it's discouraging to enter a dining room and be the only customer, stranded in an ocean of tables.

Financing

Because of the high failure rate in this type of business, bank loans are sometimes difficult to obtain, especially if your experience in the field is limited. But that does not mean that investors are hard to find. How many people do you know who have expressed a dream of someday owning a restaurant of their own? It is a rare person who hasn't given some thought to the kind of place she'd have. Take advantage of this interest and recruit these "dreamers" as investors in your business.

Determining the Type of Operation You Want

Most of the restaurant owners in our survey recommended starting out in business serving only two of the three meals each day. Which two meals you serve depends, of course, on the kind of establishment you have in mind.

"Choose a restaurant that represents something you like. If you really like cooking dinner, you should look at a small dinner house. If you really like breakfast and you're intrigued by what kinds of things can be served for breakfast, you might want to do a morning operation that goes through lunch and closes early in the day. I can't emphasize enough that you've got to look at what you like to do."

"If you operate with a limited menu, there is less worry about waste and ordering. Our ground beef is delivered fresh daily, and if, at the end of the day, we have fifteen pounds left over, we don't need to worry. Hamburgers are our main product, and we know we will use any leftover beef the next day. You begin to see patterns in your business, and your errors become fewer—not to say that they go away! When your menu is restricted, you can learn week by week and refine your skills so that your adjustments will result in very little waste."

The image of your restaurant is established not only by your decor but by the kind of food you serve. An elegant dining room with lots of crystal and silver calls for a menu that is equally elegant. A take-out sandwich shop featuring submarines and potato salad has an image all its own. The service that you offer also colors your image.

"I try to keep my restaurant a friendly, home-type operation. I have found that there is a different relationship between the customers and myself and my employees when the customers have to come to the counter to get their own food. When they are picking out their food and carrying it themselves, we are on more of a one-to-one level. There is not that servant feeling, as when you are waiting on someone."

Contrast this image with that of a dimly lit Chinese restaurant featuring exotic oriental cuisine:

"We feature gourmet dining. In Chinese cooking, when you are eating, you *are* dining. And when you are dining out, everything is done for you. Your food is already cut up; the customers do not need to cut it up themselves. We provide an adventure in dining for the connoisseur."

How do you decide what to serve?

Soups, sandwiches, quiches, and "fairly easy desserts that look as if you spend a lot of time on them."

"Simple but good food—straightforward food."

"Famous clam chowder and peanut-butter pie."

"I had no restaurant experience, but I had always been interested in food preparation. I was cooking at home for a family of eight, and it seems like anything you can do for eight, you can do for fifty. It's just a matter of multiples."

"We started with the name Potagerie, which is from the French word for soup. So we thought we had to have soup. Things have evolved from that."

"What we serve in the restaurant is totally different from the cooking I would do when I'm entertaining guests at my own home. I'd have people to my house and they'd say, oh, this is good, why don't you serve this in the restaurant? And I thought about it, and it occurred to me one day, no, even though I sometimes feel that the restaurant is like a wing of my own house, I want my home special and different from the restaurant. There are some things I do for the closest people to me that are *never* for sale. So my choice was to do something at the restaurant that is simple but good, food I can really stand behind. People say, how can you work at a restaurant and come home and enjoy cooking for friends at night? I love to cook when I go home because it's *totally different* from cooking here."

The library is a good source for quantity cookbooks to help you in your menu selections. There are also food-preparation guides that will help you convert your own favorite recipes to restaurant proportions. Nearly all the women we spoke with were regular subscribers to food magazines such as *Gourmet*, *Bon Appétit*, and *Sphere*, and cookbooks of every description were visible on restaurant kitchen shelves both for the cook's use and to encourage employees to develop their own interest in cooking. Restaurant-trade journals (you can read them in the library) are also a good source for the latest on what's cooking in restaurants across the country.

Pricing

The owner of a successful café told us: "Restaurants tend to work on a system where you can plan that a third of what you take in will go for food purchases, a third for labor, and the final third will go for your overhead expenses such as utilities and your contracted services. Finally, at the end of the last third, say 10 percent of that will be your income. So if the cost of your ingredients is one dollar, you will need to charge three dollars for the product."

We recommend that advice as a basic rule: multiply your food costs by three to determine what you should charge for your product.

"In pricing, it is often very difficult to make a big jump when the price of one of your ingredients suddenly takes a big increase. For example, a couple of years ago, all the fruits that go into pie fillings took a tremendous jump. We were really timid about raising the price of a piece of pie to cover the increase. But the public is very aware of how fast food has escalated in price with inflation, and if the food they are getting is good and well prepared, they accept those increases." This woman added, "I think we probably still underprice a piece of pie, but we pick up, or gain, in something like custard cups, for example. You may pick up a nickel here or there that will allow you to keep the price of another item down."

Several women stressed to us how very important it is to know *exactly* what your food costs are for each item that you serve. They advised taking into account all labor costs—how long it takes to prepare a dish (for example, pie is really labor intensive, because it is all handmade)—as well as waste and pilferage losses. They stressed reviewing your menu often to make sure your prices are covering your expenses.

Hard Work and Good Help

Every restaurant owner we interviewed stressed the two elements that they found to be the major factors in running a successful restaurant. These two elements are hard work and the problem of finding—and keeping—reliable help. On the subject of hard work, we heard:

"Anyone contemplating entering the restaurant business must know that initially you're going to spend hours and hours—like sixty hours a week—at work. It is *not* a forty-hour week. We had things we didn't contract out originally, because we didn't feel the money would be there for it. We were locking the door at seven P.M., then spending three more hours cleaning. And we had already been at the restaurant since five or six in the morning. That's a heck of a long day."

Even though the work is hard, restaurant owners find it very satisfying. One suggested a goal that makes the work a little lighter:

"After you have been in business awhile and have worked very hard, you will finally see a little margin in the income. Then take a look at the jobs that are to be done and say, which of these do I really enjoy and want to keep for myself? Which of these do I not mind doing? And which jobs would I like to get totally rid of? (For me, those jobs were bookkeeping and cleaning.) Then you can *hire* people to get those things done. It is so good for morale! It seems like a landmark decision when you can contract out some of the jobs that you dislike."

Hired help is the other major area of concern. We met a woman named Vida Lee who seems to have solved the employee problem with tremendous success. Vida Lee owns a restaurant that bustles with happy and efficient young employees. The feeling of cooperation, friendliness, and employee satisfaction led us to probe her on her secrets of employee management. Here is what she shared with us:

Attracting and Keeping Good Help

"I use mostly high school kids for my help, and my kids—the kids who are the most fun to work with—are kids who are really involved, kids who add on lots of activities. These are invariably kids who do everything with enthusiasm and do it well. I have never run an ad for help. Most new employees are friends of someone who works here, and most are from the neighborhood. When someone who has worked out really well suggests a friend to fill an opening—knowing my expectations and what the job entails—then that's my best information.

"I try to be very flexible in our work scheduling. For any two or three people that do a certain job, there is a set schedule, but they are free to make any trades that they want to make as long as they find a replacement who knows the things they know. I just caution against having too many new people on the same shift. I have a lot of kids who go away to college, then come back and want to work on holidays and in the summer. The younger kids who are working here, whose holidays and summers are important to them, are often happy to get some time off then, so we are often able to slip college kids in who have worked here before and are home on holiday.

"Also, when friends work with friends, they are happy, they look forward to coming to work. A lot of employee morale has to do with having people who enjoy sharing space with one another. Some people cautioned me against having too many friends working together. But if you give a lot of freedom in an organization, I think it has to be countered with expectations that are really understood by everyone. I stress that I want this place to function the same without my presence as it does when I am here. I don't want to be a policewoman. I treat the kids with respect, and I get respect back.

"Sometimes if you run a little restaurant, and you are near a school, for instance, the employees tend to draw their friends to you, and your restaurant becomes a hangout. And the kids who come in can be really intimidating to other customers. When I hire kids, I say that I won't allow this place to become a hangout. I know it's important for friends to be able to come in to leave a message or have coffee during break, but we never allow anyone who doesn't work here back in the kitchen. Work tends to stop when people stand in the kitchen."

Employee Training

"When new employees come to work, they work alongside someone who knows their job. Depending on how complicated the job is and what skills are required, they may need a week or two of this. If someone is learning to be a broiler cook, she may need to work two weeks every day beside the person who knows that job well. Then the person wo knos itafl7well will kind of pull away a little and maybe just come in for an hour or two when we're busiest, to make sure the new person is doing the job well, and if she panics, the experienced worker can help. I'm always in and out, watching, sometimes, over their shoulders."

Vida Lee mentioned the high turnover rate that most restaurants experience and noted that her record was good for having a fairly low turnover in employees. "Something that happens in restaurant work is that there is a really high turnover in those jobs that involve the lowest skill, like busing and dishwashing. And yet those jobs are essential. So I've developed a kind of 'floating helper.' In the evening, three people come in to help with the dinner busing and dishes. One is this floating helper. If the dishes get backed up, he helps there. If tables need busing, he helps out there. But his main job is preparation for the morning, chopping up onions, making apple-pie crumb topping, applesauce-cake icing, and so forth—not highly skilled things, but things you can leave if you have to go help at another job. This kind of work helps a job from being boring. We've discovered by having this third position that when the kids have a three- or four-hour shift, they can work an hour at one thing, an hour at another job, and at the same time that they wash dishes and bus, they can learn the basic kitchen jobs. Everyone who is in the kitchen now started out in this job.

"I also recommend that you, the owner, pitch in and take on any job from time to time. When somebody washes dishes for an hour or buses tables for an hour and you never go back and do that yourself, that person very easily can be taken for granted. That is hard, boring work. I make a specific effort to help out at these jobs. Be very aware once in a while to do the most menial things yourself, because when your employees say, Vida Lee does that, then they are willing to do it, too. Never forget what the real bottom is like. It makes you more considerate and aware of what their jobs are. Don't have those people be your pawns."

Profit-Sharing

The consideration that Vida Lee shows her employees is repaid to her in the responsible and pleasant manner in which her employees deal with the customers. And Vida Lee has also ensured that her employees are repaid for their contribution to her success:

"We had been putting aside a portion of the payroll each month into a savings account, which was to be for emergencies and repairs. I had hoped it would build up so that twice a year, even if it was just a token amount, we could recognize the employees' participation in the business. We have now developed our own profit-sharing plan. It pays off a little for the employees, and it pays off for me, too, if my employees feel that the place is a success, and they had a part in that success and a share of the success. You can make employees feel good in lots of ways, but restaurant pay is lousy, and those benefits don't make up for little pay.

"We made a statement to the employees that we would start out with some kind of loose guidelines, and that the system may be changed somewhere along the way if the formula needs adjusting. But originally we would include every employee, and even the shortest-term employee would see some benefit. My accountant suggested we have some kind of point system, and to pick two numbers—I picked 1 and 5—and place everyone on a scale. We took into consideration the difficulty of the job, longevity (how long they had worked here), and how many hours they worked a week. Then I assigned them a number and put the total of all those numbers into the amount of money we had to share, and then multiplied by their individual number. So the number fives had five of those portions, the number ones had one portion. It may have flaws, but it was a good way to begin. By using the point system, the most difficult-to-train jobs—the people who have invested the most effort—have the most coming back."

Good Advice

We'll pass along to you some of the good advice we've picked up about running a successful restaurant:

"More than any other business, restaurants have a high failure rate. But if you can make it profitable for a year and keep up the quality of your food and your service, business will keep coming to you!"

"Having a partner you can trust means everything to keeping your sanity and your health."

"One of the best bits of advice I received when I started in my restaurant was that, in this particular kind of business, it is wise to *pay all accounts weekly*. Don't let them pile up. And the reasoning behind this is you don't know how well you are doing if you are not paying for things as you use them. And restaurants tend to fail more often than any other business in the United States. The reason they fail is that people let their accounts build up and they think, oh, we took in all this money today. And they haven't sat down and looked at where that money has to go. First thing they know, they are over their heads."

"The owner of an independently managed restaurant must be very careful of restaurant chains in the area. Some 24 percent of all restaurants are now chains, and that percentage is constantly increasing. Because they can afford extensive advertising and promotion, chains can be a real threat to your success."

"You need to know where your business is week by week. I found that the more I knew about the bookkeeping end of the business, the more the day-to-day business makes sense to me. I know where I am, what the needs of the business are—and not just the public part of it. I do all my bill paying, my payroll, and I make a weekly report that is a little table that shows our breakfast business, our lunch business, our dinner business, and how many people we've served. I turn over all of my preliminary bookwork to my accountant, and he processes it on all of his nice modern equipment and puts it into really understandable information. He breaks things down into percentages of where all my money has gone. I have learned so much from what he does. I know when I need to make adjustments."

"Liquor licenses are expensive (they can range from $500 up to five figures), but having one is an advantage. Without a license to serve liquor, your earnings from the restaurant are certainly restricted."

"Most restaurant suppliers who call on you are quite well informed on their products, and they can help you a lot in ordering. Salespeople call on us once a week, generally, and if I'm really busy, they can pretty much look at my shelf and see what I need. They are competent."

Two restaurant owners commented on different aspects of the problems involved in expanding an operation:

"Our first restaurant was forced to close because the building we were in was torn down. We had a lot of difficulties finding a new location. Our problem was, perhaps, that we were female. I felt most of the building owners or landlords were not impressed enough with our financial statement—they didn't feel we were strong enough to expand and make it a success in a larger location. Exactly why we were rejected, quite a number of times, we can never really know for sure—except for one man whom I met with several times regarding different locations in buildings he owned. He actually did ask me why I wasn't staying home having babies! This poor man—what could I say to that? Someone that misguided."

Another woman said, "People are always saying, this place is always crowded, and it's doing well—when are you going to start another one? But I guess I'm a lousy capitalist. My income is not great, but it is adequate, and I have time of my own to do other things that I'm interested in. I have no desire to manage people managing people. I also see places that were doing so well and were so comfortable, and the attitude is, if this is good, more is better. Another place is started, and the original place is not what it used to be. And the new place is not like the original. And somehow the thing loses heart."

Here are some different types of food services to consider:

Lunchrooms

We mentioned before that when you are starting out in the restaurant business, it is wise to concentrate on only one or two meals daily. A lunchroom is often the perfect solution. There may even be other incentives for this choice:

"My sister and I had lots of restaurant experience in our teen years, because our parents owned several. Growing up in the business, we, of course, grew to loathe it immensely, as we were more or less on call weekends, holidays, and summers at any time—if we weren't *already* there working. My vow to keep away from the food business lasted about seven years. I knew that we could run a good business with good food and good service. However, things would be a little different in *our* business—no weekends, no evenings, and no legal holidays!"

Even though the hours you are open are limited (often from 10 A.M. to 2 P.M. or possibly 4 P.M.), you will most likely be working from 8 until 5, or later. The owner of a lunchroom that is open only three days a week reports putting in "about a forty-plus hour week. Very hard work physically, but great for the ego!"

Lunchrooms, like all food-service operations, must adhere to a lot of strict regulations:

"We had to obtain food-handlers' cards, which means attending a class for a couple hours to learn about certain diseases carried by food, the handling and storage of food, et cetera. We also need a license from the city and the health department, with the latter having to come and inspect the premises. The health department also grades you soon after opening. They put a visible sticker on the door or window that shows your rating. Then they return by surprise about every six months to inspect again."

Another lunchroom owner complained, "The greatest obstacles in starting my business were the various bureaucratic steps necessary to open the restaurant—the building department, the agriculture and health departments. Though they exist ostensibly to assist small businesses, their red tape and confusing regulations were only a headache."

How about expenses? "Refrigeration was our largest expense. We tried to cut down on that by buying used household refrigerators, which did not hold up well with heavy use. We learned that even though restaurant equipment is very expensive, it is built for this specific use. Stainless steel makes it costly, but it is durable and easy to keep clean."

"Seventy-six dollars on a mop bucket!"

"My expenses ran about like this: a complete kitchen with stove and hood, dishwasher, large sink, freezers and machinery, refrigerators—about ten thousand dollars. Dishes, other accessories, pots and pans—about one thousand dollars. Chairs, tables, furniture and decorations—about three thousand dollars."

What special problems might you encounter?

"Hired help, upon which you are tremendously dependent in this type of business, is the most difficult aspect of my business. One cannot usually afford to pay more than minimum wage, and you must demand a high volume of work for it. There is always the temptation to steal, and it is difficult to keep people totally accountable unless a sizeable investment is made in complicated computer cash registers and the like. My policy has been to treat hired help as kindly and sensitively as possible, to instill loyalty. It is also necessary to keep workers feeling as good and high spirited as possible so they put across a good feeling to the customers."

"The only obstacle we encountered was the surprising unwillingness to help and the unenthusiasm of the salespeople we encountered while looking at equipment. And food wholesalers acted the same way. They didn't seem to take us seriously. We don't know if it was just because we were women or because the restaurant business is so chancy they don't want to get too involved. Maybe a little of both."

Several women offered this advice: "Don't do it alone! There is too much to do, even in the smallest type of operation. It's always good to have someone around with a special interest in the place, since problems arise so often (machinery breakdowns, customer relations, quality control). Unless you can afford to pay someone *very* well to be a manager in your absence, get a partner."

One woman mentioned to us, "Being a customer in a restaurant gives you only a brief picture of what is involved in operating it." Still, the women we spoke with were enthusiastic and very satisfied with their lunchroom businesses. "The homelike style of my lunchroom has helped me to really, truly enjoy it," one woman said. Another commented on the satisfaction that comes with developing a regular clientele. "We look up and say, oh, here comes Mr. Applecrisp, here's Mrs. Cheesecake!"

Some Hot Tips

We learned of some interesting ways to vary a restaurant operation to suit your individual interests and your customers' special needs.

One woman has chosen to enlarge her business and her area of interest by combining her lunchroom with a successful gift shop. The decor throughout the shop and the dining room is homey and cheerful, with beautiful stained-glass lamps and windows that are actually consigned artwork that is offered for sale. Baskets and kitchen supplies, as well as art by local craftspeople, are available in the shop. All merchandise is selected with an eye toward the total image of the business—the placemats used on the antique dining tables and the long calico aprons worn by the waitresses are similar to items carried in the shop. The owner's flair for decorating is evident throughout the restaurant and promotes the decorating service she offers as a sideline from the shop. We were impressed by the way the owner used consigned artwork to such an advantage, achieving a very rich decor with little investment. When a painting or a hanging Tiffany-style lamp sells, she merely replaces it with the work of another artist.

The owners of another restaurant had some good ideas they thought could be turned into profit by someone willing to give them a try. We'll pass them along to you. Their first idea concerns special, "reservations only" dinner parties to be offered on limited evenings to your regular lunchroom customers. "When you make something very hard to get into," one of the women said, "then *everyone* wants to get in." They suggested trying twice-monthly dinner parties, with limited seating and advance reservations required, and a set menu. Testing this idea in their own business, they found it to be extremely popular.

Another inside tip grew out of this business's problems handling all the large, special-occasion banquets and luncheons they were called on to do. The suggestion? A restaurant open only for business and social organizations' luncheons and dinner parties. A low-rent location would be a must for such an operation, but according to our source, the demand for such facilities is great.

Delis

If you are a little timid, not the wealthiest, and have not been schooled at the Cordon Bleu, but you're still dying to try your hand at a food service, a deli may be the answer. The kitchen facilities required are much smaller than those you need for a full-scale restaurant operation, and improvements to your chosen location (including ventilation systems and so forth) don't need to be as extensive. Your local health department can answer your inquiries about the regulations that govern such an operation. In operating a delicatessen, your options include counter sales of meats, cheeses, and salads; tables where customers can enjoy prepared sandwiches and snacks; and a catering service, providing more elaborate trays of meats and cheeses for special occasions. Your own imagination will be able to supply you with even more original ideas.

"My hours are 10 to 3 every weekday. I am busiest from 12 to 1 o'clock, when most of my customers come in to get a sandwich to take out. Eighty percent of the people do not stay here to eat, though I do have a few tables. The majority of my business is people who work within three or four blocks of here. I have a simple bookkeeping system: I list all my expenses on one page, and I keep my income ledger in two parts—sandwiches, salads, beverages, and extras on one side, and deli and party trays on the other. I rarely hire help, but when I do have people fill in, I pay them with meat or cheese. When I bought the deli, I made an arrangement with the former owner to stay on for two weeks to teach me the ropes. It was a tremendous help."

Taverns

A surprising number of women have found taverns to be the answer to their business dreams. A look at the possible profit percentages may give us the reason: 35 percent of your total sales will go to cover beverage costs; 20 percent for employee wages and 20 percent for rent, insurance, and other fixed expenses. That leaves a heady 25 percent profit. (This compares to 10% profit expectation in the restaurant business.) Location is mentioned as the number-one priority in running a successful tavern.

Are there any special problems involved with running a tavern—traditionally a "man's place"?

"If you have good management, the bad types will feel uncomfortable in your place and won't feel like staying there. You have to keep an eye on what you're doing, always stand your ground. Anyway, taverns are changing today. The 'neighborhood tavern' is going out. The crowd we attract today has a certain amount of money."

We spoke with the owner of two taverns who told us, that, along with the tavern business, the games business (football, pinball, pool tables) is booming.

"All of a sudden, in the last five years, the games business in this country has become respectable. My tavern did around a half-million dollars in business last year, and $170,000 of that was in games. That means about 34 percent of my tavern business." She told us that she serves "the best hamburgers in town for a buck. We lose money on food, but if the food business is hot, the game business is tremendous and so is the beer business."

Her advice for running a successful tavern? "Cultivate your regulars—the people who spend four or five nights a week in your tavern. They're the ones who'll bring in your new business."

Got enough general information on the food business to get you hungering for a place of your own? How about some specifics—a couple of real-life stories from two very different women who are thirty-year veterans in the restaurant business.

We'll call our first tale Minding the Chips and Chowder. Meet Mo.

Minding the Chips and Chowder

In 1942, Mo and a friend bought a Newport, Oregon, bayfront café. And, "with two women and five kids trying to make a living, we soon taught five kids they didn't want to work in a restaurant all their lives!"

Mo eventually became the sole owner of the café, and for twenty-five years, she sold 50¢ ham and eggs and 25¢ hamburgers to her customers at her twenty-one-stool, two-booth café. Fish-cannery workers were her early customers. It has only been in recent years that the tourists have discovered Mo's and that the Kennedys and the Paul Newmans have not only discovered it but became Mo's personal friends.

Today, thirty-six years later, several restaurants carry her name, each with a unique, casual setting, and each serving the most delicious clam chowder you ever tasted. Her key to success?

"I set out to make a living, not a million dollars, but after almost forty years of experience, you accumulate a feel for what you're doing. I think that if you put enough into anything, you're bound to succeed."

How does doing business today differ from operating a restaurant in the forties?

"Back in 1942, business books were very simple. You simply subtracted your costs from your gross income and the rest was yours! But today, business records are beyond my understanding. I have an accountant who is in charge of taxes and quarterly reports. He even advised me to incorporate when it was to my advantage, which I did. But he never tries to tell me where or when or how I should spend my money, perhaps because he knows I wouldn't listen to him anyway. I do all that myself. I just set my prices and portions where I feel I want them."

Mo's original chowder house is a landmark on the Oregon coast, and her name is almost as well known as her peanut-butter pie. There is always a line waiting to be served in the small, bustling restaurant, and when seating space empties at one of the round wooden tables, customers from the line join whoever may still be seated at the table. No formalities, no "separate tables," just hearty, homey dining with a casual, coastal flavor.

How does she find the help that handles the overflow crowds that she feeds each day?

"I've always tried to pay a little higher than most, and I treat my people well. Kids are my most dedicated workers—kids from responsible families, who have learned a sense of responsibility. Mary, for instance, started to work for me as a dishwasher when she was twelve. She worked as a waitress all the summers of her high school and college years. And there wasn't a holiday that passed that Mary wasn't here at Mo's putting in her time. She just graduated from college with a degree in nursing, and she told me she'd be here yet if her father hadn't made her go out and find a nurse's job!"

Mo is an attractive, gray-haired woman in her sixties, candid and friendly. We asked why she decided to expand her original successful operation.

"Perhaps it was a matter of self-satisfaction. Someone is forever talking me into setting up another store, and I've found that more restaurants are just a pain in the ass! I say, 'Okay, you can set it up, but do it *this way*. Then the person I'm going in with always wants to do it *that way*. You'd think forty years of experience would speak for itself! Now I've got two gentlemen who want to set up a Mo's in Munich, Germany. Why not? What better excuse would there be to visit Europe once a year!"

Looking back over her years in the restaurant business, Mo reminisced about the many friends she has made through her work.

"Perhaps the high point of my business career, and perhaps my life, was the day Bobby and Ethel Kennedy came to eat at my restaurant. I was told a day or two beforehand that they would be coming, but I was told not to tell anyone. They arrived as scheduled in three big black cars. Everyone in the restaurant was stunned beyond belief. (One boy who was eating a hamburger was so startled at the sight of them and their crew that he got up and ran off. Bobby went over to his table, picked up his half-eaten hamburger, and took a bite out of it. He swallowed it and gasped, 'I'm starved!') I waited on them, serving them my famous chowder. They were some of the most wonderful people I have ever met. They were totally exhausted from campaigning, yet they glowed with warmth and kindness. After they left, Ethel called from the airport. 'Mo,' she said, 'we are so tired, we just couldn't appreciate your chowder enough. Would you bring some of it out to the airport for us to take on our flight to Los Angeles?' So I got three big pots ready, and a police car drove me to the airport. I delivered the chowder, explaining precisely how to serve it. Ethel told me she wasn't any good at preparing food, would I come with them and serve it to all the people aboard? It was such a shock to me that all I could think about was that I had to work the next day, I had no extra clothes, no toothbrush! I declined, and I will never forgive myself. Bobby Kennedy was killed a few days later. I have vowed never to decline a spur-of-the-moment offer again."

How can you compare a bay-front chowder house to an "uptown" Chinese restaurant in a big city? By comparing the personal satisfaction and financial success achieved by the two very distinct personalities that run them. Mo is a confident and open woman who was willing to work a second full-time job for ten years while struggling to establish her restaurant. "It was a matter of pride," she told us. "I loved Mo's and I knew I could never give it up." Ruby Chow has also been willing to work very hard. Since her restaurant opened its doors thirty years ago, Ruby has worked out front, providing the personality that she feels is essential to the success of any restaurant.

Ruby Chow's

"Thirty years ago, the public had pretty set attitudes about Chinese food. To them, Chinese food was fried rice and chow mein, and a bowl of noodles—and that's all they thought we ate. I started thirty years ago to *teach* them some of the different dishes we eat."

Ruby Chow is seated at a back table in the restaurant that bears her name, pouring tea and telling us of her experiences in running one of Seattle's landmark eating establishments. "In the old days," she tells us, "Seattle was not an 'eating out' city. It is beginning to be that now. People eat out more than they did thirty years ago."

Her restaurant experience began at the age of fourteen, working in a honky-tonk. "In the old days," she relates, "people were going slumming when they went to a Chinese restaurant." She was determined that one day she would have her own place—"and it would be a *nice* place." Her dream was realized when, with her husband serving as chef, she opened at the pagoda-roofed location she still occupies today. Living upstairs, the couple managed to build a thriving business and raise a thriving family of five children at the same time. "My last two babies were raised upstairs. I had a loudspeaker above the crib, and when the baby cried, I would run upstairs and change his diaper or feed him."

How has the restaurant business changed over the years she has been in operation? "Thirty years ago, when people came in to dine, they were all dressed up, the men in suits and the women dressed very nicely. You could usually tell just by looking at them how much they were going to spend. Now you can't. Also, today people are more willing to try more exotic food. At one time, they wouldn't try anything new or different.

"In the past, you had to give your customer quality, quantity, service, and a good price. Now it has changed. You don't have to give them service. You don't have to give them quality. You don't have to give them quantity. But if you charge them a lot and give it a fancy name and some atmosphere, you've got it made! I have found that to be. I don't know why it is. Values have changed."

Ruby commented that other women often say to her, "How do you manage all this, how can you do all that? I just couldn't possibly do it." "That's the one thing that they should get out of their minds," she told us, "that they *can't* do it. They can if they want to, if they set their minds to it. I've always gone on the basis of that. When the ball is thrown, I pick it up and run with it!"

We asked if any of her five children were involved in the restaurant. "I started my kids in the restaurant when they were eleven, first in the kitchen, then busing, then waiting on tables. But now none of them is involved in the business. They told me, 'Mother, if you wanted to give us the restaurant, you shouldn't have sent us to college!'" The problems we've heard from many working mothers were never an issue with Ruby. "You just can't say that a working woman cannot give her time to her children. You've got to show them that you love them, but you don't need to smother them. Just show them what you want."

Another issue sometimes debated among women who run their own businesses was declined by Ruby: "I feel I have gotten equal treatment from everyone over the years, and I didn't have to demand it. Men knew I was firm in what I wanted and that I would tell them the truth. I am very candid about everything I want done. I have, of course, had to raise my voice a few times . . ."

But she never raises her voice in front of the customers. "I have never scolded any of the help out in the dining room. I wait until they come back in the kitchen, and then I tell them if I feel they did something wrong. Restaurant work is hard because you have to take it from your restaurant help, your kitchen crew, *and* your customer. I just don't allow myself to get tense."

Ruby Chow's offers short-order food, gourmet dining, catering services, and hors d'oeuvres for parties and such. With these four different facets of her business, she handles nearly everything in the restaurant field. "Tomorrow," she explained, "I have a party of seventy-five coming in the back room, one hundred coming in the front room, and in between, I have a catering to deliver for five hundred people. All in one day." The work is very hard, "and if you expect to run a restaurant by coming in and watching the clock, you won't get anywhere."

Still, the years have been exciting and rewarding. The restaurant expanded as it became "the place" to go for a late-night supper. "Theatrical people like Chinese food after their shows," Ruby commented, mentioning visits from Bob Hope; Lucille Ball; Sammy Davis, Jr.; and Jack Benny. "I have so many pictures of myself with these important people that I just haven't had time to put them in a book."

And Ruby has become one of the important people, too. In addition to her role as mother and full-time restaurateur, she has added the duties of county councilwoman. These added responsibilities have made a change in her role as businesswoman. "Owning and running a restaurant is a personality business." Motioning to a number of empty tables at the height of the dinner hour, she continued, "You can see if I'm going to be putting in my time on the council, I'm not going to be spending as much time on the floor. I can't give it as much time as I used to, and the business shows it." But, after thirty years, Ruby feels it is time for a change. "Running a restaurant, raising five children, and being active in the community is quite a job," Ruby says. And it's a job she has done very well.

6 Retailing Variations

There are a number of variations in the retailing trade that offer the would-be entrepreneur some additional roads to explore. We'll take a look at some of them now. First, consider a franchise business.

Franchise Businesses

A franchise business is one in which a parent company grants an applicant the right to run a business under the company's name. McDonald's, Baskin Robbins 31 Flavors Ice Cream and Stretch & Sew Fabric Centers are some familiar franchises. Franchises may apply to a single store only, or to an entire area. In some cases, the franchisor is the boss and the individual store owner is not. If you are a strongly individualistic person, this type of business may not be satisfying to you.

Choose a franchise for the same reasons that you would choose to start a business on your own—that is, it is *essential* to follow your own personal interests in making your decision. Be sure to investigate thoroughly the company as well as the product, the territory offered, the technical assistance promised, and the contract you must sign.

Of course, there are good and bad points to franchise businesses. Here is what we have found. A franchise offers these advantages:

1. A franchisor will offer guidance and training in your new field, teaching you all you need to know about operating the business.

"Still, it's good to get a little background before you dive in. We worked in the local store for two months before we made our decision."

2. It may be possible, because of group purchasing power and company financing, to open your franchise business with a lower cash investment than might have been feasible in your own operation. (Of course, costs vary tremendously in different franchises. A rug-cleaning franchise may be purchased for as little as $1,500, but some restaurant franchises run as high as $500,000.)

3. Some franchises offer bookkeeping services, co-op advertising, technical and legal help, and group buying discounts.

"By owning a franchise, we belong to a national franchise council that meets to discuss any problems you may be having. There may be patterns you don't like or would like changed—just about any problem or complaint you may have will be handled there. So we have constant help with our problems."

4. When you operate a franchise, you are dealing with a product and a business method that are well known and have proven successful. You have a tried-and-true advantage, with the customer appeal of a brand name.

The owner of a sewing franchise put it this way: "There's a lot of security in a franchise. There's power in numbers. We're not just a fabric store, we're something special. The company gets 5 percent of our profits—a small price to pay considering we have four hundred people in the main office working for us. And it is in our contract that we don't even have to buy our fabrics from them. But we do, because we know they are the best."

5. Franchises are extremely popular. They account for 31 percent of all retail trade.

Here are some of the apparent disadvantages of franchise operations:

1. Your individuality in the business is restricted by the franchise agreement. You may be your own boss, but your independence is lost to a certain extent.

2. Too many other franchised dealers may be allowed by the parent company to establish in your area, decreasing your volume of business.

3. The reputation of one dirty or mismanaged namesake in your area may reflect on your business.
4. The franchise fees to be paid to the parent company or the required purchase of highly marked up supplies from the franchisor can lead to greatly diminished profits, even though business is booming.
5. Some franchise owners complain that, though training is offered, it is often not sufficient to prepare you for all aspects of the business.

The Federal Trade Commission has ruled that all franchise operators must give the following information to potential investors:

1. The company must provide a list of the "Who" behind the franchise business—names of key executives and their background.
2. The company must reveal all lawsuits and bankruptcies in which it has been involved.
3. The company must list the names of all suppliers that the franchisee will have to do business with and the amounts of money these particular suppliers pay to the franchise operator.
4. The company must make a full explanation of any financial assistance given by the franchisor to the franchisee.
5. The company must make a full disclosure of all money the franchisee will have to pay, both at the start of the business and throughout business operation.
6. The company must supply a full explanation of the terms under which the franchise may be revoked.

Point six is especially important. Have your attorney assist you in going over the provisions relating to termination. Can you sell the franchise to someone else or back to the franchisor if you are dissatisfied? Can the franchisor revoke your contract or fail to renew it? For how many years is the contract valid?

After weighing the merits of a franchise operation, try talking to the owners of similar franchises in your area. Better yet, work for one awhile. You may find you don't enjoy scooping ice cream eight hours a day! Another way to evaluate the benefits of running a franchise is to work up a comparison model of a similar business (using your business plan format) that would be run independently. Check the prices for supplies, services, equipment, advertising, and so forth against the charges that the franchise lists. In this way, you can see if the franchising costs are truly justified. Finally, if you are still interested, have your lawyer look over your contract before you sign, so you will be fully aware of all the details involved.

Mail-Order Businesses

The mail-order field can easily be adapted to fit almost any special interest you might have. Dee operates a mail-order business involved with the dairy-goat industry. "I was always interested in goats, and when I decided to start a business, I knew I would do something in the dairy-goat field. I did not say to myself, 'I'm going to start a mail-order business, what product should I choose?' Instead, it was 'I have a tremendous interest in the dairy-goat industry. How can I utilize that interest and come up with something that, even if it is not terribly profitable, is lots of fun to me?'

"Periodically I receive ads in the mail that say, 'Start your own mail-order business. You can push this product out the door, all you have to do is take our material, put your name on it, and start shipping!' But most of these are gimmick type businesses. It may be okay if you are *interested* in gimmicks. But I feel you really have to be interested in the product to be successful."

When Dee started her business, she was aware of the primary trade journal in the field, so she knew where to place her advertising. "My monthly advertising in the *Dairy Goat Journal* runs about fifty dollars. Of course, your advertising costs will vary with your industry. Mine is a rural industry, and costs are relatively low. In the computer industry, for example, an ad smaller than mine would cost much more."

She chose three items to promote when beginning her business three years ago, then she sought out local suppliers for her products, originally buying the finished products from them. She now produces many items herself by handling her own silk screening, printing, and award-ribbon production. "It helps if you live in a city that is large enough to offer you a selection for your supplies. You have access to many more resources in a large city." She was able to save money by locating discontinued lots of paper to use for her fliers, for example.

For her first promotion, Dee mailed out one of her calendars and a flier mentioning the other items she handles to every name that she found listed in her trade journal. (Each month, the journal carries the names and addresses of hundreds of goat breeders and advertisers across the country.) It was her first mistake. "I thought I had worded the accompanying flier so that the customers would know that they should remit money for the calendar, and that I would fill orders for others. Not only had I underpriced the calendar, but only two out of three hundred who received the calendar sent money! I immediately upped my price, but I learned a dreadful lesson: Don't ship the merchandise before receiving payment. On every calendar I sold, from the additional orders that came in, I lost 10 cents."

Still, the promotion was successful in that it did create interest in the industry for her products—so successful, however, that it led her to make her second costly mistake. "Even though only two people paid me for the calendars I had sent out, I received many orders for more of them from members of the different associations. I had originally printed five hundred calendars and had mailed out three hundred. I immediately sold out the remaining two hundred, and then I made a judgmental error—I printed another three hundred. Only experience could have stopped me from making that mistake. I sold very few of the reordered calendars and had stacks of them left. You just have to learn how to reorder. Now I feel that when I reach a point when I have to send someone's money back because I don't have the stock—then I may increase the size of my order the next time around. Until then, I will only order five hundred calendars a year, for example, until I absolutely sell out."

Dee uses six different ads, running them an average of two months each, so that she has a year's coverage in the trade journal. "There was a woman from Florida who was advertising a T-shirt and a bumper sticker when I started out. She's no longer advertising. She advertised the same product month after month—the T-shirt for about three months, and then the bumper sticker. The problem was that she saturated her immediate market. Everyone bought T-shirts who was going to. Everyone bought the bumper sticker who was going to. And then she was paying for an ad that wasn't bringing in response."

In her business, she has never used compiled mailing lists purchased from a broker. "I make my mailing list from the hundreds of names and addresses that are listed in the trade journal. I send out my catalog to everyone who orders from my ad, usually also enclosing a flier with the most up-to-date information on my product line. I maintain a customer file, marking the date the catalog was sent out on the back of each name-and-address card. I keep the file by state, by city, and then alphabetically by last name. By sending out your mailing consistently—which is *very* important—you also keep the list up to date. If the customer has moved without notifying you, you will catch the forwarding addresses while they are still valid if you don't wait a year and a half between mailings."

Dee handles all her business out of her own home, with no additional employees. She uses regular postage for her mailings. (Bulk rates are cheaper, but you need a $40 permit, you must send out at least 200 pieces at a time, and your mail must be zip-code sorted.) "In a mail-order business, you must be concerned with the breakability of your product, its size and weight, its ease of packaging."

She feels a storefront location is unnecessary for her type of business. "I would only get curious people coming in, taking up my time." And for now, she still advertises only in the one trade journal. "If I had a separate advertising department whose only function was to get the ads out, I would try to advertise in other magazines. But I am limiting myself to a size I can handle myself. You have to work to your own capacity—if you don't, all the pieces will fall apart. My time is taken up now with my two priority functions—to develop new items (I have three games in progress now) and to promote my products. My new ideas are still in the in-progress stage because I just don't have time for full-time product development."

Dee told us, "I had a large loss in my business in the first year, a smaller loss the second year, and this, the third year, I did make a profit! The profit was minimal, but it was a turning point, and that turning point is very important. It puts you on the other side of the balance sheet, and it's great to reach!"

Dee has lots of good advice for other women interested in the possibilities of mail order. "Limit the items that you handle. A huge selection requires a huge amount of capital behind you. Also, it is not always necessary to have all the stock on hand before you run an ad. You can wait awhile and judge the customer response.

"When investing your capital, you have to look at long-term returns. You have to buy in large quantities, for example, and you aren't going to sell it all at once. Your business isn't a one-time stab, it's an ongoing thing. You can't expect to get all your money out quickly."

Also, "I do all my printing at the community college. Community colleges are a tremendous resource for small businesses such as mine. By taking a printing class, I can do all my printing there. I print my own mailing labels, fliers, many other items. I think someday everything will be done on audiovisual cassettes. Then I'll take a class in *that* at the community college and make my own cassettes.

"When I started out, I had in mind that I would be handling large orders—a dozen of this, eighteen of that. Instead, I have found that most mail order business is for single items."

On enthusiasm: "The most valuable quality a businesswoman can have is enthusiasm. There are times when business can be devastating. There are times when you'll be down. The question is, will you get out? It really helps to have a shoulder to cry on (your husband's or another businessperson's)," Dee says, and she recommends getting together with others in business to keep up enthusiasm, to use each other as a sounding board.

"In the mail-order business, there is a constant battle to keep your fliers and catalog current with the materials that are available. You have to constantly update your items, and it's often hard to come up with new products that you can offer without going to a great deal of expense. Still, I would suggest to other women that they find a field that they are interested in and just go to it. It won't go smoothly, and your costs will be about one-third more than you figured. But I have a little book at home, and on the cover, it says, 'If you're not in business for fun or profit, what the hell are you doing there?' So I figure I can't lose. Even if I don't make a profit, I'm having fun!"

Additional Facts on Operating a Mail-Order Business

Your product:

1. To justify the 2- or 3-week wait for delivery of your product, it is best to choose items that the customer cannot find in a retail store.
2. Your product should be easy to illustrate, advertise, and package.
3. Products priced under $10 generally sell best through mail order.
4. Check the mail-order sections of several magazines and note which type of products are advertised the most. These are probably the type of goods that have been most successfully promoted through mail order. By looking at back issues, you can see which ads ran for the longest periods of time. The longer the ad ran, the more successful the product probably was.
5. To locate suppliers for the products you choose, check:

   a. Yellow Pages for manufacturer's name
   b. manufacturers' directories in reference section of the library (*Thomas Register of American Manufacturers* and *MacRae's Bluebook Directory* are two of the best)
   c. trade publications (most of these publications have directory issues that list the manufacturers of products in the trade)
   d. *American Register of Exporters and Importers* in the reference section of the library (for listings of product importers)

Your advertising:

1. Use magazine or newspaper ads, or direct mail advertising (utilizing a mailing list you have drawn up yourself or a list purchased from a broker), or both.
2. Promote buying convenience in your advertising, especially for rural customers.

3. Place your advertising in magazines that carry a lot of other mail-order advertising, and remember your intended market when choosing the magazine.
4. Limit the number of items you offer for sale in your ad.

Your mailing list:

1. Compile your own mailing list from past customers. Send back a catalog with every order that you fill.
2. Mailing lists can also be purchased from mailing-list brokers, who are listed in the Yellow Pages. These can be "buyer lists," maintained by large mail-order firms, with the names of previous mail-order customers; or they may be "compiled lists," with names categorized by profession, trade, business or social affiliation, with no regard to the customer's buying habits.

The national average for return on direct-mail advertising is 3 percent. In order to be successful, you *must* repeat your advertising constantly and constantly update your line of merchandise.

Two advantages of selling by mail order instead of in a retail outlet were cited by the operator of a mail-order china business:

1. "You can almost totally eliminate the cost of hiring salespeople to sell the merchandise. Our catalog sells the items, and the cost of producing a catalog and paying our packers and warehouse people to assemble orders is far less than it would be to keep several salespeople on the payroll. Also, packing and warehouse people are being paid to assemble *sold* merchandise, while salespeople must spend their time trying to sell merchandise, often to nonbuyers."
2. "Also, in mail order, the geographical location of our customers is boundless. We often get orders from countries out of the United States. If we were a local retail outlet, we would only be able to reach customers who are within traveling distance."

Exchange Businesses

Another variation in retailing is the exchange. In this type of business, your inventory is acquired totally on an exchange, or consignment, basis. Handicrafts, art, and antiques are obvious choices for this kind of shop, but again, your imagination can help you develop many other ideas. The benefit of starting this kind of business is, obviously, that your initial expense is limited to rent, advertising, employees' salaries, and other overhead—there is no investment in inventory. To be successful, though, as in any business, a sizable investment in *effort* is required.

Carole, for example, is the owner of an arts and crafts gallery. She represents more than two hundred West Coast artists in her shop. Though the artwork she shows in her gallery is taken on consignment (no financial investment involved), her personal investment in each of her artists is sizable. Aside from the *time* she spends in representing each craftsperson, she invests in advertising, mailings, and receptions to promote their works. She takes a sales commission that is typical of other art galleries. She receives 40 percent of the sale price of any paintings that the gallery sells, 30 percent on sculpture sales.

Carole notes that her relationship with the artists she represents is often very personal, though having a written contract stating the artist's agreement with the gallery is a must. Such a contract protects her from the loss of a commission if an artist sells some of his works after a show has closed in the gallery, though the purchaser first viewed the works in the gallery showing. She also asks that the artists she represents not show their work in any other area gallery.

Finding artists to represent has never been a problem. Often an artist will bring in samples of her work for Carole to view, and others she invites to be a part of her gallery showing. She prefers to see six or so items that provide her with a sampling of the artist's work. She looks for professional quality and reasonable price. ("I won't represent an artist who prices his or her work too high; I won't be able to sell the work, and the artist will resent it.") She also will not take the work of a new artist if it is very similar to the work of an artist she already represents.

She feels that education is part of her job, as well. She tells how, at one time, women wouldn't come into the gallery when she was exhibiting nudes. "That doesn't happen anymore. That's education."

Carole receives a lot of personal satisfaction from finding homes for local artworks. Though she did not take any money out of the business for the first three years, she is now able to support herself with gallery profits.

Sue also operates an exchange-type business, this one located in a fashionable converted-warehouse complex of shops, where she handles handmade children's clothing and toys. Nearly all of her merchandise is taken on consignment. "For every item in the shop, there is a signed agreement and a number and a price assigned. I charge the craftspeople a $2 bookkeeping fee the first time they bring an item in, then $2 a year thereafter. When a customer makes a purchase, I keep from one-third to 40 percent of what the item sells for. When you compare this to the 100 or 200 percent markup that most retailers use, you can see that the profit margin is not tremendous. To make good money, the selling price really should be split fifty-fifty."

Sue's policy is to reduce her inventory periodically through price-reduction sales, with the consignors' consent, and to send back unsold items to their maker after one year. Though the shop was begun with the idea of selling the things that she made herself, Sue has learned, like many other craftspeople, that "you're either going to make it or sell it. It's pretty hard to manage both." Now when she has an idea for an item she'd like to try in the shop, she contacts one of her consignees who she knows has the skills to make the item.

Sue cited "horrendous bookkeeping" as the biggest problem in her business. By acquiring her merchandise from so many different suppliers, she has "200 different accounts, which means writing between 50 and 125 checks a month to consignees." By taking items on consignment, though, Sue feels she is able to help many budding crafts artists. "We can give more people a chance, since we don't have to pay for the items in advance."

Selling Door-to-Door

She sells sea shells down by the sea shore. Only goes to show that there are other ways to operate a sales business besides sitting in a store behind a cash register. Using your imagination, you can find lots of ways to make the sale in lots of different places. Consider direct sales.

Ding dong. How about taking your products to your customers at home? Cosmetics, encyclopedias, and food containers come to mind, but they are certainly not the only things that can be sold this way.

Ginni, "The Wicker Lady," is an ingenious door-to-door businesswoman. She sells every size, shape, and form of basketry at evening home parties. Going to a different home every night of the week, she displays her huge basket stock around the hostess's home. She has never had to ask anyone to host a party, and she is now booked up nine months in advance. Party size averages from twenty-five to thirty people.

"When I decided to sell wicker products at home parties, I started out with three parties, and within three months, I was booked up four months in advance. I started with a $500 inventory, and today I've built it up to a $5,000 inventory.

"The keys to my success? There are five of them:

1. One of the main reasons for my success is that I decided on my own to underprice my wicker.
2. I always take an item back if the customer is not satisfied.
3. I bend over backward to not be a pushy salesperson.
4. Another important aspect of my success is that I offer a service with my products. I show women how they can use my baskets in their homes.
5. And speaking of helping people, I have a keen sense for tuning into the needs and interests of the audience.

"Problems, Yes, I've run into several problems, and each seemed to arise from the fact that aspects of my business conflicted with my personality. One arose when I decided to take orders for wicker at the parties and then deliver the wicker two weeks later. I did this because this was how sales parties had been run in the past, to my knowledge. I was trying to conform to tradition, and I wasn't taking my personality into account. I hated delivering orders two weeks after each party. It seemed so anticlimactic. Then I decided that I could mold the business around my personality, and I began bringing my stock to the parties and selling the items directly to the customers. One problem solved.

"Another problem was that my gregarious personality sometimes overwhelms people. I would come into a home, burst into my usual talk and chatter, and wonder why the hostess and her guests were whispering and withdrawn. It took me the longest time to realize that I overwhelm some people. Now I've learned to make myself a part of the furniture at the beginning of each party. I sit in the most inconspicuous corner and busy myself with little bits of paperwork. Then, when the guests and hostess are able to loosen up more, I introduce myself and begin talking about the items I have on display and how they might be used. Then I get in my socializing toward the end of the party."

Tips on Buying an Established Business

In buying an established business, the first thing to remember is . . . *be careful!*

Have your accountant and lawyer in tow before you make any decisions, and study all records, contracts, and figures carefully. Here are some points to be especially concerned about:

1. How long has the business been established? If any goodwill fee is being added to the price of the business, length of time in business will need to justify it.

"I had noticed a small, local, retail fabric shop being run poorly, with a lot of unsalable merchandise. I told the owner I would try to sell the merchandise for ninety days, then give him the money, in exchange for a down payment. There was no goodwill to purchase, as the former owner had huge debts, horrid credit, and was known to be unreliable with customers. I was essentially taking over a lease on space."

2. Examine any equipment that you will be buying along with the business very carefully. Was it new when purchased? Will it need to be replaced soon? (Check the recent billings on equipment service and repairs). How has the present owner depreciated the value of this equipment on his or her income taxes? By dividing the list value of a piece of equipment by its estimated life span, you can figure out how much the item declines in value each month. A business has a means of recovering its initial investment in equipment by deducting this amount from its income tax.

3. Study gross sales and net profits per month. These figures

will help you judge the activity of the business and to see if the profits make all of the "activity" worthwhile.

4. Examine thoroughly the profit-and-loss statements (income and expenses) for at least the past three years. Also ask to review the balance sheet, which lists all money invested in the business and business liabilities.

5. Examine the building in which the business is located and the lease agreement. Be sure there are no building or zoning restrictions that you are not aware of. Contact the city or county where the business is located for information. Check with the health department if the business is a food operation. Compare the rent figure to total sales to make sure that you don't exceed the recommended 6 percent per month expenditure.

6. Take note of insurance costs.

7. Require a complete inventory of business stock. "I put in a bid on a toy store that I heard was for sale. In checking out the store, I noticed the toy prices were way below what they should have been and the choice of toys could have been vastly improved. I also checked the store's tax returns, which were much lower than the owner claimed on the real-estate card. My low bid was accepted, and I was in business."

8. Make sure that the name of the business is included in the sale if you want it to be.

9. If there are sales routes, customer lists, recipes, and so forth, are they also included?

10. Will the present owner agree to spend a predetermined amount of time with you in the beginning, to help train you and acquaint you with business operations?

Several women commented on the last item in our list as being vital to a successful changeover in business ownership.

Some other interesting advice we heard:

"A business will often run on personality, and that's why it's tricky to buy someone else's business. You must be as good as the former owner, or better. Businesses run on an established clientele; you must see the same people over and over again. If you don't have the same regular customers, you are doing something wrong."

When you have studied all the details of the business carefully, have your lawyer help you prepare your offer to buy. In this way, you'll be assured of at least a few less surprises on the day the previous owner waves good-bye and you take on the business for your own.

A Village of Women Entrepreneurs

As you can see, the choice to begin a retail business is one that offers endless possibilities. There's a spot out in Issaquah, Washington, where many of these possibilities have become realities. It is called Gilman Village.

Twenty-five minutes from Seattle is a bustling, "country-place" village of specialty shops that are special in more than one way. This unique center of over thirty shops is the realization of a dream of one businesswoman who has coordinated the growth of the village from its beginnings. What makes this center so special? Nearly all of the shops are owned solely by women. (Just recently, a couple of men entrepreneurs joined the group, partially to satisfy the needs of the men who wandered the pathways of the village, apparently suffering from that "shopper's husband" syndrome often noted in shopping malls.)

Another special aspect of this women's country village is its very original style. All the stores in the village are housed in old buildings that have been moved to their present location from the surrounding countryside. Old houses, barns, a feed store, even a Conestoga wagon have been converted into a variety of shops and restaurants and a fruit stand on wheels!

How did this group of women come together with such a unique and successful idea? We learned the story of their beginnings over a glass of white wine with the village coordinator, a shop owner herself. Dynamic and enthusiastic, Betty's manner is comfortable and friendly, and her talk is nonstop! Five years ago, Betty was the owner of a handicraft-gift shop that was located in an old house she leased and converted to fit her business needs. The charm of the old house had suited the style of her shop right to a "tea"—brewed spicy hot on top of an old wood-burning stove and served to customers as they browsed through the handmade gift and decorating items.

When the lease on her shop was up, the owners of the property had other plans for it, and Betty was forced to move her business. Her desire to relocate in a shop with all the charm of the old house she was leaving led Betty to put into action an idea she had long been developing. She had a dream of organizing a shopping village out of old, converted houses and buildings. She envisioned a circle of unique yet complementary specialty shops, joined by connecting wooden decks.

Though her finances were limited, her imagination definitely wasn't. She sought out the owner of three pleasant acres that would suit her scheme, and she convinced him of the possibilities of her idea. It took more convincing on his part to get bank financing for the project that was now exciting them both. Though this man would own the property and be landlord to all the shop tenants, the shopping village they planned would be housing only woman-owned businesses. Turned down by a large downtown bank, the concept of the woman-run shopping area was finally sold to a small local bank. (Now that the village has prospered, Betty confided, women seeking financing for new businesses in the village have much greater credibility and find it easier to secure a loan.)

With financing secured, they located four charming old buildings in the surrounding countryside, had them moved to the acreage, and began construction on the site. It was not long before the village was in business. Because they were short of tenants at first, Betty quickly opened her second shop, a woman's clothing store, and hustled to find four women who, inspired by her confidence, were willing to try their "inexperienced" hands at running a restaurant. Owning two of the four original shops made Betty "half-owner" of the village during the first year of business. From this beginning, the village grew to eight shops in the second year, and now it has thirty-three in its fifth year. And the success of the independent shop owners and of the village, as well, has been tremendous.

Betty described to us the association that all village members belong to, which was organized and is governed by the women themselves:

"We are seventeen miles from town," she explained, "and we have felt from the beginning that we must work *together* to bring people out to our village. We envision ourselves as a kind of mutual support structure, that is, we feel that it is very important that we *all* do well. Each member of our association pays a forty-dollar-a-month fee. This fee covers advertising and maintenance work on the grounds. We publish a country-village newspaper, which features news about the different shops, and advertising. We had an artist design a village logo, and it is printed on all the shopping bags that each of the stores uses. Using the same kind of sacks in all the shops helps promote the kind of cohesive atmosphere that we favor."

This unified feeling is strengthened by the physical layout of all the old buildings. Working closely with an architect, they were able to position the old structures so that they loosely form two adjoining circles, with all the shops connected by decking. Parking is laid out around the edges of these circles, so that once you are in the village, you are enclosed by the old country stores, the mountains, and the sky above—no street noises or parked cars to disrupt the country feeling. Children can roam the village streets, playing safely or resting on an old bench or a cozy front porch, while their parents are free to shop. With a touch of "calico-colored" language, one village shop owner describes this feeling precisely:

"We've got a sense of the country—not 'shit-kickin' country, but classy country—with all the conveniences of city shopping."

Shopping convenience is an element that the village emphasizes. "The village is set up like a department store," Betty explains. "We have many different 'departments,' so we can draw a greater number of people by offering them more choices. We've found that a better and wider range of choices always makes for more sales."

A walk along the pathways of the village will take a shopper past a toy store, an antique peddler, art and stained-glass studios, and eating establishments with fare ranging from vegetarian lunches to European-style pastries. There are clothing shops for "every body," candies, diamonds, and enough fiber and thread shops to tie up quite a portion of the handicraft crowd.

"Sometimes the owners of small businesses worry about competition," said Betty. "We've found that the competition doesn't always compete—it often complements." Betty is able to illustrate this point with figures from her own gift shop. When she was in her original location before the village was organized, she did $40,000 in yearly sales. In the village, with thirty other shops "competing" for business, her yearly sales increased to $125,000. "Competition is bad only when shops are handling the same brands of merchandise. That's when undercutting starts to happen, and that hurts. Shops in the village may handle the same category of merchandise—clothing, for instance. But the emphasis in the shops is always different—one shop caters to women's sizes, one to junior styles, one to children's wear, and so forth. This is the way the 'department store' arrangement works."

As the paid administrator of the village, Betty is in charge of the mutual advertising and promotions, as well as doing "an awful lot of therapy" for shop owners dealing with individual business problems. "Part of my job is to talk to new prospects for the village. Many women come to us with ideas for unusual shops, or just with the desire to own their own business and hope that we might have an opening somewhere. When a woman comes to us with an idea for a shop, I first have to see if they have 'tenant mix.' That means, will the shop fit in and complement the other existing shops, or is it not in our style, or do we already have such a shop. Second, I try to determine if the woman herself is capable of opening and running her own business, both financially and personally. Most of the shop owners in the village have not owned a business of their own before, so previous experience is not a necessity. But confidence, credibility, and the willingness to take a chance *are*."

The unique and charming aspects of the village have given the different businesses there many opportunities for free publicity as well as the themes for many of their advertising promotions. "We try to get two freebies for every paid advertisement," comments the coordinator. "Every time an old building is moved onto the property, anyone with a camera is notified in advance. If our efforts net only one photo in the paper or a few seconds on the evening news, that kind of publicity is worth far more than a paid announcement. Paid advertising is helpful in getting your name recognized, but the feature stories we get for free are worth their weight in gold."

The second year the village was in operation, the shop owners invited to lunch all the women's editors from the newspapers and magazines within a fifty-mile radius. Of course, every editor didn't accept, but several of the ones that did featured the shopping concept in a story, including one article in a national magazine. A balance in paid advertising is sought among newspaper, radio, and TV spots, and a file is maintained on all the advertising the village does.

Village members pay rent, which is a percentage of their sales, generally based on the degree of markup on their individual products. For example, in a shop using a 30 percent markup on goods, rent is determined as 3 percent of sales; where the markup on goods is 50 percent, the rent is 5 percent of the sales volume. Shop owners are also entitled to a 10-percent discount in all the other shops in the village. Few businesses have failed in the five years the village has been in operation, and when we considered the national average (75–90% fail during the first three years of business), we could see what a success this shopping concept has been.

What caused the demise of those few shops that didn't make it? Betty has the answer to that question. "Our only failures were shops in which the owner was trying to live off the business in the first two to five years of operation. That is something that just can't be done. A successful business has got to reinvest nearly all its profits for the first five years or so, in order to build up the business. When the owner takes nearly all the profits out in a large salary, the business is sure to suffer."

A specialty shopping center is an exciting concept for women interested in furthering their own business ideas as well as implementing a kind of female support structure to aid in the establishment and growth of other feminine enterprises. The woman's touch is evident in this village in many different ways. Responsive to the needs of their shoppers, the village association hurried to establish three new restaurants when the volume of customers made the original restaurant unable to handle the crowds easily. Child care, often one of a working parent's greatest problems, is a common concern among the businesswomen in the village, so co-op baby-sitting and "kid-swapping" help make a shared problem not so great a worry. An out-of-town buying trip for one shop owner may give her kids a minivacation at a new friend's home. Inventory time or an off-season holiday will give the sitter an opportunity to return the favor. When women work together, kids and careers *have* to mix, and with a little cooperation, they do!

What's in the future for this little country village? An adjoining four acres has just been purchased, with expansion plans spanning the next five years already brewing on the back burner of that old wood stove.

Betty commented to us that a sales representative once looked at her curiously, then said, "That's funny, you don't *look* like a feminist!" If coordinating and working among a group of enterprising women, succeeding in the business world while remaining vibrant and sensitive, and pursuing her own very personal goals while assisting other women with theirs—if these are the qualifications, Betty *must* be a feminist! And "feminists" like her, in business for themselves, promoting unique and original projects of their own design, prove that women are coming of age in the business world. And they are doing it in style.

Some General Retailing Advice

Here is a potpourri of advice offered by some of the women running retail businesses today:

"Don't be afraid to ask questions! People everywhere are happy to give plenty of free advice."

"Your goal should be, at least in part, to make other people happy. The money part is secondary, because you have to live with yourself and not the almighty dollar."

"I've seen a lot of gals go into business in the past six years. The ones that go *out* of business don't realize how much work it takes and are not willing to give up their exercise classes and ladies' luncheons. They decide to give over the business to part-time help, giving it less and less of their personal attention. Customers want to deal with the owner, especially in a small shop. Hired help does not give the customers the attention and consideration that the owner tends to give."

"If a telephone call to the author of a bad check doesn't give you any satisfaction, you will probably have to turn the account over to a collection agency. This type of bill-collection service will charge you a percentage of its collections (often 50% or so) to chase your bad accounts. You'll justify their high take by figuring that any account you turn over to them was considered a loss anyway. Any recovery they make will be more than you had before or could have salvaged on your own."

"To be successful in a retail shop, you've got to be people oriented, but you can't be *too* nice. In my ten months in business, I'm getting on-the-job assertiveness training—to be able to say *no!* I know now that I kissed too many asses at first. A customer would say, can you hold this for me for three weeks, and I'd say, well . . . okay. Not anymore."

"To make it in business, you've got to be gutsy. If you don't know if you should do something or not, *do* it. Otherwise, you'll never know what you missed."

"One question is asked of me often by other women interested in trying their own business. How much time will it take? they ask. I feel that if you have to ask and are worried about your time, you shouldn't go into business at all."

"A final word about being independent in a small business: independence is a myth. One is more dependent than ever—on one's own mental resourcefulness, discipline, and especially on the presence of customers!"

"In my retail business, though I advertise in the newspaper and on radio occasionally, I found that direct mailings get the best customer response."

"To be a success, you have to feel confident. And to feel confident, you need to look your best. A silk blouse, a wool gabardine skirt or pants, and a wool blazer, coupled with just a touch of good gold jewelry, and you'll be ready to take anybody on!"

7 The Service Business

If you've decided to undertake a business in which service to mankind is your primary objective—and that service can be anything from midwifery to information retrieval, paper hanging to body massage, bookbinding to home remodeling—you've chosen a field of business with great variety and flexibility as well as tremendous potential. In a service business, the word "service" may be defined as "work done for another or others." The people you will be working with will be clients, not customers, because you will be offering them a service, not a product.

As we mentioned before, service-oriented businesses are the fastest-growing concerns in the country. And small-size businesses are the major element in the service industries. The old saying Let George (or Mary) do it, has never been more meaningful. With greater affluence, more women working outside the home, and fewer children and grandparents at home to perform some of the time-consuming but necessary projects of everyday living, greater numbers of people each year are "hiring it done."

Working Up Your Business Plan

In Chapter Two, we outlined a business plan for you. Turn back to it now and fill in the details for your intended service business, using the outline. It's the best means we know of to get you thinking about *all* the aspects that will be involved in organizing your business. After talking to other women in the service field, we've uncovered some information that we'd like to add to aid you in developing your own plan.

What (What will your service include?)

The importance of defining the service you provide was stated succinctly by a massage-parlor owner: "Post a sign stating what you will and will not do. And be blunt when asked. (NO SEX)."

Any business that provides a service should make sure that its clients fully understand the extent of the service, the guarantees, and any special terms of the agreement. Then, according to your own circumstances, you may or may not feel inclined to follow the last bit of advice offered by the massage-parlor owner: "Collect the money before the massage, in case 'something comes up.'"

Educating Your Clients

The service businesses we encountered educated their clients as to the extent of their service in a variety of different ways. Fliers listing payment schedule, delivery terms, job time requirements, and optional services available were a common means of getting this information out. These fliers can be simple, straightforward checklists or larger, decorative sheets that advertise as well as inform. Make them available at your shop, hand them out in the area that you serve, or mail them to prospective clients.

One woman uses a rate card in her typing business to clarify different charges as well as to advertise her other services, such as editing. The card informs the client that there is a 20-percent surcharge for "problem copy" (hard to read, frequent misspellings) and a 20-percent price reduction if the agreed-upon deadline is missed. The card reduces the room for argument if there is a difference of opinion between the typist and the client about the price or the finished product.

A women's bank, in an effort to inform potential investors about what makes their banking service unique, hired a professional consulting firm to produce a brochure for them. Illustrating their services and objectives, the brochure provided a useful promotional and informative tool in the development of the business.

One woman we spoke with suggested that many service businesses might profit from her idea of using a small presentation kit, both to inform prospective clients of your services as well as to advertise your merits over the competition. Your kit will be composed of three different elements: an introductory letter that briefly explains your business and your services; a representative sample of your work or your price schedule; and one of your business cards. Mail this kit to prospective clients, then follow the mailing with a phone call to assess the client's interest and to answer any questions she or he may have. If you add new services or expand your business in some other way, make up a new kit to notify your clients.

Your Guarantee

The guarantee you give in your service is a point to think about. Though there must be reasonable limits on the length of the guarantee, remember that your client's interests are your first concern when you are offering a service. Balance the costs of extending a guarantee beyond your usual limits against the possibility of losing an established client before you make any refusals.

Who

Your Qualifications

A service business can often be run, at least at first, by only the "resident expert." "Expert" here is a key word, however. For although your ease of entry into the field may be encouraging, you must be expert in your management ability and in your skills in order to build a successful service business.

We have learned that poor management is one of the biggest problems a new service business faces. Because the original investment in the business may be small, the overhead low, and the employees few, many new service-business owners enter the trade with little previous management experience and little formal business education (in the form of previous service experience) to guide them. No matter how small your operation is, you will profit from careful management. You must constantly study your methods of operation to monitor efficiency and to lower costs. Your management responsibilities also include effective work scheduling. To keep a tight control on your labor expenses as well as to promote the client satisfaction that is your goal, you must schedule your service appointments carefully.

Some special expertise in your chosen field is essential, though it matters little whether you are a natural-born talent or a night-school expert. You have to be good at what you do.

The owner of a catering business told us, "Anybody can platter a ham. To be a success, you have to be creative. Ten years later, if someone looks at a picture of a party you catered and all the candles on the table are crooked, you probably weren't much of a success."

In some extremely personal services (such as counseling, home-based child care, and the like) the "who" constitutes the primary element in the business. In such a one-to-one service relationship, a midwife advised us, "There is a natural process of elimination. The ones who are good get referrals; the ones who aren't drop out. Word of mouth is the only way to develop a reputation."

Giving lessons (dance, voice, musical instruments) is a popular kind of service and another one in which the name of the teacher—the "who"—is central not only to the performance of the service but to the promotion of the business as well. In this type of service, you are promoting your name, to which a certain talent is connected. Personal appearances and performances are most effective in promoting this type of business. Other services that require special schooling or training may also call for promotion of the "who" behind the service. "Twenty-five years experience," "Graduate of the Cordon Bleu cooking school," Hairdresser to the Stars"—all give identity to the expert performing the job.

Your Customers

Coleen is a Seattle woman in the fashion recycling business. She teaches women how to turn thrift-shop finds into the latest fashions, She has an idea for a new direction for her service to take. "I got my idea when I found a pure silk dress in a thrift shop—size 22. I thought I could make a skirt for myself out of the huge skirt on the dress, but before I cut anything off, I put the dress on and stood before a full-length mirror to size myself up. I took off the belt buckle and tied the large belt around my waist. The dress, with its big sleeves, large armholes, and long skirt, looked just like today's fashion. I thought how it would encourage women on weight-reduction plans to stick to their goal if they knew that their clothes would still fit—with just a little adjustment—after they lost the weight. I sent word of my idea to all the weight-loss clinics and health clubs in the area, and they all told me they would be happy to accept fliers advertising my class." By narrowing in on some "narrowing in" customers, Coleen feels she can widen her customer base and expand her original service.

Another woman, a partner in a health and beauty consultation service, told us that when they are working for the first time with a new client, their advisers "need to find out if she has an evening social life, an afternoon social life, or no social life at all. Then we can adjust her program to her personal life-style. In our business, we do a lot of listening." And in that way, they satisfy the need to find out exactly who their customers are.

To be successful, a service firm *must* establish a permanent clientele. It is only through repeat customers that a business will grow and develop to its full potential.

Where (What location will best suit your service?)

The initial investment required for a service business can be very low—often, a desk and telephone will be all you need to get started. Those who need your services will seek you out in the telephone book or in your other business advertising. In some cases, it is even to your advantage not to be too handy or visible. The foot traffic that comes with a streetside location often does little more than slow down your business operation and take up your valuable time.

In choosing your location, keep in mind the nature of your service. If you offer pickup and delivery, your shop should be located conveniently so that your travel time is minimal. If your customers will be coming to you, they will want easy parking and easy access to your shop. Says one business owner:

"The cost of your shop rent is important, but the location is much more important. I thought I had found the perfect location—downtown, close to lots of businesses, sharing floor space in a large building with other artists, graphic designers, and related printing businesses. I thought I would have a kind of 'captive clientele' in the very businesses that would surround me. But I was worried about parking. My printing customers need to drop things off and pick them up, often in a hurry, and parking downtown can sometimes be impossible. I found this other location outside of the downtown area, with a street-front window and easy parking. I knew right away it would be right for me, even though the rent was slightly higher."

Even a rural location is suitable for many services, but a remote location calls for a little extra consideration. Will you need to add your travel expenses onto your service rates? Will the money you save in rent be enough to offset the business you will lose because of your inconvenient location? Or, in a similar vein, will your savings in rent be enough to cover the extra advertising you will have to do to make the public aware of your business? Locating outside high-priced business districts has its advantages, but there are disadvantages to think about, as well.

Choosing a location for your service business also requires a study of the competition and the potential customers in the area. Determine how many customers you can expect to service within your area, and then find out who is handling these customers now. Do the firms who are servicing these customers look successful? Or have many similar operations failed in the area? Look closely at the businesses that are similar to your intended business to make sure that they are not offering services and inducements that you can't match, or at least compete with.

When (Perfecting Your Skills)

The amount of time you allow for the organization of your service venture will vary according to the expertise and experience you already have in the field. The members of a printing collective, for example, spent "two years before we opened full-time, doing printing odd jobs in our spare time to get experience rather than make money." The owner of a cooking school suggested trying a variety of experiences, from working in a cookware shop to doing in-store cooking demonstrations to teaching small groups at churches and women's clubs, and so forth before opening for business. Not only will your experience help you in meeting the public and performing in front of an audience, but you'll be on your way to making a name for yourself, as well.

Another woman, who had been operating a typesetting business out of her home, had to make further time allowances when she relocated in a shop:

"When I moved my business out of my home and into an office, I had to plan in advance for a lot less business at first. This seems contradictory. You would think that I would want to line up lots of extra work to cover the expenses of moving and office rent, and to make up for the customers I would lose in changing locations. But typesetting is a high-pressure business, and I knew with the new office, I would have to be involved in training my first helper. And training takes time. It makes it too difficult to be constantly interrupted when you are trying to teach someone new skills. I also had to allow time for a little redecorating, installation of a new phone, and the printing of my new business cards and forms with the new address on them."

The best laid plans, however, for a smooth and slow transition are often fouled up by an anxious customer. This woman told us, "The day we moved my typesetting machine into the building, one customer rushed in and asked for a rush order! I told him if I plugged in the machine and it worked, I'd work his order. I put in the plug and the machine came on, so he became my first official customer!"

Several women in the service field offered this advice: When starting up your new business, limit your customers until your feet are on the ground. It may take you longer to make your first paycheck, but it will cut down drastically on the initial confusion.

"We worked night and day the first six months without even advertising. We had so much work that we finally had to hire students to help us. And the wages and taxes nearly killed us. Now we have hired a business manager."

Special note: many services are quite seasonal—catering, house painting, and gardening, for example. Organize your business so that you have time enough to work out the initial bugs before your first big season hits.

Why

Evaluating the Need for Your Service

A woman who offers fashion advice and wardrobe counseling told us, "My business is successful because of the timeliness of it, and I think that is what every woman interested in her own service business must think about. In my case, I am offering advice to the many women who want the latest in clothes but find today's prices exorbitant."

Your lack of education or experience need not restrict your success if you can find the *right* need to fill with your business. There are many services that require no specialized training. Think of all the "match up" services that are enjoying great popularity—matching parents to day-care and baby-sitting facilities; matching roommates and apartments or rental housing and tenants; matching jobs and people. By using imagination and a knowledge of the circumstances in your own particular area, you'll find many needs that need filling.

Can Your Business Compete with Others?

Shopping around and comparing is the way to come up with a bargain. And to ensure that your service is a bargain for those clients who look for one, you will have to compare favorably with the competition. Be aware of the conveniences they are offering, such as delivery, credit terms, parking, and so forth. When you come up with all the advantages that they offer, you will know the areas in which your customers will be making their comparisons. Make a list of the special services that you plan to offer, then measure your business against the competition. The services that tip the scale in your favor will be good ones to mention in your advertising.

Betty is the "Oregon end" of a "London connexion" that offers a unique travel service. Though there are many larger, well-known travel agencies in the area, Betty and her English partner promote the elements of their travel package that are exciting and different. They arrange for Americans to travel to London and stay two weeks with an English family, paying one price for room and board, a bus/tube pass, and some first-class theater tickets. As a special service, Betty offers a "culture shock" orientation meeting for her clients before they go abroad, advising them on currency changes, how to use the tube, and other helpful information.

Bettering the competition in service and convenience is "why" your new business will succeed. We were told: "If there is a demand for your service, and you do it with enthusiasm, confidence, and knowledge, for a fair price, success will not be far off!"

How (Advertising and Promotion)

The best method of sales promotion is to provide good service to your clients. One woman told us, "In the service business, customers come mostly by referral. Recommendations are where opportunities come from." Gaining new business by referrals is a very slow way to grow, however, and most new businesses cannot afford to rely solely on word of mouth to get them established. It is very difficult to advertise an intangible product, and that is what many service businesses are selling.

Unlike a retail product, which can be assessed through a comparison of similar aspects (size, color, feel, comfort), the service you provide must often be selected solely on the merits of your advertising, your image, and your price. Quality is difficult to determine until the job is completed. Shopping services; researchers; advertising agencies; counselors on health, marriage, sex, and finances—all offer services that are hard to judge comparatively until after the service has been accomplished.

Promotion and advertising are often cited as the biggest obstacles that a new service business encounters. And the more unique the service, the more difficult it is to advertise it effectively.

Colleen, the woman in the fashion-recycling business, found herself with something "new and unique—it had never been done before"—and the problem of how to promote it. "I spoke with the director of the community college near me, and she liked my idea (converting thrift-shop finds into the latest fashion). She said I could offer a class in fashion recycling the next term. When only one or two people signed up, I was told the class would be canceled if there were not more students. So I called the fashion editor of the newspaper and told her what I was doing, and that I needed students. I took a bag full of recycled articles, showed them to her, and she wrote an article about me for the paper. Since then, I have filled my classes regularly. When I saw the continuing need for students, as I began offering the course at several different colleges, I thought, 'Well, I better hit the television stations.' I called the morning talk-show hostess and told her that I had put together an entire spring wardrobe for less than seven dollars." With her daughter modeling the outfits, Colleen was a hit on the TV show and has been asked back several times.

Most of the businesswomen we spoke with mentioned Yellow Pages ads (the bigger the better) and fliers as their most successful means of paid advertising. Distributing business cards to related businesses is also profitable. (One woman remarked on the way many men distribute their business cards—at every introduction, business and social, and at every other opportunity. We should take this hint from them, she said, and realize that business cards are a great way to spread your name around.)

Another woman mentioned again the need for a "good old girl" network, especially in service businesses, where referrals from related businesses are the best means of building a clientele. ("Contacting potential customers yourself means something," one woman noted, "but a personal reference means so much more.")

Your Image

What image do you want to promote? Speedy delivery? Twenty-four-hour service? Whatever your service, you *will* have an image. It is to your advantage to promote the personalized character of your business and to make your image precise—and concise—enough to use in your advertising.

MAKE THE LONDON CONNEXION!
LIVE FOR TWO WEEKS
WITH AN ENGLISH FAMILY
FOR ONLY
$300!

The message on the red cover of this woman's brochure states simply yet thoroughly the service that her firm offers. The image is low key, low budget, and straightforward—no glossy photos, no Old English script to glorify the message. Economy and convenience are the image, both of the service her firm arranges and of its advertising.

If you will be taking your service to the client, performing it at her location rather than in your own shop, the employees who represent you will create your image for you (whether it is the image that you desire or not.) Cleanliness, courtesy, efficiency—and likewise, rudeness, sloppiness, poor workmanship—all influence your business image. In the beginning, at least, how you manage yourself and your business will be as important as your skill. After your service is completed, your client will be the final judge of your success.

One cleaning-service owner told us how she has worked very hard to create and project a respectable business image:

"I wish to convey that I offer a professional, personalized cleaning service that is licensed and bonded.

"I am very strict about my employees, and I have very specific employee rules that must be followed. No jeans. No hair rollers. Long hair must be tied back. Name tags. No kids or husbands allowed in the client's home. When clients call me, they're inviting a stranger into their home, and it's up to me to see that the person I send is a good representative of the image I want to create for my business.

"I offer personalized service. My employees are instructed to use the customer's own preferred cleaning products and to follow the personal instructions that the customer leaves. For example, if you've always put linseed oil on your great-grandmother's hundred-year-old coffee table, we follow your instructions to the 'T.'

"Another part of my image is that I am licensed and bonded. If one of my employees accidentally swings the vacuum into your plate-glass window, I will pay for it. Few other cleaning services in my town offer this added benefit. My customers have this assurance that we will be responsible for what we do."

How Much

Start-Up Costs

The lack of adequate capital plagues many a business, services included. Start-up costs will fall into three general areas: equipment and shop fixtures, parts and materials, and general business overhead. By drawing up some charts to show what and how much you will need in the way of equipment and materials, you can estimate your expenses. Here are some samples to follow:

EQUIPMENT AND FURNITURE

Equipment and Furniture	How many needed	× Price per unit	= Total Cost

Concerning equipment and furniture:

"Get the best equipment you can afford. It helps you look professional, especially when you are operating a service out of your own home."

"Don't forget to check out ads for used equipment and office furniture. They are often reasonably priced and a much better buy than trying to use equipment that was not intended for business use. Equipment meant for use in the home does not stand up under commercial use."

PARTS AND MATERIALS

Parts/ Materials	Amount needed for initial inventory (12-month supply)	× Cost per unit	= Total Cost

On ordering materials:

Use some 3-by-5 cards to keep records for the ordering of your parts and materials. Make a different card for each of the materials you use in performing your service, and include on it your supplier's name and address, prices and discounts available, delivery times and charges, and minimum order sizes (a gross, a dozen, one of each?). Also, include information on alternate suppliers.

When you are figuring your overhead, consider all these costs:

rent
advertising
salaries
utilities
insurance
accountant
taxes
licenses
postage
miscellaneous expenses
"emergency fund"

The "emergency fund" was suggested by two women who used it as follows:

"From the beginning, my partner and I put some of the profit into a joint savings account, which would be used for emergencies (to buy new equipment, to replace old, for example). This proved to be a good idea, as our business was forced to close, and we are using it now as our own 'unemployment compensation,' since self-employed persons are not eligible for regular unemployment compensation."

Break-Even Point

In setting a price for your service, you must be aware of your "break-even point"—how much you have to make in order to cover your expenses, with no profit or loss. Because your profit depends on your volume of sales, your costs, and your selling price, by determining your break-even point, you can see what a change in one or more of these elements will do to your profits.

The Small Business Administration (SBA) offers this formula to help you determine your break-even point:

$$\text{Break-even point (in sale dollars)} = \text{total fixed costs} \div 1 - \frac{\text{total variable costs}}{\text{corresponding sales volume}}$$

Let's look at an example of how this formula works:

Helen owns a hand laundry. She needs to know how many shirts and slacks she must launder each year to break even in her business. First she made a list of her fixed business costs:

rent	(\$150/mo. × 12)	\$1800
utilities	(\$120/mo. × 12)	1440
taxes and license		260
insurance		500
interest		100
depreciation		400
total		\$4500

Then she added up the percentages of her total business that were represented by her variable, but controllable, costs. In working up these percentages, she followed the guidelines suggested for her type of business operation in the *Barometer of Small Business*, published by the Accounting Corporation of America. (Locate this in the reference section of the library.) By knowing the recommended percentages allowed for each of her areas of expenditure, she adjusted her spending to follow the norm.

Variable Costs

operating supplies	6.90% (of each sales dollar)
outside labor	5.32%
gross wages (not including owner)	41.51%
repairs and maintenance	1.63%
advertising	1.43%
car and delivery	2.43%
bad debts	.03%
legal and accounting fees	.72%
miscellaneous	2.71%
total	62.68%

By adding up the percentages represented by her variable costs, Helen can see that 62.68 percent of her total sales, or about 63 cents out of every dollar, is spent on variable costs. By rounding off the figure to 63 percent, she is able to work out the formula to figure her break-even point (BE) like this:

$$\text{BE point} = \frac{\$4500}{1 - \frac{.63}{\$1.00}} = \frac{\$4500}{1 - .63} = \frac{\$4500}{.37} = \$12,162$$

By using this formula, Helen knows that she must make at least $12,162 a year in sales for her business to break even. In order to show a profit, she'll need to work even harder.

A relatively small difference in one or more of your fixed costs makes a significant difference in the amount needed to break even in your business. For example, if Helen chose to locate her laundry in a different part of town, where rents are lower, here's how the formula would work:

Fixed Costs per Year

rent	($100/mo. × 12)	$1200
utilities		1440
taxes and license		260
insurance		500
interest		100
depreciation		400
total		$3900

With her variable cost remaining the same (63 cents out of every dollar), the formula would work like this:

$$\text{BE point} = \frac{\$3900}{1 - \frac{.63}{\$1.00}} = \frac{\$3900}{1 - .63} = \frac{\$3900}{.37} = \$10,541$$

Now that you've worked out the elements of your particular business plan, you might enjoy hearing how one woman turned her special talent into success. We ran an ad in the university newspaper:

Wanted: Interesting women with interesting businesses of their own. Tell us about it!

Pamela was one of the women who responded to the ad. The tale of her business venture gives new meaning to the expression, Service with a smile. Pam smiles all the way to the bank! We'll entitle this story:

The Smooth Ones Are Nails, The Wrinkled Ones Are Screws

"Being a contractor is very much like running a house. You have to organize, shop around to get things at the best price, cook up a variety of ingredients, and get them all to the table at the same time! I think women are culturally adapted to doing this kind of work, and we do it well."

Pam is a high school art teacher turned carpenter turned contractor turned rental manager turned tax-investment adviser. Her energy is matched by the services she can provide, and business is booming! How did it all come about?

An interest in woodworking and the desire to work with her hands led Pam to take a summer job as a shingler. Next she bought an old house and remodeled it herself, with knowledge gained by taking community-college woodworking classes at night and using an occasional subcontractor to handle jobs she felt she couldn't yet tackle. For other prospective home remodelers, she advises starting this way. "Buying an old house and remodeling it is a great way to start, if you don't mind living in sawdust for a while. Even if you were to hire all the work done, with you acting as the contractor and 'subs' doing the work, you can sell the house for an eight- to ten-thousand-dollar profit easily in two years, with you only working it as a quarter-time job. The profit you make is called sweat equity, and that's what it really is, but the effort is more than worth it."

Because she enjoyed her own remodeling, Pam bought another old Victorian-style house as an investment, to fix up and sell for profit. A friend was impressed with her work and introduced Pam to a doctor who was interested in investment property. With an eye toward the future, Pam scheduled a pair of important appointments—one with a lawyer and one with her accountant.

Together they worked up a scheme that has paid off handsomely and has opened up several areas in which Pam's business can grow.

"With the help of my advisers, I worked up a plan in which I would locate old houses for remodeling. After the investor approves it, I put up 10 percent of the down payment, and he puts up the other 90 percent. For example, if the down payment is $10,000, I only have to put up $1,000 and the investor puts up the rest. This made it easy for me to start my remodeling-investment business, as my part of the investment is quite small. Then we usually rent the house, as is, for one year. (The investor gets a tax break and I get a 10% rental-management fee.) At the end of a year, we refinance the property (property values will have increased during the year), and we use the money that is realized to remodel the house. I do the design work, and I still like to have a hand in on some of the woodworking. (I'm great at carrying the other end of a long 2-by-4 on a piece of siding!) We hire subcontractors to do the rest of the work to get the house in shape. Then we sell the property. I receive 50 percent of the capital gains made on the sale."

Pam sold her business scheme to that first interested investor, and then to seven other clients as well. Together they work in a continuing buy-sell agreement, with Pam running the business entirely by herself. The contracting business led into her own rental-management firm, for she felt that she needed the 10 percent management fee as her portion to offset the fact that her investor-partners were getting all the tax breaks.

Pam's business, which has grown from a personal home project to a full-time job, is especially fulfilling in three ways. With a little planning and foresight, she has been able to utilize her art training in designing and decorating; she is still able to get in there and work with her hands, which she enjoys thoroughly; and she finds it intellectually stimulating to plan and initiate schemes for tax advantages, property investments, and the like. Each of the jobs she has undertaken has had many different facets. Hearing about just two of them showed us how much variety is involved.

"In one case, I bought an old house and rented it to some students, who offered to do some work for a portion of their rent. I've found students to be very good tenants, by the way. I bought the materials they would need and supplied the plans for them to follow in their work. In fact, I even paid for a course in remodeling for one student-tenant who was interested in, and talented in, carpentry work. The students enjoyed the cheap rent while they lived in the house, and I got the house renovated with very little effort and very little expenditure.

"Just recently I purchased an old fourplex. Three of the units were occupied, but we let a carpenter move into the empty fourth unit. In exchange for rent, the carpenter is remodeling his unit according to my specifications. When he completes the work, we are going to use his unit as a model, and we will sell the four units separately as condominiums."

Pam is a very busy woman, but she has time to offer encouragement and advice to other women who might be interested in the contracting business. "Investing in property is a great way to make money, especially since the government strongly encourages the profits made in real-estate investments through their offer of tremendous tax advantages. If you can stand to sell something that you've put so much of yourself into, then sell your remodeled home, take your sweat equity, and buy two more houses—one to live in and one to use as a rental. You'll make nothing but money, and the challenges and fun make it a great business!"

Pam's success story is very encouraging, yet it is evident that her success is due to much more than a lucky break. She didn't take a course in organizing a business, but if we analyze her approach, we see that she covered all the necessary bases in developing her business. First, she began her initial project in the same spirit that she advises other women to employ: "Look around and see what you're doing that has commercial value, and find someone who is willing to pay for it." (Or, in other words, check your own abilities and set some personal goals.) She knew that she enjoyed woodworking, she had artistic talent, and she increased her skills with night-school classes. Her work on her own house, coupled with the interest expressed by people who saw what she could do, convinced her that there was a market for her abilities.

Second, Pam made some sound plans for her business development through early planning and organization, using the professional advice of a lawyer and a CPA. She was able to enter the field with a very small initial investment, operating with low overhead and only occasional employees until her reputation was established.

Finally, she has ensured an interesting and profitable business future by allowing her business to expand in a number of different ways. She is capitalizing on a popular trend, the renovation of older houses and buildings. Her remodeling business has offered her the flexibility, however, to further her other interests in investments and property management. Her business is free to develop along with the changing tastes of the public, as well as her own changing interests.

8 Five Popular Service Businesses

In our survey of service-related businesses, we found that many women are involved in five large areas: cooking (in this category, we will include cooking instruction and catering); teaching (skills, languages, the arts); child care; secretarial services; and sewing. It is interesting that, liberated and innovative as we are today, women still often prefer to develop and excel in the traditional "womanly arts." This is certainly not the only direction in which our own businesses can take us. But since so many women are choosing to go into these areas, (and, we might add, with so many untraditional ideas that the fields take on new direction), we want to pass along some general hints and warnings that we have gathered.

Catering and Cooking Schools—The Moveable Feast

A catering business can be run from your own home kitchen or from a storefront location. You may be a "food specialist," merely providing the foods and their delivery, or you may choose to extend your services to setting up the meals at your client's location, supervising the service, and possibly supplying special equipment. You may feature a specialty, such as picnic lunches, ethnic foods, desserts, organic meals, or special-occasion parties. Or you may change your menu for each customer's individual preference.

"It is difficult to start in the catering business," one woman told us. "If you are working out of your own home, your business will probably be part-time at best. You really need a storefront or your own deli to get enough exposure to operate on a full-time basis.

"The best way to gain new customers in the catering business is, of course, by word of mouth. When you do try to solicit new clients, you should go to them with a formal presentation—like an advertising layout—complete with pictures of what you have done, sample menus, and so forth. I also leave my business card at new businesses, office buildings, and the openings of banks."

Other women mentioned free samples as a good way to promote your new catering business. (One woman packaged bite-size portions of her holiday fruitcake and delivered it, along with a flier, to schoolteachers and shop owners in her area.) Also try direct mailings, letters to the managers of large offices, and Yellow Pages ads. Planning advertising promotions before special holidays is effective.

As with any food service, the caterer must be fully aware of all special zoning laws and permits required from the health and labor departments. Prepared foods cannot be eaten on your premises, or your business will be classified as a restaurant. The number of regulations your catering operation will be subjected to is lessened if you perform your "personal service," cooking at someone's request, in your client's own kitchen.

Start-up costs for your business can range from the cost of the foods for the first luncheon you cater to an investment in five figures. By sharing kitchen facilities with a restaurant, a bakery, or even another caterer, you can significantly lessen your investment, allowing for a minimum overhead until you build the faithful clientele that such a business requires for survival. You will probably only need to keep staples on hand, purchasing your other foods as needed for each job. Usually, most of the serving pieces, linens, and glassware that you need can be rented, with the rental fee included in the client's bill. Many caterers encourage clients to use their own liquor and wines. Using disposable packaging for foods to be delivered eliminates the need for returns.

A good catering rule of thumb is to multiply your costs by 2 to figure the total price to charge your client. Several women mentioned allowing a $2-an-hour wage for their own time, then adding a 40 percent profit onto the total food costs. When figuring your time, however, don't forget to include all the elements that are necessary to complete the job: preparation time; travel time to and from the job; setting-up time; reheating time, if necessary; serving time; clean-up time; loading and unloading time.

"It is very hard to figure out an hourly rate when you are just beginning in catering. The customer shouldn't have to pay for the extra time you take to do a job because you are still learning. On my first big job, I got a comparison bid from another caterer—I called up and inquired what the competition would charge for the special dinner my client was planning. It is often helpful to talk to others in the business, to see what they are charging."

To be successful in the catering business, you must have a love of food, the ability to work with other people (remember, it's *their* party, not yours), and a location in which there is a suitable market for your service. You need a creative flair and the ability to remain calm when the hostess is panicking. You will have to manage large quantities of food (get a good quantity cookbook to help you estimate recipe changes for different size groups), and you will need the means to transport this food, delivering it hot and unscrambled.

When you are starting out, you need to contact a grocer, a butcher, possibly a source for gourmet items, and an equipment-supply firm for your paper goods. If a food wholesaler will work with you, you are in luck. Otherwise, check to see if your supplier will offer you a discount or possibly a thirty-day account for payment. When a client accepts your bid for her large party, it is customary to ask for one-third or one-fourth of the total bill in advance, as a deposit. Several women mentioned that it is helpful to keep a job envelope for each account handled, including in the envelope all purchase slips, rental bills, menu plans, and special requirements for each job.

A cooking school is often the result of a successful catering business, either formed after the business "retires" or run in conjunction with the catering. You will need adequate kitchen facilities (either your own or rented) and all the equipment that a well-stocked kitchen can hold. Self-confidence and a little theatrical flair will be appreciated by your students, and your knowledge of foods and their preparation must be thorough—from the fundamentals to the gourmet. In teaching, you can use a demonstration method, or, if your facilities allow, you may want to offer class participation. The rates that you command will be partially determined by your name and expertise in the field, so there are no definite rules to follow. Consider your time and your overhead expenses, then add on the total cost of the ingredients that you will use in the course, averaged out among the number of students you have.

Earlier in this section, we related the advice of one cooking-school owner who advised getting as much experience as you can *before* opening up for business. Don't discount any opportunity—demonstrations for church groups, schools, on the local TV show, in a department-store kitchen department. Each appearance will introduce you to more potential students and will help you polish up your delivery, as well.

Your school or series of lessons will profit from adopting a theme or specialty. Like a caterer, you may choose to concentrate on ethnic dishes, gourmet or peasant recipes; and yet you still have the freedom to change your style with the changing tastes of your clients.

Teaching

In this section, we are concerned primarily with women who wish to teach privately or small groups, in their own home or in a studio. Dancing schools with hundreds of students or the Berlitz School of Languages are not what we have in mind here. Most of us, especially in childhood, have taken lessons of one kind or another, and many have gone on to perfect their skills to such a degree that they, too, feel qualified to teach them to others. How do you go about it?

First of all, you will need a suitable space in which to teach. If you are going to work out of your home, you must be professional. Keep your work area separate from your family area, in a place where "people traffic" won't be an interruption. If you are able to arrange a room for your work only, then you will gain a tax advantage, as well. If the telephone rings often at your house, have an answering machine installed. And remember to dress in a businesslike manner—your clients are paying for your professional services, and it is important that the impression you make is in line with your skills.

Several women recommended making up a course outline when first getting underway. Use this guide for your own planning and to show prospective clients what your course covers. Decide what type of students you want in your classes, considering age, level of skills, and so forth. You will then know where you should advertise. For instance, if you are interested in teaching children, business cards or fliers placed in children's-wear shops, day-care centers, and other schools would be appropriate. If you teach advanced languages, a card tacked up in the foreign-language departments of local colleges may reward you with many tutoring jobs. If you offer music or dancing lessons, try to obtain a mailing list from the local musical-instrument shop or dancing-supply store, and send out fliers advertising your business.

Rates, again, will differ with your expertise and your renown. "When teaching a language," one woman told us, "if you are teaching your native tongue, you can charge more. That is, if you are a native of France, you can charge a higher rate for lessons than an American can for teaching French."

We suggest checking with others in your area who are offering similar lessons, to see what rates they are charging. Many women we spoke with who teach—and the lessons ranged from languages to music to fashion coordination—expressed disappointment in the financial compensation they could demand. In cases where a university education is a prerequisite for teaching or tutoring in the field, instructors are especially discouraged by the rates they can charge. Unless the classes are offered regularly through a school or college, most women agreed that giving lessons could never be a full-time business, especially if you operate out of your home. One woman advised that the teacher should just consider her work as a supplement to her income and do it for the enjoyment that it brings.

As with any home-operated business, you must check with the local business-licensing bureau to obtain the necessary approval and get tax information. (In many cities, for instance, if you charge a fee for a service, you need to be licensed. Licensing for "home occupations" may include stipulations about the type of sign you use to advertise your business, how many students you may instruct at a time—no more than two music students at a time, for instance, and no more than six craft students at one time—and regulations against causing abnormal automotive or pedestrian traffic or creating objectionable noise.) City and county zoning laws also vary, so be sure to check with your local zoning board.

When you are giving craft lessons in your home, if there is any danger of injury to your students, you should check the extent of the liability clause in your home insurance policy. Policies vary, and if your craft is particularly hazardous (using excessive heat, chemicals, and such), it might pay to incorporate to protect yourself, as an individual, from liability.

Child Care—Hugs, Kisses, and Act-of-God Insurance Coverage

"A basic requirement is that you love kids," says one operator of this kind of service business. And if you do, a child-care business can be very satisfying. Child-care operations include baby-sitting in the home ("family day care"), day-care centers housed in their own separate facilities ("group day care"), and nursery schools, which may occupy their own building or space leased from churches or other businesses. We also learned of a woman who operates a baby-sitting service that is primarily a telephone operation. She has a baby-sitting referral agency, in which she connects clients needing child care with women who are experienced sitters.

Not only does the need for child care exist, but it increases every day as more and more women seek employment outside the home. Nearly twenty million mothers today are working outside their homes.

Mothers with small children of their own, ex-teachers, and women with grown families find that their own personal experiences with children have equipped them with the most important qualifications they need for success in the child-care business—maturity, energy, reliability, and the ability to cope with many "small problems" at a time. These qualities, along with your love for children, form the foundation for your success. But what else do you need?

Location

You need a good facility in a good location. And the development of your facility, whether it is in your home or in another building, can be your greatest obstacle. Government regulations concerning day-care operations are lengthy, confusing, and often overwhelming. We don't want to imply that government regulations should discourage you from operating a day-care facility. We just want you to be aware that there are many more rules and restrictions than you might have imagined. In general, most requirements concern:

1. the ages and number of children allowed in a group
2. the ratio of children to adult helpers
3. building requirements and restrictions
4. space requirements for the number of children under your care
5. age and qualifications of your adult staff

Here is what one woman told us:

"I have been caring for children in my home for years, and when I decided to become licensed for day care, I called and got a list of the requirements. I intended to remodel my garage into a large play area for the kids, and I wanted to be sure I met all the government specifications. I had the remodeling done, bought cots and all the materials that I needed to become legally licensed. Then I began running into problems.

"All the red tape involved in getting licensed made me wonder if I was running my own business or, rather, running an offshoot of the state and federal government. To begin, I had to get a zoning variance for a conditional use permit to operate my day-care business out of my home. You pay $35, then they set a court hearing date. You speak before the court hearing officer on that date. I told him I wanted a day-care facility in my home. They wanted to know how many children I was going to have and everything I planned to do. They okayed me on the condition that I follow their eight rules—such as I must have a fenced yard, couldn't hire help, and couldn't erect a free-standing sign.

"With my zoning variance in hand, I applied for my state

license. This involves a state fire and sanitation inspection, and then finally an inspection from the state licensing bureau. What surprises me is that each department has its own list of specifications and rules. One inspector tells you to do one thing, and the next inspector tells you to do the opposite. I managed to obtain my license, but I've found that I am open to 'pop' inspections. I had two last week. The whole system of licensing intimidates me. All I wanted to do in the first place is take care of other people's children. I have been doing it for eight years, and I really think I know more about it than all the inspectors put together."

Because regulations are so stringent, we recommend that you obtain a copy of the rules you will be required to follow before going any further in your plans for a day-care service. The Children's Services Division of your state government will supply you with the information you need concerning state and federal day-care requirements. Upon our inquiry, we received a hefty envelope filled with detailed standards and statutes concerning the regulations governing infant and toddler care, school-age day care, and rules governing standards for day-care facilities. Health, sanitation, and safety regulations are extensive, as are the other requirements for certification. There are certification workers in the local regional offices who will help you decipher the regulations, if necessary. (One woman commented that she wondered if state governments were not hoping to take over the child-care business in this country by making it next to impossible for individuals to meet their requirements!)

Satisfying government building codes and space and safety requirements (regulations specify a minimum square footage allowed per child, both indoors and out) is not your only concern when selecting your location for your day-care operation. When you find the perfect building with plenty of outside play area, you still have an additional element to consider, and that is the particular needs of the families in your area. Check out the neighborhood you will be serving, and get an idea of the number and ages of the children you will be caring for. The occupations of the parents in your area may be a determining factor in the hours that you set for your operation. A location near public transportation may also be necessary. Know who your program will serve and what their needs are.

When you have solved the problems concerning your location

and have satisfied the zoning regulations in your area as well as your building, fire, and health inspections—you've come a long way! Now you can concentrate on some of the things that you *originally* thought would be your greatest concerns—like costs, developing your program, recruiting children and employees! Let's take a look at some of these elements in your planning.

Costs

The costs involved in setting up your program will vary tremendously with the size of your operation, the services you offer, and the staff and the equipment you feel you require. By operating out of your home on a small scale, you may be able to begin your business with an investment of $2,000 or less. If you set up your operation in another location, however, your expenses can be much higher. Rent, utilities, the transportation you provide, and the meals you serve will all influence your budget. Investments in play equipment can range as high as you allow them to.

Regulate your spending by following a carefully planned budget. Know what you have to spend, then stretch your budget as far as you can. When the costs of developing your own facility prove prohibitive, for example, consider sharing space with another community organization or business. If a hired staff is too costly, try a cooperative approach, in which parents assist the full-time teacher. And don't forget elderly volunteers. Bypass strict food preparation regulations and the expenses of equipping a kitchen by dividing your nursery-school program into morning or afternoon sessions or by having children bring their own sack lunches. Be creative in your use of throwaways, materials scraps, and recycled toys and games to help cut investment costs in expensive equipment and supplies. By using your imagination and a little ingenuity, you can trim your budget to a size you can handle.

Your Program

Developing your program involves paying attention to the well-being of the whole child—both physically and psychologically. As one woman said,

"I provide for their physical needs first—I see that their pants are dry and their stomachs are full. Then I go about caring for their minds!"

Adele has been operating her Musical Kindergarten for over twenty-five years. Her program is quite structured, based on a course that she studied in music school. From 9 until 12 each weekday, she teaches approximately twenty-five preschool-age children. They learn rhythms, sing songs, play simple instruments, dance, and follow the musical commands that she plays on the piano. "I try to have a balance between seated activities and physical activities," Adele told us. "Each activity lasts about twenty minutes, because that is approximately the length of the children's attention span. I feel that it is very important to follow a set program with the children."

Adele, who is a former opera singer, recommends to other women that they develop their own child-care programs from their personal interests—be it art, music, gymnastics, or even a scholastic interest, such as reading-readiness training. Children enjoy having a routine to follow, and though much day care is more "caretaking" than "educational," there is no reason your program should not be enriching to the child as well as fun. Organize your program to include learning time as well as sleeping, resting, and eating time.

The equipment that you need, as well as your space requirements, will follow along with your program. It is helpful to have different areas for different activities. If you are caring for children whose ages vary significantly, it is also good to have different play areas for them. If the outdoor space in your facility is limited, you will need to have a larger amount of space indoors to accommodate all your activities. You can plan field trips and walks to provide children with the outside activity that they need.

Recruiting Children and Employees

All the women we spoke with said that the need for good child care is great, and there is little problem recruiting all the children you can handle. Again, word-of-mouth advertising is the best, although you can also use newspaper ads, Yellow Pages ads, fliers in your neighborhood, or small notices of your service tacked on bulletin boards in shops and schools in your area.

One woman commented, "I'm as choosy about picking my customers as they are about picking me. A new customer calls and tells me she wants steady day care. She asks me how long I've been in business, do I smoke, and do I go to church. I turn around and ask her the same things. I ask if she plans to work steadily or just part-time. Later, if I find that I cannot work with the parent on certain matters, I give up taking care of the child."

We mentioned earlier that your staff can be volunteer parents, elderly volunteers, or paid instructors. Often a pleasant personality is a much more valuable asset than a college degree. Check your state regulations for definitions of what constitutes "adequate staffing."

Some Problems—And Some Good Advice

"In order to get my license, I had to meet all the specifications, some of which seemed ridiculous to me. For example, I was not allowed to have children under the age of 2½ years old, so I had to get special permission to have my own child in my day-care group. The rules and regulations I must follow to maintain my license are only important bureaucratically; otherwise, they're needless."

"Insurance is a major cost in your day-care operation. Find out what your costs are going to be before you try to draw up your budget. You'll need every type of liability coverage—accident, fire, flood, and damage."

"Use a little imagination when trying to raise funds for your child-care operation. Local businesses and religious organizations are often a good source of equipment or inexpensive space. Small fund-raising activities, often involving the children, are also a source of additional funds when you are trying to expand or add new equipment."

"When looking over a building site, keep in mind what renovations will be required to bring it up to government standards. Also remember your own needs—is there plenty of storage space? If rooms are small, are you close to any parks or other recreational facilities? Is there convenient parking space for parents who will be dropping off their children?"

"I've learned to tell all the mothers who come to me that they have to have a back-up baby-sitter if they want to use my service. I used to be a nervous wreck when I had to call mothers and put them on the spot when I was sick and couldn't care for their kids. I still don't feel that I can take a day off, but if I'm sick, I do call the parents. I'm not like a teacher, however. I don't get paid for the days I have to be home sick."

Secretarial Services

For many women, the opportunities in a small secretarial service seem custom-made: Such businesses are convenient to run out of the home, the investment is relatively small (often a typewriter is the only equipment you'll need), and the hours can be very flexible. We spoke to many women in this field (finding most of their names in the "Services For Hire" section of the newspaper), and they had lots of advice to share. General typing was the most common service offered, so we'll begin by listing some of the steps to follow in organizing this type of business. Most of our examples come from secretarial businesses run out of the home. When the business volume grows enough so that office space outside the home is required, organization should follow the steps that we've already outlined for general service businesses.

Operating a Home Typing Service

"Have the integrity to really know what you are doing before you try to sell your service." This was the advice we received from a woman who operates a successful home typing business, specializing in school typing (theses, manuscripts, term papers, editing) for college students.

"A good typist needs a solid understanding of the English language. You must know the meanings of words. There are 'sight' typists and 'content' typists, and a content typist—one who can edit and make grammatical corrections in the manuscript—is by far the most efficient."

1. Polish up your skills. The first step in the organization of your business should be to polish up the skills that you already have, and then you should "educate" yourself about the needs of your intended market. When typing for university students, for exam-

ple, you must follow the style and format requirements set by the university. Obtain a style sheet from the graduate office of the university or from the college bookstore, and familiarize yourself with it. Scholastic works often also require special paper, so acquaint yourself with the types of paper available. When you accept jobs from students, it is also wise to ask them to furnish you with a copy of the format requirements that they expect (including margin specifications, footnote procedure, bibliographical arrangement, etc.), so there will be no room for error.

A good set of reference books will be well worth their expense—a dictionary, a zip-code directory, a secretary's handbook, an almanac, and any specialized works that pertain to topics you will be frequently dealing with. (A typist who specializes in medical transcription, for example, will need an up-to-date medical dictionary.) The cost of your reference materials is tax deductible.

2. Organize your office. When you feel your skills are in order, it is time to organize your office.

"You need a desk of *appropriate* height and a *good* chair. Your efficiency will increase with your comfort. Adequate lighting is a must, and a typing stand, even if you haven't used one before, is very helpful."

The most important item in the office, of course, is the typewriter. Obviously, if you already own a typewriter, you do not need to invest in another one. But if you are going to select new office equipment, pay attention to some experienced advice:

"When you are buying a new typewriter, you need to consider the reputation of the company that manufactured the machine, the quality of the machine and of the print, and the kind of service contract that is offered. Never buy a used machine—you can't afford to wait for repairs when it breaks down in the middle of a job. You can rapidly make back your investment on a good, new typewriter.

3. Publicize your service. "I get the most response from my business cards, which I put in a little pocket on the bulletin board at the local college."

"I make up 3-by-5 cards advertising my business and put them up at the college. I also put my name in at the graduate office and at the department offices for each of the major areas of study (at the English department, the foreign-language department, and so forth). I would never recommend advertising in the daily paper. It is far too expensive for the return you receive."

"I have learned of a very good source of typing jobs. Go to the local Small Business Administration office and ask them how to obtain contracts with government agencies. There is a lot of work available in this field."

"Another way to earn money by typing at home is to work for a secretarial service. These services often contract out work that needs to be done overnight or over the weekend. Check the listings in the Yellow Pages for the services in your area. The work they handle is often specialized (medical and legal transcription, for example), so expertise in this area is helpful. Put your name on their lists to be called for their overload work."

"As with most businesses, word-of-mouth advertising is your most helpful promotion."

4. Set your rates. General typists we interviewed offered rates varying from 50¢ a page (usually student typists and part-timers) to $1.25. Thesis typing was more expensive, averaging $1.50 per page, and other specialized typing commanded much higher rates ($2.50 per page for medical transcription, for example). Most typists charge different rates for typed and handwritten copy. Regarding quoting rates over the telephone, we were advised that you should state your standard rates, but inform the client that you will have to see the copy before you can give a firm price. The use of tables of numbers in the text, for example, will slow down your typing speed, and you will need to charge a higher rate to compensate for the extra time that you spend.

"If you are going to be doing a lot of typing for engineers, business students, and others who use a lot of tables in their work, an electronic typewriter would be worth the investment. It is the best for column work and for repetitions, because it has a small memory bank. It will help ensure that you make the money you should be making in this type of work, by increasing your working speed."

Accuracy is important in this kind of business, and most typists include one proofreading in their rate. Spelling and punctuation corrections are also included in the price per page, but major editing jobs are figured on an hourly basis, ranging as high as $7 an hour.

"Many home typists make the mistake of not figuring their

overhead when setting their rates. You must remember to include service-contract costs, your supplies (ribbons, correcting tape, paper), and a portion of your utilities. When you are starting out, you should figure the minimum that it costs you to live each month. Then figure out your typing speed, and see if the rate you are charging will enable you to make it. You may need to reconsider."

In general, the market in your area determines what you can charge. When you are typing for students, we were told, you cannot command the highest rates. One woman offered a valuable suggestion:

"It would be extremely helpful if the typists in a particular area got together and organized themselves so they might set minimum rates for typing. When there is a fair amount of competition in an area, often all it does is drive the price down on your work. We need to organize!"

Drawing up a price list that shows rates, correction policies, and payment requirements will help you avoid disputes over charges.

We also learned that it is helpful to devise a standard form to use on each job, listing customer name, address and phone number, special job instructions, and charges quoted. Here's a sample form you can follow:

Date 8-12-81

Name Mary Smith
Address 210 N.W. 13th St. City
Title of Work "Faulkner's South"—term paper

Deadline 8-19-81

General Instructions:
Follow attached style sheet
Include 2 tables in appendix

Charges: 15 pgs. text at $1.00, $15.00
2 tables at $1.50, 3.00
Total $18.00

This form can be used not only to record all of your jobs, but as your billing record, as well.

A note on record keeping: be sure to keep all your receipts for supplies, as well as all your job records. If you drive your car to pick up or deliver work, keep track of your business mileage. And if you buy some new equipment for your office, check Internal Revenue Service allowances for investment-credit deductions and depreciation.

Other Secretarial Services

General typing is the most common secretarial service we encountered, but there are other related services that are profitable and relatively easy to organize. Typesetting businesses are often begun in a basement home office, and we spoke to several women who had developed such businesses into full-scale office operations outside of the home. An office machines salesperson can help you with the questions you have about buying or renting the machinery you need. By obtaining a Composer on a trial rental basis, you can see how the work suits you as well as obtain a few initial clients before you make a large equipment investment.

We spoke to a woman who developed her own telephone-answering service business in a small office building she owned. Seeing the need for some centralized phone service for her office tenants (some of whom did not have private secretaries), she invested in a switchboard with sixty buttons.

"I got to know the tenants in the building and saw the services that they needed. Because I have a small operation, I can adjust my service to their particular needs. For example, I can take messages for them if they are out of their offices, I can make calls for them, I can accept orders for the ones who do not have their own secretaries.

"After establishing my business with these first clients, I bought a mailing list of all the businesses in my vicinity from a direct-mail company. I had a brochure printed and mailed out over a hundred of them, advertising my 'customized service' and offering a special introductory rate—first or last month's service free.

"There is a lot of competition in the answering-service business, so rates must be very competitive. I only want to operate my service during business hours, from 8 until 5, and there are some people who want their service to run until 10 at night and on Saturdays. I just refer these people to another service.

"I think running an answering service is a perfect business for a woman. I would recommend that people who are interested check around at nearby small office buildings, see if they have reception area space, and then check into starting a business there, as I did. If the building owner is willing to let you establish there, you'll have a ready-made clientele. The building tenants will love your service."

The switchboard required to operate an answering service is expensive, with installation fees and monthly charges varying with the size of the board. The marketing department of your telephone company can answer your questions concerning this equipment.

Advice for Small Secretarial Services

"Office equipment is a favorite for burglars. Be sure everything is adequately covered by insurance."

"When you first start out operating in your home, you should be willing to take evening and weekend work. After you are established, you can afford to cut down on your working hours if you want to."

"A very good market exists for specialized typing services, such as legal and medical typing. I took a one-term class in medical terminology at the community college, then worked in a doctor's office as a typist. When I decided to start working out of my home, I was able to continue typing for my former employer. I also went around to other doctors' offices and left my name. In deciding on my rates, I looked at what the large, professional typing organizations were charging for the same work. When they were charging the doctors $3 per page, I set my rate at $2.50 per page.

"The only equipment I needed besides my typewriter was a tape recorder. The doctors would record at their offices, then I would pick up the tapes and play them and transcribe them at home. I made more money working at home than I did working full-time in the doctor's office, because at home I didn't need to pay for child care."

"When you are a small business offering a service, you can afford to offer your clients customized service. Find out what they really need, and suit your business to those needs. Large secretarial services are so cold, so cut and dried in their service. Adjust what you have to offer to create new jobs."

Sewing

One Oregon woman has taken her interest in sewing and developed it into an amazingly successful home sewing corporation. From her beginning on an old treadle sewing machine, she increased her talents until she was able to organize classes to promote her special sewing techniques. The success of her classes led her to begin licensing instructors to teach others her techniques. Then came her own fabric centers and a sewing-instruction book that sold a million copies, and from there, a five-year national TV series and extensive diversification that includes her own franchise stores.

Encouraged to promote your own sewing talents? You can do it, as many other women have proven. But we'll start you off in your planning with some of the good advice we have collected. It may not help you achieve the amount of success of that woman we were telling you about, but it might help you avoid taking on the nickname that her sprawling and extensive business has earned in the trade—"Stress and Strain!"

Your Skills

"Anyone who advertises as a seamstress must be able to do *all* basic construction features. I've had customers tell me that they have called women who advertise sewing in the newspaper who cannot handle the project they needed. You will not be successful as a seamstress if you can't do bound buttonholes."

"I have been sewing for years, and I have developed lots of special techniques that make my hand-sewn garments look professionally made. I started teaching my friends how to sew, and they suggested that I offer sewing classes built around the innovations and shortcuts in sewing that I had developed."

To promote your skills as a seamstress, your garments must not look homemade. As one woman told us, "You have to have confidence in yourself and in your skills to sell yourself to others. You have to make your customers feel that you are capable. And that feeling only comes when you have the skills to handle the job."

Different Ways to Develop Your Talents

There are a variety of different ways to promote your talents as a seamstress. In your sewing, you can either create a product (made from yardage goods) or you can provide a service (by altering or changing an existing garment), or you can do both. Creating a product includes not only custom-sewn garments, but also sewing handmade craft items. We spoke with one woman who had tried a number of outlets for her sewing talents:

"When I started my business full-time, I wanted to hit as many different markets as possible. I concentrated on four different areas. First, I advertised sewing classes—lessons for beginning and intermediate sewing and for beginning quilting. I have had little response for these classes, however.

"Second, I advertised my services for custom sewing. (I have found that most people who need custom sewing are either very big or very small, by the way.)

"The third area I tried was sewing for boutiques. There are several boutiques in the area that take items on consignment. I've found there are three main drawbacks to this kind of sewing, however:

1. It is expensive—you have to invest a lot of time and labor, with no guarantee of a sale.
2. Boutiques often sell their things for less than the big stores are charging, and also they take from 30 to 40% of the sale price. Because of this, I haven't been able to make more than $3 an hour, on an average, for my work.
3. There is a big risk when you make up an item for a boutique—you have to hope there will be a buyer, in that size, who will like that particular style!

"Fourth, I tried a line of children's crafts. This, again, requires a significant investment, and it is often difficult to anticipate the market. I also found that many shops want an exclusive on your work, which may limit your sales. I've learned that the primary competition comes from craftspeople who are not trying to make a living on their work. This drops the price on the items, and I was only making about $1 an hour on some of my work. Of a hundred dolls I made for Christmas, I only sold ten.

"After trying these different areas of sewing, I find most of my business is in custom sewing."

One other way to obtain sewing jobs, we learned, is to offer your services for tailoring in local stores or cleaners. You may find full-time work, or you may catch their overflow at peak periods in the year.

One woman told us, "I specialize in expensive, high couturier sewing. I draft and design my own patterns, and I limit my jobs to my own interests. I don't accept work from everyone who calls—only the jobs that are interesting to me."

In a similar vein, another woman said, "I am more interested in doing unusual, high-quality sewing, customized for the individual. I copy designer clothes, sometimes from photographs, and I specialize in fine fabrics. I prefer new construction and offer alterations only to former customers. Though the market is big for alterations, it is close to the same for new construction. I find there is still plenty of work when you choose to limit your jobs to your own interests."

Working Out of Your Home

Home sewing businesses are traditional, for a good reason: The work is easily handled out of a room in your home, and the personalized character of the business makes a home location a natural. Convert a spare room into your studio, oil up your machine, and you're nearly started. Keep in mind, though, that this is a business that will involve lots of personal contact. You must have the ability to get along with people—to be polite and discreet—and to not get upset when the customer does! When you choose a home location, your business will be primarily local, so check the demand in your immediate area and make sure you have a market for your service. Many women we spoke with averaged around twenty to thirty hours a week when working out of their homes, but several felt that their work could be full-time if they advertised more extensively. Also, remember to check local licensing and zoning regulations when you plan a home business.

Setting Your Prices

Custom sewing prices vary. We noted hourly charges ranging from $4 an hour to $6.50 an hour and up. One woman who has developed her dressmaking business into a full-time operation employing eight seamstresses explained her pricing in this way:

"Originally, I charged by the hour, but I found that it would scare my customers when I said that it would take four or five hours to do something! They think that since we are professionals, we're supposed to do everything in fifteen minutes! So I began keeping a complete log of how much time each employee took to make each garment, and I made a specific rate per pattern piece, taking into consideration each main pattern piece, each lining piece, and each interlining piece. Now the women can choose patterns within their price range. For example, we have some women who bring in thirteen- to fourteen-piece Vogue patterns, and we also have retired women, who can't afford too much, who specifically choose a pattern with only a few pieces."

Another woman suggested checking with other established dressmaking and alteration services to assess the going rate.

Advertising

"Get your name out any way you can to people who might need your services. I offered to help with sewing demonstrations at a fabric-store opening, and so the store became familiar with my work. Because they know I am qualified, they have agreed to carry my card and to recommend me if a customer asks for the name of a seamstress. I would recommend this idea to other women wanting to develop their businesses. Take a sampling of your work around to different fabric stores and show them your abilities. Then ask if they would be willing to display your card."

"I placed three different ads in the Yellow Pages. They are expensive, but it is a good place to advertise. I have found, though, that I usually get only one piece of business from about every ten calls."

"I receive most calls from the business cards I have displayed in the fabric shops. Next to word of mouth, this seems to be the best form of advertising."

Problems and Advice

"I think it would take at least five years to establish a reputation that would allow you enough business to support yourself with custom sewing. And you would need to have a lot of money saved to carry you through in the meantime. If you really want to develop the business, you can't work another job, because half of your customers will want to come in the day and the other half at night! You also have to be home when the phone rings. If you advertise in the phone book, people expect that you will adhere to traditional hours—that you will be available from nine to five."

"Many seamstresses dream of developing their own shop, featuring clothing they have made. But it is impossible to turn out enough merchandise to stock a shop and to be the clerk and the seamstress at the same time."

"I thought I could create an alternative for those people who don't like big sewing classes or lecture classes by offering private sewing instruction. But the business was just not there. The only possibility I see now is to try to teach sewing classes through a fabric-store outlet."

"The most important thing to remember is—don't get discouraged! Be prepared to wait awhile for your business to develop."

Midwifery—The Second-oldest Profession

Whenever someone mentions midwifery, we think of the scene in the movie *Tom Jones*, in which the highwayman jumps out from behind a tree, stops the stagecoach by waving his very long pistol, and yells, "Stand and deliver!" Whereupon the old woman, outraged, leans out of the coach window and cries indignantly, "What do you take me for, a traveling midwife?"

But the services of midwives are increasingly in demand. There is a very new look to this very old profession, as many couples seek to arrange a more personal and satisfying beginning for their families. The number of women using the services of midwives has doubled in the past ten years. (One midwife we spoke with delivered 5 babies her first year as a midwife five years ago, and in the first few months of this year, she has already delivered 65!)

Women interested in performing this service of "women helping women" train in a number of different ways. One woman we spoke with studied under a naturopath, others served apprenticeships under practicing midwives. Specialized birth clinics and women's health clinics offer birth education classes, reference libraries and midwifery referral systems.

Hazel, an established midwife, told us, "You can't be a midwife and hold another job. It's impossible to schedule labors!" Midwives often operate in a gray area, providing their services without a license or special insurance. They are neither legal nor illegal. Midwives can provide prenatal care, and set their fees according to their own requirements. Hazel adjusts her fees according to how far away the mother-to-be lives, usually charging between $250 and $350 for the birthing, with prenatal-care charges added on to that fee. All of her clients come from referrals, and each case is different, as each couple may choose the services they want.

Hazel maintains a waiting list for her apprentices, never taking more than one at a time. Each apprentice serves one and a half to two years with her, observing thirty or so births, then delivering five or six babies on her own, under Hazel's supervision, before setting out on her own practice.

Midwifery is a very intimate and personal service, very different from most of the services we have discussed. Still, as women's businesses go, it is one of the oldest professions, and, according to the women we spoke with, it can be one of the most emotionally satisfying. For more information on this field, contact your nearest women's resource center.

Problems Your Service Business May Encounter

We have mentioned some of the reasons services are such popular business ventures. These businesses can often be started with a minimum investment (though this is certainly not *always* the case), and they can be run from the home in many instances. Many times one person can operate this type of business in the beginning, allowing for flexibility of hours and causing a minimum of the expense and paperwork that additional employees involve.

Still, service businesses are not without their own particular problems. We've already noted the difficulties involved in advertising and promoting, especially with unusual services. What are some other problems?

High Insurance Rates

When performing a service for a client, liability insurance can be a vital—and expensive—element of your business.

"See your insurance agent first," a caterer told us, "and that may determine if you can really undertake the business at all. Check what your overhead will really be when high insurance rates are included. You may find the hidden costs make the price of going into business prohibitive. Still, insurance coverage is imperative. You must realize how suit-happy some people are. If a candle drips on an antique dining table or if someone gets stomach flu and calls it food poisoning, you've *got* to have plenty of liability insurance."

We encouraged you in an earlier chapter to find an insurance broker you trust before you even begin your business. Insurance rates vary considerably according to your exposure, and your premiums will likely be based on your payroll, as an indication of your business activity, or on your gross sales. Kinds of liability insurance range, too, from liability against physical damage, bodily injury, product failure, and even "completed operations," which would protect you if you finished and left the site of a job and *then* something happened. Those in the building trades and sometimes landscaping and cleaning services, among others, also are required to obtain a fidelity bond. This bond guarantees that a firm's employees, as well as others with whom the firm does business, are honest and that they will fulfill the obligations of their contracts. The state sets the bonding figures and the limits of liability.

Costly Equipment Repairs

Equipment-repair costs are often tremendously high:

"Mechanical repairs are so exorbitant," one woman told us, "that we try to do them ourselves—after spending our first year trying to find an adequate repair manual for our equipment!"

Many women offered this advice: Insure your major equipment investments with regular maintenance. If your equipment supplier offers a service contract for cleaning and repairs, take advantage of it. It may well be worth the expense.

"Some people feel that used equipment can be a good buy, but I much prefer to buy new equipment so that I can get a service contract from the company. I want that contract from day one, because it's far too expensive to repair and replace equipment in the middle of a job. For a yearly fee, my contract includes everything from service to parts. And the repair service is very prompt—I have never been without my equipment for more than half a day."

Luxury Image

Many services fall into the category of luxury, and it is the job of the proprietor of such a business to convince the public that hers is a luxury they can afford.

"Languages are a luxury in this country. The client must be found who is prepared to pay for it," a German language teacher told us.

"Catering is not a necessity service, so clients must be developed from the limited percentage of people who can afford it."

"The market for custom sewing is there, but it takes time and effort to reach that market. The reputation that custom-sewn articles are very expensive is hard to overcome. So far, it's only by word of mouth, from one customer to another, that my clients come to realize that a custom-sewn wardrobe from me is expensive, but it is no more than clothing from a fine quality department store."

Webster defines a luxury as "the best and most costly things that offer the most physical comfort and satisfaction . . . usually something considered unnecessary to life and health." How do you go about convincing people that they need your service? Thumb through some magazines and you'll see how luxuries are promoted by the big-time operators. They sell convenience, status, glamour, prestige, luxury "with a compact price." Isn't it time that your clients, too, "had the very best"? Promote your service that way.

Setting a Price

Be especially careful when setting a price for your service. There may be no "recommended price" listed anywhere for your service, but that doesn't mean guidelines don't exist. We've said before that your competition will play a large role in setting your price, but don't undersell yourself just trying to beat them. No one will ever thank you when the job's over if you've lost money because of poor cost figuring. All your overhead expense, labor, and materials costs and profit expectations have to be taken into consideration.

Your rates may increase with your expertise as your business progresses. "When we began, we made so many mistakes that we felt it was unfair to charge our clients an hourly rate. Until an hour's work was *really* an hour's work (and not a period of time split between working and correcting), we used a flat rate per job."

Another woman advised new businesswomen to keep in mind the current federal minimum wage, then add to that overhead costs and compensation for skills and experience.

Several women we encountered used a bartering system in their businesses, trading services for services. In a one-woman operation with minimum overhead, this sytem of exchange works well.

A midwife explained, "I have been wrestling over my price for some time. I have such an intimate relationship with the people I work with that it's like charging my friends. The price I charge is often determined by the people I'm dealing with. One couple I'm working with now is helping me get my chicken coop together!"

Allowing for Change

We've told you that service businesses offer an amount of flexibility that some other types of businesses do not. Adapt this element of flexibility to your entire business scheme and you will avoid the problems encountered by many service operations whose services become outdated. Many linen suppliers (at least the ones who are still showing a profit) now find themselves very much in the paper products business. Floor-maintenance services have gone from working on hardwood floors and oriental rugs to wall-to-wall carpeting and back again. Don't limit your growth by limiting your service. Note changes that may affect your customers, then adjust to those changes.

One woman commented that, once your business is growing, you'll find a demand for your other skills as well. Another wisely advised: "Once you get your foot in the door with just a few clients, then it is *you* who must listen to *them* and to their needs. If you can meet their needs, then you've got yourself a going concern!"

Advice from Women in the Service Field

"You must learn—and eventually you will or you'll have a nervous breakdown—not to take things personally. You cannot please everyone. I know that's an old saying and we all know it's true, but sometimes it's hard to remember when you really *do* try to please everyone. You don't have to justify the why's and rules of running your business to anyone else. If you know why you're doing something, that's all that matters. Many times the customer just wants something to complain about and doesn't care why he's not getting his way. Accept your performance as the best you can do, because it *is* the best you can do."

Other advice we received:

"Respect your client's time. Be realistic in estimating the time needed for job completion and allow a little extra time for unexpected problems. It's bad business to be late with an order—but you'll look great if you finish ahead of schedule."

"My business (arranging an English holiday for visitors from the United States) benefits greatly from a kind of symbiotic relationship with a Vancouver travel agent," one woman told us. We think her efforts at services sharing show how two businesses can work together for mutual benefit. "By choosing a single travel agency to work with, we can take advantage of co-op advertising with the agency. In our brochure, we mention that air travel is not included in the package, and we suggest contacting this particular travel agent. In our newspaper ads, we list the travel agent's phone number to call for additional information. The agency, in return, often suggests our plan to clients considering a London holiday." By working together, both services enlarge their market. Consider such an arrangement when making your plans.

An important aspect of any business is record keeping: "Once you've found your first client, start keeping a job book," advised a woman. "Give each job a number. Record for each job the client's name and address and phone number, and write down a description of the job you are doing. Note any special instructions, and when the job is finished, write down the itemized bill."

It seems as though, if everyone followed our advice, there would be Gideons *and* a 3-by-5 file box at every bedside. But we've learned that, especially in a service business, your customer records are the most important things that you have. And a handy way to keep those records is to file a card with each new job (including customer's name, address, phone number, as well as the date and service provided). Then update the cards with each new service that you provide for a customer. This way you'll know who your customers are, what services and products they are using, and how to reach them in the future for promotions or sales specials. Use your records *aggressively*. Remember, your customers—and their records—can tell you more about your business than anyone else, suppliers and hired consultants included.

9 The Manufacturing Business

Got a great idea for manufacturing doormats in the shape of a male chauvinist pig? Before you go into production, keep this point in mind: You are not ready to promote and sell a product until you can produce it uniformly, at high quality, at a price that will appeal to the buyer. When you feel you have reached this point, you are ready to try manufacturing in quantity. In this chapter, most of the manufactured products we refer to fall into the categories of clothing and crafts. (The problems involved in manufacturing precision instruments and nuclear warheads will require further, independent research.)

When a craftsperson goes from the individual production of handcrafted items to the mass production that manufacturing requires, there is naturally a sense of creative loss—your feelings on the unique aspects of your art must change. But manufacturing offers a new challenge to a craftsperson: the challenge of arranging the production of an item in the most economical way while retaining its character and quality. Your creativity will be channeled in a new direction.

The facilities that you need, as well as the equipment and number of employees, will vary according to your kind of business. In a small manufacturing business, sales help and your own shop are often unnecessary. One of the most vital areas of consideration in manufacturing any item, however, is setting your price. Before going any further, let's look closely at the way you arrive at your price.

Setting Your Price

The cost of any item that you produce is much more than just your labor plus your materials. There are several channels your product can go through before it reaches the customer, and your wholesale price (the price at which you sell your item to someone else, who in turn plans to sell it for a profit) must be sufficient to cover all possible costs. Many craftspeople make a mistake when first starting to market their goods through a variety of outlets. They are used to selling their items themselves, at retail price. When they have to allow a 50-percent discount to wholesale buyers, they soon discover that they have not allowed for *selling expenses* in their price structure. Don't make this costly mistake!

Keep in mind these elements when working out your wholesale price:

1. Shop and business overhead. Included in your business overhead is your training time, designing time, ordering and organization time, as well as all shop and office expenses.
2. Materials. Even if your materials are free, it takes time for you to gather or locate them.
3. Labor costs. Labor costs equal your hourly rate multiplied by the amount of time it takes to complete one unit. In setting a figure for your own hourly labor rate, remember that the minimum wage represents the hourly rate that an unskilled worker can command. Your hourly rate, as a skilled craftswoman, should be at least twice that figure. Don't shortchange yourself or your skill.
4. Your selling expenses. Include all commissions charged, delivery charges, entry fees for fairs and exhibitions, etc.
5. Administrative expenses. Include any office help.
6. Finally, your profit expectations.

Point number 4 is where many problems arise. There are many different ways you can market your product, and with each different way, there are certain costs involved. If you choose to sell through a wholesale distributor, for example, he may be able to make many additional sales for you, but he will also demand a commission (a percentage of your wholesale price) for his services.

Your price must have taken this commission into consideration, so that even when this percentage is deducted, your selling price still covers your expenses and profit demands.

Justifying Wholesaling Expenses

In working out your price, it may appear to you that it is more profitable for you to sell directly, at retail price, rather than giving percentages of your selling price to the various distributors and wholesalers. These percentages are justified, however, when you consider that the valuable time you spend contacting buyers and taking orders could be spent in actual production when others handle your sales functions. The commissions you *saved* by distributing your own products, you *earned* by assuming the role of salesman. When you are first starting out in business, you may elect to sell as much as you can at retail and merely sell what remains to wholesalers. This is perfectly acceptable. When business picks up, however, you may find your time is more profitably spent in production, and it is well worth the commissions charged to have someone else handle sales.

Your Best Price and the Price-Volume Profit Relationship

Several women offered this bit of folk wisdom from the manufacturing trade: *If you can't make it as fast as people are buying it, you are selling it too cheaply*. Look back to Chapter Three now and read again the section on pricing—how to determine your best price, and how to arrive at the most profitable price-volume relationship. We cannot stress too greatly the importance of a correct selling price. As your business grows and you expand your market through the use of product distributors and wholesalers, remember this: If you are selling at a loss because of careless cost figuring, there is no way that you are going to improve the situation merely by selling in greater quantity.

Five Important Aspects of Manufacturing

Your manufacturing business must be organized around a careful business plan. We've already given you the elements that you need to consider, but since manufacturing your own goods offers some very unique challenges, let's get more specific. There are at least five important aspects of a manufacturing operation that deserve special consideration. They are all in our general plan for beginning a business, but in this kind of business, we feel they merit additional attention.

1. Know your market area. Market familiarity concerns not only the territory in which you plan to sell your goods but the customers who make up that territory, as well. Before you set out to manufacture a product in a certain area, you *must* be aware of who is providing that product now, how much of the market they are covering, if the demand in the area is holding steady or increasing, and also what kind of customers make up the market. You should determine the geographical size of the area you hope to cover, which will influence the ultimate size and shape that your business will take.

Keep in mind these two things about your product market. First, it must be large enough to provide you with enough sales to recover your costs and to earn a sufficient profit. Second, you should have a broad customer base within your market area. That is, don't place all your hopes on a single type of customer. A diversified customer base is a valuable business safeguard.

2. Check out the competition. Mary Ann, a designer of table linens, offers this "how to" for marketing handmade items:

"Check the kind of items you plan to market at the local department stores. See what people are buying and what they are paying. Note the quality they are getting. If you think you can compete, go ahead. You can also talk to the suppliers who call on the local shops."

It is helpful, in assessing your competition, to actually make a list of the features of their product, comparing these features to the qualities, and maybe the weaknesses, of your own items. Noting such details as price, size, style, quality, and so forth, you become aware of helpful selling points for your product, as well as discover areas in which your work could use improvement. The more competition you have in your area, the closer you must watch your quality, terms of sale, delivery scheduling, and any other aspects of business which may affect your relationship with your customers.

Nearly all our advisers offered this suggestion: "Constantly examine the competition!"

3. Anticipate your volume of sales. You've already researched your market and your potential customers, so before throwing the switch on your Mighty Manufacturing Machine, you had better figure out what kind of sales volume you can achieve with your product. Now is the time to make some predictions, especially before we get to step number 4, which is how you will manage your production line. Make up a chart for yourself, projecting what you feel to be reasonable goals for your business for the next couple of years. The SBA suggests you outline the sales you expect to reach something like this:

	total sales	product(s) 1	product(s) 2
first year	$________	$________	$________
units	________	________	________
second year	$________	$________	$________
units	________	________	________
third year	$________	$________	$________
units	________	________	________

4. Organize the elements of your production line. "Production" is the key word in a manufacturing business. It includes all the steps that are involved in making your finished product. When you are planning your business, the elements in the production of your item must be determined with precision. A mistake in the figuring of the time needed to complete one unit, or the costs of raw materials, or the wages of the labor involved could cost you your business. Keep this in mind as you follow these steps in planning production:

a. First make a list of all the steps that will be involved in producing your item. These are your "manufacturing operations." By having a systematic record of your entire operation, you will have your "business pattern" available if it becomes necessary to apply some "alterations." For example, if your product fails to compete successfully in the market, you may see the necessity of reducing production or handling costs.

The owners of a wholesale natural-foods warehouse commented on the necessity of watching handling costs: "When we first started out, our warehouse was in a funky old wooden three-story building. As much as we loved the place, it was just not economically wise to stay there. We couldn't use a fork lift there, and we had to handle the items physically three and four times before they sold. Handling costs money, and the less you handle, the better off you are."

Other ways of reducing production costs may include increased mechanization or a more efficient work-flow pattern. Sometimes an increase in the cost of your materials will need to be overcome through a modification in your operations. This type of balancing is all in the line of "stayin' alive" in business.

b. Now list all the materials you need to produce this item. We recommend listing your raw materials on 3-by-5 cards, including for each item such information as quantity price, address and phone number of supplier, delivery and credit terms, colors and sizes available, and so forth. Also list some alternate suppliers, in case of emergency. Keep those cards in your handy file box.

In some cases, storage of your raw materials may need extra consideration. Are the materials perishable? In order to be properly supplied, will you need special storage facilities? Are these materials readily available only in certain seasons? Your finished product can only be "finished" when all of its parts are complete. You must have the resources to provide *all* the parts, and backup suppliers to help out in emergencies.

Your inventory of materials is vitally important in a manufacturing operation. You must anticipate price changes in the market, holiday interruptions of your suppliers, and any possible shortages so that you always have plenty of raw materials on hand. However, you do not want to have too much of your operating capital tied up in your inventory of raw materials. If you do, and prices drop, your product price will still be fixed by your high materials price.

Your choice of materials may also in some way be determined by your competition. If their price for a similar item is better than yours, you may be forced either to find a way to buy better at the market (buying in larger quantities, for example), or you may have to substitute less expensive materials in your product when you can (taking care not to alter the primary features of your item).

c. Equipment requirements in your manufacturing business may vary from a single sewing machine to a machine shop full of metal commotion. Will you buy it or rent it? How much money should you set aside for maintenance and repairs? What will you do if something breaks down in the middle of production of a large order?

Most manufacturers establish a system of preventative maintenance to keep their equipment in top working order, to help avoid costly breakdowns. Keep records on each piece of equipment, showing its cost, the purchase date, its use and storage schedule (if applicable), the facts on depreciation, and its maintenance dates and repair record.

d. How much labor will be involved in the production of your product? You need to determine how many workers will be needed, how much training they will require, how much pay they will earn in the production operation. (In a manufacturing business, the "time-cost factor" is very important. This is the amount of work that can be produced in a given time.) Other indirect labor may also be involved, such as office help, maintenance crews, and the like.

An organization chart is helpful in determining how many workers are required to handle all the production elements. As your manufacturing operation grows, your chart will sprout additional boxes to handle increased work and responsibilities. For now, page 286 shows an example of the organization of a small manufacturing plant.* The woman at the top will probably handle the tasks in the first few branches of the organization until business growth demands that these responsibilities be delegated to others down the line.

*This chart was compiled with the help of information from the SBA. Draw up your own chart, filling in the boxes to suit your own manufacturing needs, to determine the labor force your operation requires.

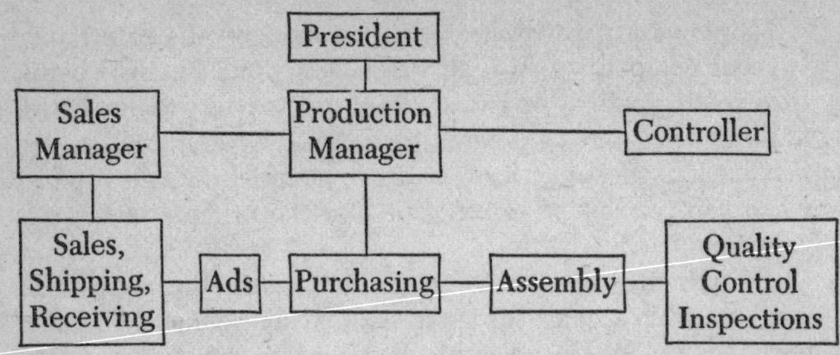

e. The information you have gathered on production goals, equipment, and labor will determine your space requirements. In figuring the amount of space you need, don't forget to allow for storage of raw materials as well as completed inventory. Remember that you need plenty of room for the handling of each step in the manufacturing operation. Time means money in this type of business, and if your workers have to clear off their tables after each step before they can go on to the next process, you are losing both time and money. If your workers have to move from one location to another in the production process, make sure their path is direct and convenient.

The space that you utilize may be in your own basement or it may be in a separate building. Will you rent or buy this business space? What will it cost you?

f. Finally, there are some other overhead items that will figure into your production costs. These items will vary according to your business, but include such things as salaries for managers, utility costs, special tools and supplies, and so forth. In developing the total picture of your manufacturing process, account for all the elements that will be involved, however they may be related. When you have itemized costs of all your production needs (supplies, machinery, overhead, etc.), you will be able to see how each of the component parts contributes to the total cost of your product.

5. Assure distribution of your product. Although consumer advertising is usually unnecessary if you are selling an item that you manufacture, you'll still need to get your product known in order to encourage wide distribution. There are a variety of

methods of contacting your potential customers. Some methods are better suited to the sale of manufactured handcrafts, while others will work well in the distribution of other types of products. Let's look at several of these methods of selling and distributing what you have produced.

Fairs and Exhibitions

A good place to begin marketing your products, especially handcrafts, is at local arts and crafts fairs, trade shows, or other public exhibitions of related goods. Ask other craftspeople, and suppliers in your field, and read craft magazines to learn when such fairs are to be held and how to go about entering them. County, state, and regional fairs are also a possibility. Sometimes a fair is a one-time event, but others make a regular circuit that you can follow.

"If you've noticed a show in a shopping center at which you feel your work would sell well, contact the shopping-center office to see who manages the show. Then contact them for details of exhibiting."

"Fair" Facts

Fairs and their exhibiting requirements vary. We've learned that:

1. You should check to see how long the fair you are considering has been in operation. Reputations develop over a period of time, and your efforts will be better spent on an established fair.
2. Location plays an important role in the success of any exhibition. Before selecting a rural or remote location, determine if your kind of goods will market well in such a setting.
3. It is common to be charged two different fees when you enter an organized fair—a registration fee (we've heard of them ranging from $10 and up) and a commission to be paid to the fair organizer on all the sales you make. Such commissions vary with the exhibitors, some charging as low as 10% and some up to 40%.
4. Talking to others who have shown previously at a certain fair will let you in on much valuable information—whether it is a "buying" or a "looking" fair, which booth locations are the best, how much merchandise you should bring with you, and the like.

5. The sponsor of a show or fair plays an important role in your satisfaction (financial and otherwise) as an exhibitor. Many crafts people recommend fairs sponsored by the business community, commenting that when businesses feel the fair will boost their sales, they are anxious to accommodate exhibiting craftspeople. Shows backed by art groups were also recommended. When the craft exhibition is used as a form of fund raiser for some group or charity, however, sales are often reported to be low. These fairs often serve more as a social event than as a shopper's market.

To Market, To Market, To Buy a Fat Hen . . . and Just About Anything Else . . . at the Saturday Market

In Portland, Oregon, the Saturday Market provides a lively mix of color, smells, and people every Saturday and Sunday from April through December each year. Handcrafted goods, sold *only* by the person who handcrafted them (you can't buy someone else's goods and sell them), are displayed in casual array in heavily trafficked open-air booths no larger than 8 feet by 8 feet. Run by a nonprofit corporation, the Market takes 10 percent of each vendor's daily gross sales, a minimum of $2 or a maximum of $15. ("The rent is not quite as cheap as it sounds," one woman commented. "When you figure you may pay $30 for a weekend, it works out that your shop rent is $120 a month for an 8-by-8 booth.")

Potential displayers may wait years (*at least* one) for a permanent spot to peddle their wares. In the meantime, they are advised to go to the Market office the morning of the sale, review a copy of the vendor guidelines, show Market managers a sample of the product they hope to sell, put their name on the reserved-spot waiting list, then hope for an opening among the many locations throughout the Market that are not reserved.

"Corner spots are the best," one craftswoman told us. "It's also good to be near the food stalls." This woman explained that the original Market vendors chose their locations by lottery. Vendors now take their chances as to whether they will be located under the protection of a nearby bridge or out on the fringes of the area, depending on daily vacancies.

The casual atmosphere of the Saturday Market may deceive shoppers who believe the weekend booths provide merely a social and creative outlet for talented craft artists who are otherwise "gainfully employed."

"I support a family of seven with my booth at Saturday Market," one woman told us. "I have worked here for four years, and when you figure out all the hours I spend during the week to prepare my things to sell on the weekend, I am working far more than the hours required in a normal full-time job. I have one other wholesale outlet for my items, but I do far better financially here at the Market."

Another woman vendor told us, "I don't make the minimum wage from my booth, but it sure beats typing in an office or being on welfare! I support myself and my child on what I make here. Because the Market is closed from Christmas to April, in the past, I have worked at temporary jobs in that time. This year I hope to have budgeted better so that I won't need to do that kind of work again." She advised that other craftswomen just starting out in their own business should "keep a regular paying job until you are *really* established in your craft business."

"I like the Market because it is good advertising, and it is very useful to me while I am trying to develop a larger wholesaling business."

"Saturday Market is good for craftspeople, because they can often work on their items while they are sitting at their stalls and selling. It's not like a shop, where you just have to stand around all day waiting for the sales."

"I started out my business at the Saturday Market, and now, even though I have my own shop and a full-time business, I still enjoy selling there. I do it now more for fun and publicity, but if I had to (and I've done it in the past!), I could live on what I make at the Saturday Market!"

The only drawback to the Saturday Market approach to selling was voiced by a woman who noted, "The Saturday Market is okay, but there is no protection there for your work. That is, you have no guarantee that your booth will be under cover if it rains or hits 110 degrees. There is also no guarantee that there won't be twenty other craftsmen there selling the same kind of things that you are."

Setting Up Your Booth

Usually, craft fairs and other exhibitions last only a couple of days, and you are responsible for setting up and decorating your space or booth. Booth requirements will vary, but it is always imperative that the booth you outfit be attractive, easy to set up and take down, and a sturdy and safe display area for your goods. Costly items should be carefully placed at the rear of the booth or in cases, where shoppers won't be tempted to "lift" them; while inexpensive, touchable items are best grouped in quantities and put where passers-by can handle and admire them. Putting your big sellers out front will draw attention to the other work in your display.

If you can work on your craft while managing your sales booth, so much the better. A visual demonstration attracts an audience of potential customers.

Two other things to include in your sales booth—plenty of change (you can't afford to run out when customers are waiting) and a large stack of your business cards.

"Fair" Advantages

Exhibiting your new product at a fair has the distinct advantage of offering you immediate feedback from your intended customers. Shoppers passing your booth will let you know in a hurry what they think about your product, its quality, and its price. Keep your ears open and learn from all their free advice. You'll find out quickly which of your items will carry your business and which should be eliminated.

The managers of some craft shows maintain mailing lists that will help you plan for future events. It is also a good idea to make up a mailing list of your own by keeping track of the names of your buyers—those customers who purchase articles from you at one fair may be interested in knowing where they can find an exhibition of your goods in the future.

Saturday markets, craft fairs, and other new-product exhibitions are a good way to make your first contacts, gain your initial following, and earn enough money to give your small business a successful start.

Manufacturers' Gift Shows and Trade Fairs

The manufacturers of some unique calligraphic designs told us of their experience at a gift show:

"We soon decided that local craft shows were not enough; we wanted to distribute our calligraphy nationally. Renting a booth at several West Coast gift shows was the beginning of our education about gift shows. Shows cost money, from $350 to $450 dollars and up for booth rental. Travel, restaurant, and motel expenses make the ventures very expensive. We also discovered that the newer you are to the shows, the less desirable a position you get in the building. We were put way upstairs, away from the main floor, at our first show. We also learned that instead of renting a booth, you can give your product to a representative who already has a prime location. You give him or her a percentage of the sales. After several show experiences, we have decided to go through a representative—a far less expensive and more profitable venture for us. I am not a salesperson, and I'm certainly willing to pay someone to sell for us who has twenty to thirty years' of experience behind him!"

To find out about the shows and trade exhibitions that would be good exposure for your type of merchandise, read the trade papers and magazines in your field and related industries. They will give notice of upcoming shows and events. Not all small manufacturers feel that trade shows are the answer for their distribution needs, however:

"I started out selling my products through individual shops and at local craft fairs. Then I considered displaying my things at the twice-yearly gift show in Seattle, where gift-shop owners from all over the country would come to buy merchandise for their shops. It would cost me $350, however, to rent a tiny space and be one of two thousand exhibitors for four or five days. Several gift-shop owners told me that I would probably do much better selling my own products, in person, to the various stores. I think now I have worked out the best arrangement. I set up the initial orders, in person, at the individual shops, then I send out spring and fall catalogs to these customers to show my new fabrics and designs. I have cut down on fairs and sell 90 percent of my things wholesale to gift shops."

Selling to Retailers

Contacting Buyers

When you've tried out your product on the public in some way, and you've learned what goes (and what went!), you are ready to try selling directly to shops and wholesalers. Don't be afraid of your first contact with the business world—the buyers you encounter will be real people, just like the customers you've had so far. And even though the buyer represents a giant department store or wholesaling business, the sale will be made on a one-to-one basis—the buyer and yourself—just as if you were dealing with a single customer.

Begin by checking the Yellow Pages of your phone book, and make a list of businesses that carry products in your field. Then visit the shops you have listed—you may find they are not the kind you want to carry your merchandise. When you have decided which shops you would like to contact, it is best to call and make an appointment with the buyer in advance. Describe the product and set up a time to show it.

You must do plenty of homework before your first appointment. Don't take up the buyer's time by being indecisive about your terms, your delivery, your production schedule, and the like. Here's a list of facts to have clear in your mind (or in your notebook) before you keep your first appointment:

1. Have a firm wholesale price (the retail price for a handcrafted item is generally not less than two times the wholesale price). Don't be caught quoting different prices to different customers. If the item is very inexpensive, give the price per dozen.

"And never undersell yourself! I value my time very highly. When I have figured out how to put together an item the best and most efficient way possible, I feel I should be paid for doing so. I mark my products up three times the cost of the material. If I can't sell for that, I won't market it."

2. Know when and how you will deliver. You'll need to be very sure of your production times and your inventory. You will also need to know whether you will mail the product, deliver it yourself, or use a delivery service—and who will pay for this delivery.

3. Decide whether you will sell your samples outright to customers or whether they have to place an order. It is recommended that with one-of-a-kind items, you should offer them for sale at that time. But if you are selling an item in quantity, you should ask for an order, because the buyer will possibly order a larger quantity than you have with you.

4. Have an easy and precise ordering system. If you are offering a variety of items or products in different sizes, colors, etc., give each a different number, color code, or classification so that you can take orders quickly and correctly.

5. Decide in advance if you would agree to offer a product to one store only in an exclusive agreement. Figure out the terms you feel would justify such an agreement.

7. Determine whether you are willing to consign your merchandise. Many gift and craft shops prefer to acquire their stock in this way. You will not be paid for an item until the shop sells it. If your product is expensive, this may be the best way for you to promote. If your product is quite inexpensive, though, it would probably be best to be paid outright.

Consignment Selling

Consignment selling presents some problems for you, the manufacturer. Here are a few things mentioned frequently by manufacturers of handcrafted items who had consignment arrangements with a number of shops:

1. Sometimes, because there is no "out-front" money involved, a shop will take an item on consignment that really does not follow the store image (beauty shops or restaurants that take artwork or flower arrangements on consignment, for instance). Shoppers in those particular stores are not looking for your kind of merchandise, so your sales may be slow. And your merchandise (and the money spent in the production of the merchandise) is tied up, with little reward. Beginning manufacturers commit themselves to this kind of arrangement because it is often one of the few ways they can get their product out on the market.

2. Once your items are taken on consignment by a shop, it is easy to lose track of their progress—the shop may be far away, the payments from the shop to you may be slow in coming. You are

unaware of customer response to your items. To avoid such a loss of control, you should establish from the beginning a system of exchange and replacement with the store. Don't let your merchandise sit in the shop for months getting dusty and shopworn, eventually to be shoved under the counter or into a corner. Service your consignment accounts regularly to replace items that have sold and to exchange popular goods for things that aren't moving. Don't leave this responsibility for replenishing your stock to the store owner—it's not his worry.

3. Be sure to get a signed accounting of the merchandise you have consigned, its retail value, and your percentage agreement with the shop.

Your Sales Presentation

By the time you arrive for your first appointment, you should have worked up a little presentation to display your product to its best advantage. Velvet-lined boxes, colored photographs, and printed brochures all play a part in selling your product. Don't show your entire line if you manufacture a hundred articles, but don't show too little, either. Move quickly and smoothly, and don't be too discouraged by a deadpan reception. Offer suggestions for display or promotion, if you have them. If the buyer looks doubtful, suggest placing a small order at first, to see how the product is received.

In some cases, with very large businesses or out-of-town stores, it is better to make your first contact by mail. Write or inquire about the store's buying schedule and policies about receiving samples or brochures on your work. Then follow their instructions on presenting your work for consideration.

Sales Materials

A trip to an office-supply store will fix you up with all the forms you need for billing and shipping. You'll need:

1. Invoices, which tell which items you are sending the customer.
2. Packing slips, which list exactly what is packed in each box. (If you are sending four boxes, for instance, you will send one invoice and four packing slips, one in each box.)

3. Statements, which are your bills. Include on these the invoice and purchase-order numbers, if there are any.

Of course, you will keep duplicates of all your ordering and billing forms. Later, if you feel that store-bought slips with a stamp-pad endorsement are not classy enough for your business, you can have some made up by a printer. In the beginning, though, why not economize?

Try, Try Again

If at first you don't make any progress in promoting your product to stores in your area, don't give up! Try changing your price, altering your presentation, or perhaps contacting different types of stores. And after you've set up a few initial accounts, don't forget the next important step—servicing those accounts! Follow up on all the customers you've acquired, taking reorders, exchanging popular items for those that are not moving as well, and showing any new products that you have added to your line.

Selling to Wholesalers

After contacting different stores in your area, try selling to wholesalers. Often shipping costs, salespeople's salaries, and showroom expenses are higher than a small manufacturing business can justify. In this case, a wholesaler may be the best person to get your product to the right customer. Wholesalers often come in two varieties, stationary and traveling. They have the knowledge of the product markets in different areas, and they can often reach markets that you, as an individual producer, could not serve.

Stationary wholesalers usually maintain a permanent showroom in which they exhibit different products from individual manufacturers such as yourself. Some of these agents work on commission, and some work on a consignment basis. They will promote your product to the different store buyers.

The traveling wholesaler will reach many more customers than you could in person. In selecting such a wholesaler, you should make sure she has a familiarity with your particular product market. Also, keep in mind that this person will be representing your business, just as your own salesperson would. Select someone who meets the standards you would set for your own sales staff.

Once you have established on your own even a small amount of business in local shops, it will be easier for you to find a sales representative to market your goods around the country. You can get the names of these representatives from the buyers at the stores where you are already doing business. Showing them your sales records may entice them to take on your product line.

Dealing with wholesale buyers brings into question the many options open to you in setting quantity prices. Here again the special consideration you gave to your pricing system will be of value. Your price, if you followed our recommendation, has been adjusted to cover all forms of marketing, so that your profit is ensured in whatever means of selling you utilize. The wholesaler's commission may vary as to the extent of her services, but remember that a larger percentage is justified by the removal of sales responsibilities from your domain. The more the wholesaler does, the more time you have to devote to production.

Wholesale accounts are commonly handled in one of two ways. First, wholesalers may receive a 15-percent discount on your wholesale price. Wholesalers earn this discount because they make the sales contacts for you, and through their wider range of contacts, they are probably able to sell a greater quantity of your product than you could. With this discount rate, you handle the billing and shipping to the individual shops.

The second alternative is to give wholesalers a 33-percent discount on your price, with you shipping the product to them and billing them for the total. They service the individual customers. This method is easier and less time consuming for you.

To see how this system of discounting to different buyers works. let's take a look at Cathy's candle business and see how she sets her prices:

One of Cathy's decorated holiday candles sells for $12 at the annual Christmas bazaar that she holds in her own home.

$12

Direct Sell — Cathy ◀ .... ▶ Customer

Cathy also sells her candles to local shops at a 50-percent discount. In this case.

	$6		$12	
Store Accounts	Cathy ◆ .... ◆	Store buyer	◆ .... ◆	Customer

Cathy has a contract arrangement with one gift-shop wholesaler, whereby he receives a 15 percent discount off of her selling price, so that,

	$5.10		$6		$12	
Wholesale @15%	Cathy ◆ . ◆	Wholesaler	◆ . ◆	Store buyer	◆ . ◆	Customer

(note that the price to the store buyer, either from you or from the wholesaler, is the same)

Another agreement was arranged with a different wholesaler. This wholesaler receives a 33-percent discount on Cathy's candles, but he handles all the shipping and billing expenses to the individual accounts.

	$4		$6		$12	
Wholesale @33%	Cathy ◆ . ◆	Wholesaler	◆ . ◆	Store buyer	◆ . ◆	Customer

Other Distribution and Promotion Ideas

Mail-Order Advertising and Catalog Sales

Distributing your product through mail-order advertising or catalog sales is one way to reach a large market. We discussed the operation of a mail-order business in Chapter Six, and if you think this marketing method would be suitable for your product, look back at that section now for some general information.

In selling an item that you manufacture through magazine advertising or the use of a catalog, you must determine first who your target audience is. Then direct your advertising and your mailings accordingly. If you choose to advertise in magazines, select only those that carry a large number of other mail-order advertisements. It is recommended that you run your ad in at least three, and better still, six, issues to build up some reader confidence.

Even if your product line is extensive, limit the items that you mention in your ad—it will make for stronger appeal. And always offer your customers an unconditional guarantee.

The response that you get from mail-order advertising may just be enough to enable you to break even on your advertising expenses, but it will help you develop a mailing list of interested customers. This mailing list will prove valuable in developing the repeat customers who will help your business grow. Send your catalog or brochure to the names on this list to advertise the other products in your line.

Using a direct-mail catalog or brochure to sell your products is an expensive method of distribution, but many different kinds of businesses have found it satisfying. The mailing list that you use can be your own, compiled from past sales and mail-order advertising response, or you can obtain the names of potential customers from professional mailing-list brokers. Check your Yellow Pages under Mailing List Brokers for the names of local firms that handle mailing lists compiled from different professions, trades, and business and social affiliations.

If you sell your manufactured products through the mail, keep in mind that you must repeat your mailings frequently to develop enough business to justify your expenses. You must have the ability to update your line of merchandise and to add new items to create interest.

One-Woman Shows

Another way to start your business off and get some quick response from the public is to hold your own sale or show. A sidewalk sale, a special showing in your home, or an exhibit in the foyer of a large office building will draw attention to your work and stir up some interest. Be sure to check in advance if a permit will be required (from the city, the building manager, etc.), and then use a mailer to notify friends and past customers of the event. If the idea appeals to you but you don't feel you have enough to put on a one-woman show, ask another craftsperson or manufacturer to join you. Double your interest, and maybe your customers!

One woman who produces fresh and dried flower arrangements sells her items primarily at craft fairs, in fine department stores, and through custom orders that she receives from people who have seen her designs. In addition, she offers an individualized service that promotes her product and advertises her business at the same time. At the client's request, she goes into the home and creates decorations for parties and special occasions, coordinating her designs to the individual decor. In developing her arrangements, she uses the client's own vases and containers whenever possible, increasing the personalized touch. Word-of-mouth advertising from party goers and others who have enjoyed her work have made this business so successful that she was invited to Washington, D.C., last Christmas to provide decorations for one of the historic government houses. An expense-paid holiday trip is an exciting way to stage a one-woman show!

Specialty Shops

We learned of another unique way for handicraft producers to market their items. In a suburban shopping mall, there is a shop which features sixty different craft artists, who rent display space by the month and pay a percentage of their sales to the shop owner. Craftspersons who use the store to sell their items advised us that only tried-and-true items are a good bet in their limited shop space—items that are proven good sellers, that will help cover the rent and management percentage.

Demonstrations

Another way to promote your products and gain some publicity is to offer to share your talents by addressing groups who secure speakers for their regular meetings. Pass out plenty of business cards, and demonstrate your product or craft, if possible. Or offer minitours or demonstrations in your own home studio or production plant. Creating an awareness of your product is your primary objective.

"My partner and I manufacture a number of different herbal items—breads, vinegars, salts, dried seasonings, and teas. We have given several talks to local garden clubs and women's organizations. We demonstrate how to make some of the products, but we do not give away special recipes. We've found when they've seen the involved procedures we follow in making our products, many people are interested in buying them."

One woman has really taken her lumps in the manufacturing business. She's the big-time manufacturer of a teeny-tiny item, and we'll call her story Chickens Are Popular, Mushrooms Are Out.

Chickens Are Popular, Mushrooms Are Out!

Paulette's house is a mess. A week's worth of her husband's ironed shirts are hanging across the workroom doorway. Yesterday's clean laundry is in a pile on the living-room couch, and when we shove it aside to sit down to talk, last month's peanut butter cookie flips out from between the couch cushions. Three sixteen-year-old girls are giggling around the kitchen table, painting little red aprons on Christmas angels, while a TV soap opera blares in the background. The phone rings, the kids come home from school and a three-foot-by-four-foot fort of building blocks collapses of its own accord in a back bedroom. We're here to learn about running a small manufacturing business out of your own home.

Impossible? It's delightful! Where else can you open a door on a dreary winter day and find a room up to its ears in dried flowers, bursting with colors from baskets and bunches along the walls, from floor to ceiling? Gingham fabrics and rickracks fill a section of drawers, and grocery sacks full of ribbon bows crowd the workbench, along with trays of miniatures—wine bottles that are one inch high, broomsticks, tiny eyeglasses, and mortarboards to fit the head of a three-inch-tall graduate. Such is the stuff that dough art is made of, and Paulette is an expert at the craft.

"I tend to do what has to be done, and the rest can wait its turn," Paulette explains. What has to be done is stock twelve different stores and twenty assorted crafts shows with her dough figures and plaques, manage the mall showings of groups of local craftspeople at six large shopping centers, teach workshops in creating dough decorations, and write a book on the art of making baker's dough decorations. All this to be done, by the way, after the needs of her husband and two young boys are taken care of.

"I started making dough-art items six years ago, when the craft was very new. There were no books on the subject, no recipes to follow. The mushroom theme was popular then, so I worked up a group of dough mushrooms, glued them to a board that I painstakingly stained and rubbed by hand, and began selling them at craft shows. It took me two years to learn that I could dip the boards to stain them just as effectively, in a fraction of the time. Learning to mass produce is a process that just takes time, and mistakes.

"I have no formal artistic training, so developing new designs in the dough takes lots of time and work. Still, I feel that if you set yourself up to sell something, you are saying, in effect, that you are a professional, and therefore you should never just copy another person's designs. Everything you sell should be your own. When I was starting out, I would just make a few of an item; then I'd take it to a show, and if it sold well, I'd go home and make some more. You learn quickly that purple isn't a big seller, but yellow, orange, and green are."

Paulette continued, "The good thing about starting your own craft business by appearing in craft shows is that the feedback is immediate. When the traffic is good through a show, you'll hear remarks that instantly let you know what the public likes and what they don't. An enthusiastic compliment can make your day, but hearing, 'Oh, look, Susie, you did that same thing in Brownies last week,' is enough to make you want to fold up your table and go home!"

Paulette's designs are unique, and her prices are very reasonable. "I made the decision that I would rather sell lots of inexpensive items than a few twenty-five-dollar items. Most of my things sell for between one and eight dollars, usually depending upon the size of the board they are on. I've made one twenty-five-dollar item—just for my own ego, to see if I could sell a dough creation for that price—but I carted it around to four different shows before it sold. Last Mother's Day, I wanted to design something that cost a dollar, so children could afford to buy it for their mothers." That's when the Lumpy was born. These charming lumps of dough are billed as "happy little people who serve no useful purpose." They are accessorized in a variety of ways, from bridal veils to ski poles. "I made four Lumpies and took them to a shop to see if they would sell. They were gone immediately. Then I made eight more. Then I made six thousand."

Another decision had to be made. "As the business grew, I had to keep asking myself, what are my priorities? I did not want to slight my family, but I had made so many valuable contacts in my field, I hated not to pursue them all. When you are working in a creative field, you have to keep coming up with new ideas. New things have to be working themselves out in your mind all the time, or your business won't grow. If I had stuck with mushrooms and not developed new designs, I would have been out of business long ago! So I decided to hire some girls to help out with the mass-production aspects of the business. I teach them how to make one portion of a piece, and they make that part until I have plenty in stock, and then I teach them something else."

Efficiency is the key to mass production. "My husband used to make my plaque boards for me, but it seemed whenever I had a rush order, he'd have to work overtime at his job. So I fired him! I learned to cut and do the routing on the boards myself, and I'm teaching one of the girls how to handle the saw, also." When Paulette's craft projects went from a part-time hobby to a full-time business with paid employees, cost analysis became a major factor in her business.

"When you are manufacturing a product, you have to analyze costs every step of the way, especially if you plan to sell your product at a discount to a variety of shops. Usually a shop will take an item on consignment and keep 30 percent of the sale price. Or they may buy the item outright at a discount of 40 percent. Pricing, therefore, is vital, for even a couple of cents' error can ruin your profit if you're selling an inexpensive item."

Paulette pays her employees by the piece, which is called contract labor. This kind of pay structure allows for a simpler bookkeeping system, as no withholding taxes are figured into the paychecks. "I started out paying my girls an hourly wage and found myself watching over them every minute, feeling uneasy if they took time out for a Coke or a chat. Paying them a predetermined price for each piece they complete is much more satisfactory. I take the item that I need worked and time myself when I make it. If I can make one a minute, I figure that the girls, who are less skilled than I am, can make one in two minutes."

Figuring out what each step in the production of an item was worth took some time and experimentation. It takes 3 minutes to make a Lumpy, for example. It costs 8 cents an hour to run an oven at 300 degrees, and eighty Lumpies make an ovenful. Baking costs of one batch of Lumpies = 32 cents.

One popular item is a small wooden wall plaque that features a dough basket filled with dried flowers, beneath which is a note pad and pencil. "After you've made a hundred of the baskets, they go pretty quickly! After you've made two thousand, they're pretty boring." Repetitions are where the girls' help is really valuable. The day before our visit, one girl had earned $30 making tiny ski caps for "sports-minded" Lumpies.

Paulette still does the designing herself, usually trying out a new idea, then letting it sit on a shelf for six months or so to make sure time and the weather don't cause cracking or other unforeseen problems. One of the biggest problems that a craftsperson has to deal with is other people copying her original designs. "I have seen people at a show photograph one of my items and then run away down the mall. Or someone will bring a sketchbook and stand there drawing my things. I resent this kind of intrusion, and I always tell these people that I don't allow it. Often they don't realize it, but what they're doing is stealing. I feel that I worked hard to develop my designs, and I tell them to go design their own. I have taught dough-art classes since I started in this business, and I have always instructed my students that the designs I use are my own, and though I may use them as illustrations, the students are not free to copy them or use them in competition with me. In one instance, I took a selection of my things to a jurying that was held before a craft show, where I was competing against other craft artists to have my things selected. My designs were turned down because the judges had seen all my work before—one of my former students had taught my designs to a group at a benefit workshop. I could have easily made $400 at that craft show." Now Paulette has copyrighted her most popular designs. (See p. 305 for a discussion of patents, trademarks, and copyrights.)

Paulette's experience organizing a benefit craft show led to the service aspect of her career—managing the craft fairs that are held in a variety of shopping-center malls throughout the year. "I began charging $5 a table, not screening the crafts at all. Exhibiting in the malls now involves a larger set fee for each booth and I screen the crafts closely. I'm careful to protect the interests of those craftspeople who have shown with me before. This means that I won't put eight potters in a show when experience has shown that two potters are generally enough to handle the business adequately. I always try to be extremely fair, and I've found that when the manager is not getting a percentage of the sales, it is easier to treat all of the craftspeople alike."

Working as a show manager has been challenging and a little scary, Paulette admits. "When you try to sell a craft that you make and a shop owner turns you down, you can easily say, 'That's his tough luck!' But when you're trying to sell *yourself* to a shopping-center manager and you're turned down, it can be difficult."

Developing a manufacturing business from an enjoyable hobby has a drawback that may not be evident in the early excitement when business takes off in a rush. Paulette commented on this aspect of the business as we stood surveying the cardboard boxes of plain Lumpies and pieces of projects that crowd the floors, countertops, and shelves of her home. "I've reached the point," she says, "where often I've personally made only a small part of lots of the things I sell. I have to ask myself, do I want to be a factory? I also question the value of the mass-production pricing system that is often discussed in my home. Recently, my ten-year-old spent some enjoyable time working on a little project of his own. Then he turned and asked me, 'How much do you think this is worth?' You can't put a price on everything, and I don't want my children to grow up thinking that you can."

Still, there are elements that are very satisfying. "I always get a little glow from talking to a friend who started in dough with me. Her husband made her give it up because 'there was no money in it.' I've pointed out to her many times how much she could be making now if she had stayed with me as a partner. I've got lots of things going well for me, and I'm enjoying all that I do. Maybe I'll have to cut back on some of my activities in the future, but right now, I don't want to give anything up." Looking around at the unfolded laundry, she checks her watch and sees it's almost time to start dinner. "When I have a really good day, I'll call my mom and say, 'Hey, guess what? I made $500 today.' She always says, 'Yes, Paulette, but is your housework done?'"

Patents, Trademarks, and Copyrights

When you are developing a product for manufacture, you should be aware of the methods of protecting your original work: patents, trademarks, and copyrights. Remember, though, that you cannot legally protect an idea; you must have something tangible.

Patents

If you are working on a technical item, you should get your plan on paper and then have an engineer study it to be sure the idea is workable. The next step in acquiring a patent can be costly and very time consuming. You need a patent attorney to make a patent search through the records of the Patent Office Search Center, located in Virginia. This is to ensure that there is not already someone else holding a patent on the same thing. This search can cost you $1,000 or so, a fact that serves to discourage weekend inventors from trying to patent every gizmo that pops into mind. We've learned that out of approximately 100,000 patent applications that are made each year, about 70,000 are accepted as original, and only about 2,000 ever get to the marketplace—and just a very few ever make any money. After you have applied for a patent, there is still a three-year wait, during which time your product is protected by a "patent pending" listing. The patent you obtain will be effective for a number of years, depending on the fee you are assessed. When *all* these details have been handled, it is still up to you to develop, finance, promote, and sell the item. Any second thoughts about patenting your Whatchamacallit?

Trademarks

Associated with securing a patent is the registration of a trademark. A trademark lasts for five years, and it protects the snazzy name that you choose for your product. The lawyer who helped you secure your patent can handle the trademark search and application for you. There is a fee for this name search, as well as a filing fee. Then, periodically, you must pay trademark-renewal fees.

Copyrights

A third method of protecting your original work is with a copyright. One woman described the process of copyrighting to us in this way:

"New copyright laws guarantee that when anything new is created, it is automatically copyrighted. In order to get it in writing, however, you need to contact the Library of Congress in Washington, D.C. For an art-medium copyright, you just send along a photo of the item, a form from their office that you have filled out with all the pertinent information, and a small fee."

Copyrights are valuable for written work, games, music, original artwork and photos, even containers or special gift boxes. Your copyright is dated from the time it is registered and there is no search involved, as with a patent. A copyright cannot be obtained on a title or an idea. One craftswoman explained the limitations of copyright:

"Even though you have obtained a copyright on an item, it is still up to you to see if someone tries to copy your idea. A copyright doesn't automatically protect you—you have to protect yourself."

Five Areas of Special Concern

It's evident that your manufacturing business may take any one of a thousand directions (anything from soup to nuts, literally). Still, in talking to many small manufacturers, we've learned that there are at least five important things you should watch out for:

1. You must carefully manage your inventory. Your business will grow only if you provide your customers with the service they require, and good service means prompt and efficient handling of all orders. Your aim should be for a rapid and constant turnover of inventory. The smaller the amount of working capital that you have tied up in materials and finished products, the better off your business will be.

2. As we've said before, watch every aspect of your production operation closely. Modify and update operations as often as necessary to maximize efficiency. Remember that lost time means

lost profits. Raw materials that are late in arriving, assembly lines that are short of workers, production areas that are not easily accessible—all these, and other factors in your operation, may add up to make your production costs too high. High costs here mean lower profits for your business. Try for a system of responsibility in the production of your item, grouping jobs in operational units. Organizing along these lines makes it easier to control costs and productivity and to supervise worker efficiency. An organizational chart of clearly defined worker functions will also make it easier to fill employee positions when necessary.

3. In a manufacturing business, quality control is very important. Quality is the primary aspect of your product that will contribute to repeat customers. Always deliver what you have promised. If sacrifices have to be made to cut costs, make them in your packaging, or in other areas that are not vital to the quality of your merchandise. Constantly evaluate and study your production methods, with the aim of increasing efficiency and eliminating waste, as well as lowering costs.

Once a customer has been disappointed in the quality of your goods, it will be hard to win back his confidence. To ensure that you avoid unintentional alterations in your product, and to provide a clear blueprint for your employees to follow without possible misunderstanding, put down in writing all the specifications for your product, whether it be a metal fitting or a wedding dress for Barbie.

4. Sales are the fourth area in which your business strengths will be constantly measured. As the owner of a manufacturing business, you will have to be continuously aware of what is selling well and what isn't, what your best price is, what terms and credit you are willing to offer, what your schedule of delivery is, and the state of any old or overdue accounts.

The profits from your sales actually reflect two different markets, because your business itself is a kind of bridge between two markets. First, there is the market you buy from—where you purchase your raw materials. Then, there is the market that you are selling to. And one market reflects the other. If your materials costs are high or your materials are in short supply, then your sales and profits may suffer. You must be able to make adjustments in one market when you experience changes in the other.

Your profits depend, in large part, on three things: the market demand for your product, the competition in that market, and the customer's choice of your product to fill her need. Make sure to have all the facts that make you confident you are satisfying your business needs in each of these three areas. This knowledge will help you respond to the internal and external changes and developments in your field, and will give your manufacturing business the flexibility it needs to grow and succeed.

Some manufacturing firms are closely related to and dependent upon larger industries in which they play a part. If you are in this type of business, you must keep an eye on the economic situation not only in your particular area, but in your industry as a whole. An awareness of the state of all the links in the chain in your field will enable you to prepare your business for changes in supply and demand.

5. Finally, pay special attention to budgeting and disbursements. The smart businesswomen always take advantage of suppliers' discounts, knowing that over a year's time, even very small percentages add up fast. And a small emergency cash fund can often be a lifesaver—especially at tax time, when you've forgotten all about it!

Pitfalls

In speaking with women in the manufacturing trade, we learned of assorted problems and advice that they would like to pass on to you, a newcomer to the field.

"I can't sell my handcrafted goods to the stores, because I can't compete in the organized manufacturers' market," said one craft artist from her own experience. "I'm not a woolen mill, and I can't produce my woolen items fast enough to fill large orders. My price would have to be far too high in the shops, after the store owner added on operating percentages. My hats would have to cost two times as much in a store as I can sell them for at a craft sale or Saturday Market."

What can a small manufacturer do when faced with this kind of situation? There are a number of possible solutions:

1. Try marketing your product for a while at the price that you

feel is too high. Craftspeople sometimes don't place a high enough value on their work—they are as often guilty of underpricing as of overpricing. The buying public will determine what they feel your product is worth, and you may be surprised.

2. Attempt to lower production costs either by lowering the cost of materials (through quantity buying or substitution of less expensive materials) or by reducing time spent in production.

3. Upgrade your product, through the use of better materials or designs, to justify the high price you must demand.

4. If you've studied every aspect of your production and still find it impossible to lower costs to a customer-appealing level, you may determine it is just not economically profitable to produce the item.

5. You may choose to limit production in order to maintain artistic standards.

"By limiting myself and avoiding mass production," one woman explained, "I feel that I am able to maintain a certain aesthetic quality in my work. I may not be a great success at manufacturing, but I am, you know, working my way to being an artist!"

Other advice?

"Some timid beginning craftspeople try to sell their goods at garage sales, bazaars, and such. This can be discouraging, as most of the shoppers there may not be looking for handcrafted items. Also, your feedback won't be particularly good. If you're shy, try an out-of-town fair or show first. Your friends and neighbors won't see you, and you'll gain the experience you need."

"When you are producing a handicraft in quantity, remember that you don't want it to look like it was pressed out by machine. The handmade quality is important, so let the personal touch show."

"One of the first things you should do in setting up your manufacturing operation is have some business stationery, with your letterhead, printed up. You'll need to use this to look official when contacting suppliers, and, in fact, it is often a requirement when dealing with wholesalers."

"Even the smallest, home-based manufacturer can benefit from buying in quantity from wholesale suppliers. To do business with these wholesalers, you often have to give some proof that you are engaged in retail selling. A letterhead, a sales-tax license, or something of this sort will usually do. Also, by reading your particular trade publications closely, you will get information on different suppliers and where you can write for their catalogs."

We also recommend again the use of the many trade directories in the reference section of the library. They list names and addresses of suppliers of every imaginable product and component.

"I have a big manila envelope for all suppliers that I buy from. All the information on their products is kept in the envelope, as well as every bill I ever get from them. I file the envelopes alphabetically. I have found this easy system saves me a lot of time when I'm ordering supplies or when I have a question about a bill."

"Joining a regional or local crafts group is one way to keep in touch with others in your field and to learn what's happening. Sometimes there are other benefits, too. For instance, you, as a group, may be able to take advantage of quantity buying from suppliers. The group may sponsor classes or speakers that are of interest to you. There are some regional groups, such as the organization of Appalachian Craftspeople, who have really worked to further the interests of all the members. If there isn't such a group in your area now, think about starting one."

Go To It!

Manufacturing a product requires planning, precision, and skill. And once the production aspects of the manufacturing processes are completed, the job is still only halfway done. Getting the product to the right customers at the right time for the best price—only then will your manufacturing business succeed. Got your Mighty Manufacturing Machine in gear? Good luck!

10 Second Careers and Reentry Women

There is a new class of women emerging today, in business as well as in other areas of society. She is sometimes called displaced, due to the sudden circumstances of divorce, the death of a mate, or her children growing up and moving away. Her husband's job may have required her to move from the town she considered home. She may have been forced to retire from another job. She may have reached a point in her life when she would like to quit an unsatisfying job and begin something more personally rewarding. Or she may have discovered that volunteer work and tennis afternoons are not enough. Whatever the particular circumstances, these women, usually in their forties or fifties, often decide to reenter the business world, which they might have abandoned when they married. These reentry women, as they are called, are becoming a visible force in the network of women's business.

If you feel that you fall into the category of the displaced, don't be disheartened! With just a little extra preparation, you can change your sense of insecurity and your feelings of being out of touch into a state of confidence. It's just a matter of recognizing that all the experiences you've had in the past have prepared you for what lies ahead. And, possibly with a few specially directed activities, the skills you possess can be sharpened while you rebuild your confidence in your abilities.

If the plans we've outlined for starting your own business sound exciting, but you feel that your age or the length of time you have spent behind the stove instead of in the store renders you ill equipped to undertake such a venture—don't give up your dream. Take a little extra time and try some of these confidence builders to give your morale and your plans a boost:

Go back to school. Just getting out and back in the swing of things is an important first step. Check the local universities and community colleges and see what they offer that sounds interesting to you. Many colleges today are offering a variety of classes for women, and specifically for women reentering the work force, such as career workshops and seminars, assertiveness training, and forums in which women who have successfully begun new careers share their experience and their advice with other women. In these classes, you'll not only benefit from the information and guidance that is offered but you'll meet other women like yourself, who are seeking a new career and setting some new goals for themselves.

Try volunteer work. But be selective in your volunteering. Offer your services in a field that holds a business potential for you. While you're building your confidence, you'll be making contacts that may be valuable to you later on. You'll become acquainted with the network in the field at the same time that the people in the network become acquainted with your skills and capabilities.

Join or organize a women's consciousness-raising group—or, if the term bothers you, call it a once-a-week morning coffee. Get together with other women in similar circumstances. Nearly every woman we talked to, whether she was young, business-wise, inexperienced, or president of a corporation, stressed her need to communicate and share with other women in her circumstances. They don't have to be women in the same kind of business or in the same income-tax bracket—just other women who are involved in business, setting business and personal goals for themselves, dealing with the problems of job and family, and so on. Talking things over helps. And the problems of getting back into the world of business won't seem half so insurmountable when you learn they are shared by many others. Listening and sharing are some womanly traits that can be very helpful right now.

Get yourself a part-time job. It's not your own business, but it's a start in the right direction. By working in the field that interests you, you'll learn if you really enjoy that type of business. You'll see firsthand how the business is run, what the problems are, how much work is involved, whether the demand is great enough for another operation of its kind. And you'll renew your acquaintance with the day-to-day aspects of working for a salary—there will be customer relations, paperwork and finances to handle, time scheduling, and deadlines to meet. Part-time work or a temporary job will help you make the adjustments that you need to make your reentry easier.

The benefits of starting a second career in mid-life can be enormously satisfying. After filling a role as mother, wife, and "bosom of the family" for many years, a woman often feels she has lost her ability to act independently, lost the power to seek some kind of satisfaction that is wholly self-centered. Yet it is precisely at this time that many women especially need to experience a challenge, to feel useful and fulfilled. Betty, who had no previous work experience (aside from raising three children!), found that owning a franchise business was the perfect answer to her need for a second career, especially because her business experience was very limited. She told us:

"An ice cream store franchise was the perfect answer to the empty-nest syndrome. They teach you exactly how to run the store—everything from how to scoop to keeping the books, appeasing and pleasing the customers to janitorial duties, how to hire and fire employees, how to decorate cakes and the store. It was an all-around education!

"A franchise is good for someone like me, who wants the guarantee of a proven plan. I could have never opened my own little ice cream store. I would not have had the confidence I needed, and I would have failed the first month. But I can follow directions down to the letter. And my franchise includes a monthly plan—new signs and suggestions and game plans for each month of the year.

"Getting out and having an interesting job to work at after my children were grown has been very satisfying. The store has a pleasant atmosphere—everybody is happy to come in for an ice-cream treat! And it's a really good way to be popular with your grandchildren!"

Another woman we spoke with, who is sixty-two years old, has created her own business (an answering service) and a new life for herself at a time when many other women are feeling that they're just growing old. "My business has been great for me," she said. "It makes me get out, makes me get going! I had never worked before. Now I see that I really did need some discipline."

Don't feel that your age will inhibit your success. Build on the many advantages that your maturity gives you.

"I am fifty-eight. I have four children, and I was a homemaker for thirty-five years before starting my business. I've done a lot of volunteer work. That, and homemaking, provided management skills, money-management experience, buying know-how, experience as an employer and user of help. I believe many women could do what I've done if they needed or wanted to."

You're more experienced than a younger woman, and your years lend you added authority. More than half of the women in the United States between the ages of thirty-five and fifty-four are in the job force, so you are certainly not a minority.

"I have always wanted a business of my own," Abby told us. "In fact, years ago, I took out an insurance policy so that when I was sixty, I could have a shop. I felt my community also needed what I had to offer. We have always had very little money, and whenever we went into an antique store, my husband and I could never afford anything. I felt what this community needed was a good, cheap antique store, offering old things that clever people could do things with, things with a lot of possibility."

Abby keeps her shop open two days a week, and at other times by appointment. "I'm a selfish shopkeeper," she says. "I do just what I want to do when I want to do it!" Aside from that asset of being her own boss, Abby comments, "There are always a lot of little pluses in this business. I have really had some delightful experiences with people I've met."

Dorothy owns a gallery in a small town. "This is my second career," she says. "My first was in education. For well over thirty years, I was the director of the lower school of a large private school in California. Things got kind of rushed, and my husband said he had to make an appointment to see me, and he was not very happy with the way our life was going." Dorothy and her husband owned a little house in a country town, so they decided to "ditch the rat race and move up to it. I felt, if my husband was that unhappy, why not?" She went back to her old hobby, painting, but soon discovered that it wasn't enough.

In a painting class one day, she commented, "I think I'll open a gallery." Her instructor overheard her and gave her a lot of encouragement. "I went home and told my husband, and he said, go ahead if you want to, but this time get a partner so you won't have to be there all the time. I asked another painter, a casual acquaintance, if she knew anyone who might like to go into partnership with me. Her eyes got big and she said, 'Like me?' The partnership was formed, and the business has been growing ever since."

Peer Problems

Along with the tremendous satisfactions, of course, reentry women face problems that are somewhat unique to their station. One woman said: "When I first started, I got a lot of static from my friends. They treated me like it would go away, like a cold. Some of them said, why would you want to do *that*? No one else is doing *that*. Now, nine years later, things have changed somewhat. Another one of my friends has just opened a shop."

Peer pressure was mentioned several times as being an obstacle these women had not anticipated. Friends feel deserted and hurt by your new interests. Things shared in common are diminished, and new friends, possibly business acquaintances, take the place of the friendships that fade away.

"I was a housewife for ten years. I played tennis, was a member of the Junior League, and did a lot of volunteer work. Then I started a little printing press with a neighbor and friend. We didn't worry about making any money; we had a good time. From that, I went on to open my own kitchenware shop. I had no idea that people in business worked as hard as they do! Now when I see friends my own age who don't work, I look at them totally differently. I long to say to them, I wish you could understand what your *husband* is doing. They are impatient with their husbands' weariness at the end of the day, and it is because they have never worked, never had their own business.

"They are also impatient with me now. My own peer group

really does not understand me or what I am doing. And that's hard, because you need people in your peer group to understand what's happening in your life. I have one friend who has gone into business for herself, and it's fun. She comes down about twice a week, and we have coffee and talk taxes and all that stuff, and it's wonderful for me now to have a friend I can do that with. Otherwise, it is very difficult for me to communicate with our other old friends. Our social life has become about nil.

"Still, having my own business is very satisfying—so much more so than doing charity work and volunteering, for instance. It is satisfying because it is *mine* and because I know that *I'm* doing it, and I love it. I'm completely involved. You know, I wasn't supposed to do these things. I was raised in an era when women were expected to be mothers and schoolteachers, and my own mother has never really forgiven me for not doing that. Those were suitable occupations for a woman, and they were *all* that were suitable. But I didn't want that. I've always been rebellious enough to want to do what I wasn't supposed to do! But being in business for yourself is a measure of your own worth, in a way. Because you do know what you can do, and if you haven't had that measured somewhere along the way, for your own satisfaction, then you feel frustrated. Your own business provides that daily measure, and maybe I'm just insecure enough to need that."

A daily measure of your own worth—this woman's comment capsulizes the motive, realized or unacknowledged, that is the very foundation of many women's businesses. And for the reentry woman, this motive often has special significance.

Our Conclusions

The stories we heard and the experience we shared in developing this book were truly exciting, sometimes funny, and very fulfilling. Women in their own businesses are extremely interesting. In our search for advice and information, we found ourselves everywhere from the cool, carpeted offices of bank loan officers to the crowded sales counter of a porno shop (red-faced and clutching a tiny "novelty" purchased solely in an aim to support women's business). We lingered in quilt shops, in boutiques of every description, and over six-inch-high cream puffs (dripping with fresh raspberries) prepared by women chefs. The willingness to contribute and the enthusiasm of all the women we encountered were inspiring.

The women were radiant with excitement, self-esteem and self-satisfaction. Though their businesses and personalities varied tremendously, they shared a certain something that was, at first, indefinable. Then one day as we stood in the midst of one woman's personal creation and listened to her incredible success story, we began to realize that the elusive element we had been searching for had something to do with creativity and recognition. We began to see each business as a unique personal creation that was recognized as such by friends, customers, and others in the business community. It was this recognition that provided the women business owners with such fulfillment and delight. We realized, through our discussions with these women, that our need to create and to be recognized for our creative efforts is as much a part of our human makeup as our need to eat and to sleep. Acknowledging this need and satisfying it through the development of a business is an exciting goal to strive for.

Looking back over the conversations we taped, the notes on everything from check stubs to sales receipts to bona-fide notebooks, we are constantly reminded of the importance of goals. Goals are the essence of success, and a written goal, in the form of a well-devised plan, is the passport that sends you on your way. Without a goal, your movement is sideways. You shuffle to the left, shuffle to the right, always waiting "until . . ." Until your kids are grown, until you get your degree (or the next degree . . .), until you lose five pounds. A goal gets you moving in the direction you need to go—forward and up.

We have noted that women working together is one way to promote and develop the strengths of women's business. Through a network of contacts, both personal and in the business community, we can provide mutual assistance through referrals, information sharing, personal guidance, and positive reinforcement. An invaluable resource for any woman striving to satisfy a goal is the establishment of a relationship with a mentor—a person who is interested in your success and willing to serve as a sounding board in the development of your plans and the solution of your problems. A mentor need not necessarily be in your own field but should be wise in the ways of the business world, positive in her suggestions, and confident in your abilities.

It is our impression that the world of women's business is intrinsically different than the male-dominated realm of business we have known in the past. Each woman's business we saw had a more personal foundation, a basis in an individual goal of independence and self-expression. The business does not represent an end in itself. It symbolizes a liberating means of development, of achieving that "measure of success."

Start your own business planning today and take the first step toward owning your own business. And when you do take that first step, don't be surprised if it changes your life.

Glossary

Accounting—the system of keeping, analyzing, and explaining business accounts. It is a statement of debits and credits. An accountant is the person who inspects, maintains, and adjusts the account.

Accrual—a system of accounting in which income earned and expenses incurred are recorded at the time the sale is made or the expense is incurred. This system provides an accurate and up-to-date statement of profits.

Advertising—the impersonal presentation of a sales-generating message to large groups of people, utilizing the mass media (such as radio, TV, newspapers). Doing business without advertising is like winking in the dark—the businesswoman knows what she's doing, but potential customers do not!

ACC (American Crafts Council)—a national organization designed to assist American craftspeople. The ACC works to create an awareness of the value of individual crafts in our modern society. It publishes *Craft Horizons* magazine, a bimonthly newsletter entitled *Outlook*, and an annual list of the names of shops across the country that market craft items.

Barometer of Small Business—published by the Accounting Corporation of America, this reference guide lists the average operating ratios and financial trends of hundreds of different kinds of businesses in the United States. By showing the recommended average operating-expense percentages in various businesses, an owner can judge, for example, if expenses are excessive or if they fall within the suggested norm.

Barter—to trade goods or services in return for other goods and services.

Bonding—an insurance contract in which a bonding agency guarantees payment to an employer in the event of a financial loss caused by the actions of a specified employee, or by some contingency over which the payee has no control. When an employee is "bonded," his or her performance is secured by such a bond.

Break-even point—the point at which a firm can begin to earn a profit.

Cash flow—the movement of funds into and out of the business. Your records will tell you the rate at which money comes in, where it is going, and when.

CPA (Certified Public Accountant)—an accountant who has received a certificate stating that she or he has met all the requirements of state law.

CETA (Comprehensive Employment Training Act)—a federal program organized to help economically disadvantaged people who are unemployed and age twenty-two or over. Local offices maintain lists of individuals who are actively seeking employment and on-the-job training. When an employer provides job training for at least three months, CETA will pay a negotiable percentage (up to 50%) of the employee's salary, providing that the employee is hired full-time when the training program is over.

Collateral—security given as a pledge for the fulfillment of an obligation. It is returned to the debtor when the obligation is fulfilled. Often property, stocks, and bonds are used as collateral for loans.

Collective—a type of business that is owned and controlled by members of the group.

Consignment—a system in which merchandise is turned over to an agent (who may be an individual shopkeeper or a wholesaler) for sale, with the understanding that payment to the person who produced or owns the goods will not occur until they are sold; the consignee is the agent to whom the goods are consigned.

Contracting out and contract labor—an agreement between two parties in which one party agrees to do a specified job for a predetermined wage for the other party. Often a portion of a large job is contracted out to a professional who specializes in that aspect of the job.

Contribution—the selling price of an item, less its direct costs (labor and materials), results in the amount of contribution that item provides. This contribution is used to cover manufacturing costs such as machinery expenses and maintenance, and non-manufacturing costs such as salaries, advertising, and so forth, and also to cover profit expectations.

Controller (or comptroller)—a business officer whose job includes the regular examination and checking of the financial records.

Cooperative advertising—a form of advertising in which manufacturers may pay up to one-half of your advertising costs when you advertise their products. Often the manufacturer supplies the advertising "copy," with a space left open where the name of the business can be inserted. Cooperative funds are used in all the different media.

Corporation—a legal person and a business entity. A corporation can sue and be sued, hold and sell property, and engage in business operations stipulated in the corporate charter. It is a creature of the state, and it is the corporation, not its owners, that is responsible for debts contracted by it. Ownership in a corporation is shown by stock certificates. An advantage of incorporating is the limited liability of the corporate owners of the firm's debts. Ownership in a corporation is easily transferable through exchange of stock.

Credit—(1) Credit is the selling of goods or services subject to some kind of deferred payment. Consumer credit is given by retailers to consumers purchasing for personal use. Trade credit is often extended by wholesalers or manufacturers to other business firms who are their customers. (2) Credit is also the acknowledgment of payment of a debt by the entry of the amount on the right-hand side of the account ledger.

Debit—an entry on the left-hand side of an account, showing money owed.

Direct mail—a method of advertising and promotion in which both established and potential customers are mailed fliers, brochures, and other printed materials in an effort to acquaint them with business operations, new merchandise, changes in hours or services, and so forth. A business may compile its own mailing list, or lists can be purchased from mailing-list brokerages.

Dogs—merchandise that has been in the shop for several months, receiving little favorable customer response.

Dollar-control records—records that show an estimate of anticipated sales, often over a six-month period, based on inventory estimates and purchases and integrated with sales and profit goals.

EDP (Electronic Data Processing)—a computerized information system. Computers can be purchased or rented, or small businesses can also benefit from the use of a data-processing center, a service organization which provides processing services for a fee.

Exchange—a type of retail business in which most of the merchandise offered for sale is taken on consignment basis, involving very little capital outlay for inventory. Consignors receive payment for their goods only after they have been sold.

Fixed costs or expenses—the costs or expenses for a fixed period and a range of activity. These costs do not change in total but become progressively smaller per unit as volume increases.

Fliers—a small handbill, used in advertising.

Franchise—a legal agreement by which a franchisee agrees to conduct a business in accordance with certain methods and terms specified by the franchisor. The franchisee owns her own business and contracts to distribute or sell goods or services in a given area. In other words, a franchise is a right granted by a manufacturer to market a product in a specified area.

Goodwill—derives from the loyalty of customers or other business advantages that cause earnings to be exceptionally high in view of the physical resources involved. Though it is intangible and somewhat fragile in nature, goodwill is a business asset, and when an established business is offered for sale, financial compensation for the established goodwill is often requested, and justified.

Gross—total income, or sales, or profits, with no deductions—as opposed to net.

Guarantee—a pledge of assurance that something is as it was represented and that it will be replaced if it does not meet specifications.

Image—the symbol of, or the conception of, your business idea. Your image is the impression you make.

Inventory—an itemized list of the stock of a business.

Liability insurance—insurance that will make good any loss or damage that occurs in a business transaction, which is especially important in the service businesses. Liability insurance ranges from protection against physical damage done, bodily injury done, and product defects, to protection against a mishap which occurs after a job is completed.

Logo—short for "logotype," a typeface, character, or symbol used to represent your business name, which may include a certain lettering style.

Manufacturers' directories—located in the reference section of the library, these catalogs list the names and addresses of the manufacturers of almost every product imaginable. Also called trade directories.

Manufacturers' representative or agent—an independent sales agent for a group of manufacturers in a certain sales territory. This agent may represent several noncompeting producers of items that are purchased by one type of trade.

Markup—the percentage added to the selling price of a particular item to cover operating expenses, profit expectations, and any subsequent price reductions (for example, markdowns and employee discounts).

Media—various means of mass communication, such as newspapers, TV, and radio broadcasting.

Mentor—a wise and loyal adviser who is interested in your personal and business success and achievements.

Merchandising—buying and selling, carrying on trade in some kind of goods.

Newsletter—a regular printed bulletin carrying recent news of your business, items of interest to your customers, pertinent information on your product or your service.

Old Girl Network—an emerging system involving guidance, information-sharing, and mutual support in which older, established businesswomen are helping beginning entrepreneurs up the ladder. Serving as role models and pooling their experiences and their connections, established businesswomen are endeavoring to provide for other women what young men have enjoyed for years through the benefits of the "old-boy network."

Overhead—costs such as rent, office supplies, utilities, taxes, and salaries. Most are fixed charges in that they don't change, regardless of the amount of sales.

Partnership—a voluntary association of two or more people to operate a business as co-owners for profit. Partners should be honest, capable, and compatible, and should make both capital and management contributions to the business. Partners share equally in profits and losses unless there is a pre-agreed profit-and-loss-sharing ratio. Put your contract of partnership in writing, with the help of your attorney, to avoid problems in the future.

Profit—the necessary return to an entrepreneur for her services and risks of doing business. Profit represents the difference between income and costs, both direct and indirect.

Profit sharing—giving employees a share in the profits of the business, in addition to their regular wages.

Projections—plans and proposals in business. Budget projections, for example, are a proposed scheduling of your intended, or estimated, costs of doing business.

Promotion—includes advertising and a wide range of activities and techniques designed to build sales of products and services. Promotions include contests, window and counter displays, publicity.

Publicity—any information, usually in printed form, that brings your business to the attention of the public. By definition, publicity is free (as opposed to paid advertising). The event you stage to acquire the publicity, however, may be costly.

Quality control—the attempt to ensure the presence of qualitative factors in a product or to set standards of performance in a service.

Retail—selling goods or articles, individually or in small numbers, directly to the consumer (as opposed to wholesale). Retailers are the merchants who sell these goods to individual customers.

SCORE (Service Corps of Retired Executives)—a task force of volunteers working with the SBA who offer their experience and their expertise to new business owners. Mostly senior citizens, these volunteers may be old-fashioned in some ways, but they know the ways of the business world and can be of great assistance. If your first SCORE contact is unfamiliar with your type of business or incompatible in some other way, try another one. Their services are free.

SBA (Small Business Association)—listed in the phone book under US Government, the SBA was formed to aid small business in four principal areas: obtaining credit; getting their fair share of government contracts; handling management and production problems; and providing financial assistance to small businesses damaged by "acts of God." The SBA seems most successful in helping with management and production problems. They offer a wide variety of printed materials on every aspect of starting and running a small business, as well as materials on specific businesses and their individual problems. Most materials are free from your local SBA office or can be obtained through the mail by calling their toll-free number and requesting the materials you want by individual title or number.

Sole proprietorship—a business owned and operated by one individual. A sole proprietor has title to all business assets and is subject personally to the claims of all creditors. She owns all profits and assumes all losses.

Suggestion selling—offering related items to a customer when she has selected a certain item. For example, if a customer buys a lawn mower, the clerk might also suggest a rake, some grass trimmers, and a hose! Suggestion selling also includes encouraging the customer to "trade up" to higher quality merchandise. If she selects a push mower, offer to show her the latest in power lawn mowers.

Trade journals—listed in the periodical catalog in the library, these are the magazines that serve or cater to particular industries. They contain timely information on all aspects of the industry and help keep businesspeople up to date on the happenings in their field all across the country. Many of these trade journals also publish directory issues, which contain listings of the manufacturers of different products in the trade. They are a very valuable source of current information. If a subscription to the journal in your field is too costly right now, make it a point to read it thoroughly at the library.

Turnover rate—the frequency with which an inventory of goods is sold and replaced over a given period. The rate is usually determined by dividing the net sales for a given time by the average retail value of the inventory during the same period.

Wholesale—the selling of goods in relatively large quantities to retailers, who then sell them to individual customers (as opposed to retail). Items are usually sold in quantity and usually at a lower cost per item.

Withholding tax—the amount of income tax paid by employees through the employer's withholding of a portion of their wages.

Worker's compensation—compensation to an employee for any injury or occupational disease suffered in connection with employment. It is paid under a government-supervised insurance program contributed to by employers. The amount of worker's compensation paid per employee depends upon the safety factor of the occupation.

Market—(1) A geographical area that includes a significant number of potential customers. (2) People who have the abilities and the desire to purchase a product or a service. (3) An estimated or actual demand for an item or a service, or a place of business or trade activity.

Unit-control records—records listing the quantity of goods bought, sold, in stock, and on order, with additional breakdowns as needed.

Variable costs or expenses—costs or expenses that are uniform per unit but change in total in direct proportion to changes in the related total activity or volume.

Resources

Chapter One

Superwoman, for Every Woman Who Hates Housework, by Shirley Conran (Crown Publishers, New York, 1978). A lighthearted "how to" book on managing your time, based on the premise that "life is too short to stuff a mushroom." Full of organization, shopping, and house-management tips. The section "How to be a working woman, wife and mother" is of particular interest.

How to Decide—A Guide for Women, by Nelle Tumlin Scholz, Judith Sosebee Prince and Sordon Porter Miller (College Entrance Examination Board, New York, 1975). If you are having trouble setting goals, making and evaluating your decisions, recognizing when it is right to take a risk, this book will be helpful. Using exercises and tests that force your active participation, it illustrates some decision-making patterns that will be useful to you in personal and business situations.

"Provides a plan of action for women who aspire to business advancement," states the blurb on the first page of Margaret Hennig and Anne Jardim's best-selling book, *The Managerial Woman* (Anchor Press/Doubleday, New York, 1977). In their book, these two women attempt to give some insight into the behavioral patterns of men and women in the business world. In comparing the two, the authors note that when things go wrong, men usually blame the boss, the business climate, or the system, while women often place the blame on themselves. Men assume their own competence, while women often spend much of their time on self-improvement. Self-confidence, it is agreed, is a businesswoman's greatest need. Interesting reading.

Chapter Two

Several women told us they had profited from reading a sixteen-page handbook that was reprinted from *Ms.* Magazine's April 1976 issue. You can read it at the library or write to the magazine (370 Lexington Avenue, New York, NY 10017) for your own copy. Entitled *How to Start Your Own Business!* the handbook covers planning, professional services you will need, general advice, how to raise money, keep your books, and some good publications and other sources for information.

Claudia Jessup and Jeanie Chipps are the authors of another business guide that was recommended by several new businesswomen, *The Women's Guide to Starting a Business* (Holt, Rinehart and Winston, New York, 1976).

When you are developing your business plan, you might profit from some of the publications offered by Dun and Bradstreet (write to their Dept. of Public Relations and Advertising, 99 Church Street, New York, NY 10007). Topics include reports on business credit; management pitfalls; and the cost of doing business for partnerships, proprietorships, and corporations.

When you go from being an employee in a large, organized business or system to being your own boss, you don't have to give up all the fringe benefits you were enjoying as a member of a group. Check the *National Trade and Professional Associations* of the United States listing in your library, and you may locate a club or society that offers group rates in medical, disability, and life insurance to related businesses in your field.

Another way to protect your old age while running your own business is to instigate a profit-sharing plan or a Keogh pension system. (The first is effective in your own corporation, while the second plan is for those who are not incorporated.) Ask your accountant to fill you in on all the necessary details.

In planning and running a business of your own, it pays to keep up with what other women in business are doing, as well. Here are some magazines that deal specifically with women who work:

Working Women magazine (Hal Publications, Inc.) is a timely and helpful monthly. Articles range from legal advice and working mothers' problems to how to entertain a crowd of twenty on a minute's notice.

Women's Work is a bimonthly magazine that deals with the problems of women in business—money managing, locating job help and information, and other current topics of interest to women.

Enterprising Women: A Business Monthly (New York, Artemis Enterprises) is the third magazine we would recommend to owners of new small businesses. Each issue features a firsthand story of the development of a different woman's business.

The National Association of Women Business Owners is working to develop the "old-girl network." Offering career counseling; job referral; and an information, idea, and service exchange, the NAWBO is striving to form a support system for women in business. The goal is to provide role models for other women to follow. Consult your telephone directory to locate the nearest branch of the association, or write: National Association of Women Business Owners, 2000 P St N.W., Washington, D.C. 20036.

Chapter Three

The SBA offers a pamphlet entitled *Checklist for Going into Business*, which lists the steps necessary to open a business. It is SMA (Small Marketers Aids) 71, and it provides you with a simple guideline reference. Ask for a copy at your local SBA office.

When you are selecting a location for your business, check with the local chamber of commerce for information and statistics on the economy and population of the area you are considering. They have facts on the local business climate and may also be able to refer you to other sources of information. For a personal consultation, it is wise to make an appointment in advance.

For help with your business management, public relations problems, marketing and personnel questions, check the local trade associations in your field of interest. Organized to serve different business interests, they are listed in your telephone book, or you can learn of them by talking to people in related businesses in your area.

Chapter Four

Minding the Store, A Memoir, by Stanley Marcus (Little, Brown & Co., Boston, 1974). This is a classic retailing story that should not be missed by anyone interested in the trade. Stanley Marcus tells the fascinating story of the growth and prosperity of one of the most innovative and successful retail stores in the United States.

Based on the philosophy that "there is never a good sale for Neiman-Marcus unless it's a good buy for the customer," the book includes business and selling expertise that is invaluable for any size of retail operation. Marcus includes tales of his retailing experiences that range from arranging for a custom toupee for a mounted lion with a moth-eaten mane to the promotion of His and Hers mummy cases in his famous Christmas catalog to the reproduction of an entire store-window display as a gift for the wife of a wealthy customer who couldn't make up his mind on a single gift. An example of his selling approach: "As long as the customer is alive, you have a prospect."

For some help arranging merchandise and creating attractive displays in your retail shop, consult *Create Distinctive Displays,* by Kenneth H. Mills and Judith E. Paul (Prentice-Hall, Englewood Cliffs, New Jersey, 1974). This book includes how-to work sheets to aid in problem solving and planning.

A Handbook of Retail Promotion Ideas, by David D. Saltz (Farnsworth Publishing Co., Lynbrook, New York, 1970), provides a wealth of merchandising ideas that cost little or nothing, which a small-business owner can utilize to compete successfully with the bigger stores. The book includes contest ideas (a make-up-an-ad contest, a sale-naming contest) and ideas for building up store traffic, using direct mail, cooperative promotions with other local merchants, and so on. Advice is offered on getting rid of old stock, decorating windows, cutting costs. There are 1189 ideas in all, and you're sure to find some that you can put to use.

To find out more about the possibilities of using a computer to help you in your record keeping, ordering, inventory management, and so on, consult a computer-service organization, listed in the Yellow Pages of the telephone directory. Your banker, accountant, or trade association may also be able to give you the names of service bureaus they have worked with.

Apparel Stores, a twenty-page guide to operating any type of clothing store, is available from the Small Business Reporter, Dept 3120, PO Box 37000, San Francisco, California 94137.

Chapter Five

There are many books available on the restaurant and food-service trade, so check your library sources. On the planning and development of your business, look for *Restaurants and Catering,* available free from your SBA office, and *Planning and Operating a Successful Food Service,* by William L. Karhl (Chain Store Age Books, New York, 1973).

For a really charming and fun to read book, look at *My Life as a Restaurant,* by Alice May Brock of Alice's Restaurant fame, together with Her Friends (The Overlook Press, in association with the Bookstore Press, 1975). Alice gives the feel, the smells, and the excitement of owning your own restaurant. She includes her favorite recipes (cheese and spinach pastries serving 100), tips on equipment and atmosphere, personal sketches by the people who make the whole thing work (the food prepper, the floor people, the baker, the "Suds Buster"), information on soda cups and lids that don't fit, making work lists ("Sauté onions . . . scrub clams . . . divan sauce . . ."), and coping in general.

Chapter Six

For a free government handbook listing the background on hundreds of franchise operations, write: U.S. Department of Commerce, Industry and Trade Administration, Rm. 1104, Washington, D.C. 20230.

How to Start and Run a Successful Mail Order Business, by Sean Martyn (David McKay Co., New York, 1969), contains helpful information, with special attention paid to locating products, designing and writing effective advertising, and the actual handling of orders.

Chapter Seven

Complete Guide to Selling Intangibles, by Abbott P. Smith (Parker Publishing Co., West Nyack, New York, 1971), describes the "selling state of mind" you need to sell intangibles, whether they are a service or a product (insurance, for example). Smith includes in this state of mind three necessities: (1) You must be your prospect's representative—satisfy her needs, solve her problems. (2) You must put your client's interests in the center of your presentation. (3) You must have a constructive reason for every client contact that you make.

Smith also offers advice on managing your territory and your time, your approach to sales, prospecting for potential clients, sales presentations, and follow-up calls.

A woman in the advertising business stressed her feelings that, when selling an intangible product such as advertising and advertising production, it is essential that women use every means at their disposal to appear as efficient, businesslike, and professional as men who are in the same business. If you are too cute, too aggressive, even too manly, it will work to your disadvantage when you are trying to convince potential clients of your abilities. She highly recommended that women in business secure a copy of John T. Molloy's *The Woman's Dress for Success Book* (Warner Books, New York, 1977). Being appropriately dressed in your business life is one relatively easy way to boost your self-confidence and your image.

Malloy believes that American women dress for failure, and he sees the need for a women's business uniform. He stresses that women should not wear their uniform socially until it becomes established as universal female business attire. Regardless of how you feel about wearing a uniform, we recommend his book as supplemental reading.

Chapter Eight

One of the most comprehensive and informative books on the subject of child care is *Day Care: How to Plan, Develop, and Operate a Day Care Center*, by E. Bella Evans, Beth Shub, and Marlene Weinsteen (Beacon Press, Boston, 1971). We recommend it highly to anyone interested in entering this field.

For further information on catering and other food-related services, consult *Planning and Operating a Successful Food Service*, by William L. Karhl (Chain Store Publishing).

Chapter Nine

In the manufacturing business, your equipment and operation methods must meet the standards of the Occupational Safety and Health Act of 1970. You can obtain a copy of the *Standards for General Industry* from the Superintendent of Documents, US Government Printing Office, Washington, D.C. 20402, or from a field office of the Occupational Safety and Health Administration.

When you manufacture a product that is a component part of a larger field of industry, you will find yourself relying on a number of indicators that tell you of the conditions now and in the future for your field. These indicators may be economic (revealing the economy in your area or in the industry as a whole) or demographic (indicating social and economic patterns in your population area), or they may be financial (concerning interest rates, loan situations, money supply, etc). You can obtain information on these various indicators from a variety of sources. Your local, state, and federal governments publish demographic and economic indicators. Labor publications may indicate the manpower supply in your area. Also, the publications of the different business and trade associations in your area, as well as the manufacturers' and suppliers' news publications, will furnish additional business indicators. You should make use of these indicators to plan for your business future.

The *Standard Industrial Classification*, or *SIC Code*, for short, is a listing of broad industrial groups, broken into specific industrial groups and also into types and levels of businesses within larger groups. When you are involved in the manufacture of a product which plays a part in a larger industry, you should find your specific code number in the *SIC* book at the local library. Your classification will provide you with data concerning your area, as well as certain other economic indicators.

For the manufacturers of craft items, there are many good books available offering how to's on production, marketing, pricing, and so on. Here are a few of the titles that were recommended to us.

How to Start your Own Craft Business, by Herb Genfan and Lyn Taetzsch (Watson-Guptill Publications, New York, 1974), includes everything from pricing, packing, and payrolls to profit and loss. Very informative.

Selling your Handicrafts, by William F. Garrison (Chilton Book Company, Radnor, Pennsylvania, 1974), is a very helpful book on how to market your handmade goods. It includes valuable information on wholesale pricing. Easy to read.

How to Make Money with Your Crafts, by Leta W. Clark (William Morrow and Co., New York, 1973), is a very informative, basic text for the craft business; which includes comprehensive appendices on reference sources and materials.

The American Crafts Council is a national organization whose purpose is to assist American craftspeople. The most prominent organization of its kind, the ACC publishes a bimonthly magazine entitled *Craft Horizons*. This journal, as well as the ACC itself, aims at promoting the development of crafts and stimulating an awareness of the value and contribution that craftspeople make to our society. The ACC also publishes for its members a bimonthly newsletter, *Outlook*, which lists current developments in the field as well as upcoming exhibitions. Another helpful service of this organization is its annual list of craft shops that either accept crafts on consignment or buy them wholesale. To find out more about the ACC, write: American Crafts Council, 44 W. 53 Street, New York, New York 10019.

An informative and very enjoyable resource is the *Goodfellow Catalog of Wonderful Things: Traditional and Contemporary Crafts*, by Christopher Weills (Berkley Publishing Corp., New York, 1977). There are lots of photos showing crafts produced by individuals around the country, listing what they make, their names and addresses, and prices of their work. Artists describe their items, their life-styles, their terms. Also includes information on funding for crafts, national crafts organizations and their addresses, and government arts organizations.

If you are interested in a fashion career, check *Your Future in the New World of American Fashion*, a book authored by The Fashion Group, an organization of women fashion executives, that is available by mail only from Richards Rosen Press, 29 East 21 St., New York, New York 10010, or at your library.

The Thomas Register, found in your library, lists the names of the suppliers of raw materials and almost anything you need to complete a job.

For copyright information, write: Library of Congress, Washington, D.C. 20540. Ask for the *General Information on Copyrights* booklet.

For patent information, check the phone book under US Government, Department of Commerce. Ask for booklets on obtaining a patent.

Index

ABOUT THE AUTHORS

Marjorie McVicar, Director of Member Services, Oregon Newspaper Publishers, and editor of the *Oregon Publisher* Magazine, lives in Portland with her two children.

Julia Craig lives in Seal Rock, off the rugged Oregon coast, with her husband, children, books and typewriter.